The Essential Guide TO

Surviving Infidelity

by Liz Currin, Ph.D.

ALPHA

A member of Penguin Group (USA) Inc.

ALPHA BOOKS

Published by the Penguin Group

Penguin Group (USA) Inc., 375 Hudson Street, New York, New York 10014, USA

Penguin Group (Canada), 90 Eglinton Avenue East, Suite 700, Toronto, Ontario M4P 2Y3, Canada (a division of Pearson Penguin Canada Inc.)

Penguin Books Ltd., 80 Strand, London WC2R 0RL, England

Penguin Ireland, 25 St. Stephen's Green, Dublin 2, Ireland (a division of Penguin Books Ltd.)

Penguin Group (Australia), 250 Camberwell Road, Camberwell, Victoria 3124, Australia (a division of Pearson Australia Group Pty. Ltd.)

Penguin Books India Pvt. Ltd., 11 Community Centre, Panchsheel Park, New Delhi—110 017, India

Penguin Group (NZ), 67 Apollo Drive, Rosedale, North Shore, Auckland 1311, New Zealand (a division of Pearson New Zealand Ltd.)

Penguin Books (South Africa) (Pty.) Ltd., 24 Sturdee Avenue, Rosebank, Johannesburg 2196, South Africa

Penguin Books Ltd., Registered Offices: 80 Strand, London WC2R 0RL, England

International Standard Book Number: 978-1-61564-119-2
Library of Congress Catalog Card Number: 2011910188

14   13   12   8   7   6   5   4   3   2   1

Interpretation of the printing code: The rightmost number of the first series of numbers is the year of the book's printing; the rightmost number of the second series of numbers is the number of the book's printing. For example, a printing code of 12-1 shows that the first printing occurred in 2012.

Printed in the United States of America

Note: This publication contains the opinions and ideas of its author. It is intended to provide helpful and informative material on the subject matter covered. It is sold with the understanding that the author and publisher are not engaged in rendering professional services in the book. If the reader requires personal assistance or advice, a competent professional should be consulted.

The author and publisher specifically disclaim any responsibility for any liability, loss, or risk, personal or otherwise, which is incurred as a consequence, directly or indirectly, of the use and application of any of the contents of this book.

Most Alpha books are available at special quantity discounts for bulk purchases for sales promotions, premiums, fund-raising, or educational use. Special books, or book excerpts, can also be created to fit specific needs.

For details, write: Special Markets, Alpha Books, 375 Hudson Street, New York, NY 10014.

Publisher: *Marie Butler-Knight*
Associate Publisher: *Mike Sanders*
Executive Managing Editor: *Billy Fields*
Senior Acquisitions Editor: *Brook Farling*
Development Editor: *Ginny Bess Munroe*
Senior Production Editor: *Kayla Dugger*

Copy Editor: *Cate Schwenk*
Cover Designer: *Rebecca Batchelor*
Book Designers: *Rebecca Batchelor, William Thomas*
Indexer: *Brad Herriman*
Layout: *Ayanna Lacey*
Proofreader: *John Etchison*

This book is dedicated to my loving husband, Tom. His faith in me and support of this project have made this a labor of love. This book is but one of a number of grand adventures we've shared in our precious time together.

This book is also most lovingly dedicated to my daughters, Elyse and Sarah. They are my inspiration and my beautiful shining stars.

Contents

Introduction

This book is about a topic that makes most adults in committed relationships very uncomfortable. It's about infidelity. For those of us who have stood before family, friends, and clergy, and have taken a vow to "forsake all others, 'til death do us part," the thought of our spouse becoming intimately involved with someone else may be almost incomprehensible. Many of us approach the subject with a sort of naïve assumption that infidelity is someone else's problem. It couldn't possibly happen to us. We don't enter into marriage thinking that one or both of us will cheat. And yet that's exactly what the statistics tell us may well happen.

Infidelity and divorce are, to a large extent, a numbers game. Take the case of divorce, for example. It is widely held that approximately half the marriages in this country end in divorce. Reliable numbers for infidelity are hard to come by, for statistical and other reasons. Infidelity is by its very nature a secretive enterprise. People are generally reluctant to admit to it, except in rare circumstances. Either their betrayal is discovered, or they become so wracked with guilt that they feel compelled to confess. Perhaps they seek confidential help from a therapist, uncertain as to how they feel about either the marriage, the affair, or both. Perhaps they participate anonymously in an online survey or take part in a research study. And for everyone who engages in infidelity and either admits it or is caught, there are those whose infidelity never comes to light.

Infidelity author Peggy Vaughan estimates that 50 to 65 percent of men and 45 to 55 percent of women will engage in adultery before the age of 40. Other sources put the numbers as high as 75 percent for men and 60 percent for women. And while precise numbers are elusive, the estimates make it clear that infidelity is a significant factor in American marriage—and divorce. Some sources point to adultery as being responsible for 65 percent of divorces, while others suggest that couples are more likely to simply drift apart over time. When this happens, a marriage becomes more vulnerable to infidelity, and so affairs may be more likely to occur in the waning days of a marriage. In this situation, placing blame on an affair for the dissolution of a marriage may not be entirely accurate. Instead, the marriage was virtually over, due to a variety of circumstances, and the affair was not to blame, but rather was more symptomatic of the very fragile state of the marriage. However, many of these relationship forces act simultaneously or overlap, and it becomes impossible to point to a single event or cause of a divorce.

How are we to make sense of this? We pledge one thing when we join our lives with another, and we intend to honor that commitment. We certainly expect our partner to honor his or her promise to be faithful. Americans are among the most conservative of nations when it comes to attitudes about extramarital sex. In a survey of attitudes toward nonmarital sex in 24 countries, researchers found that 80 percent of Americans thought sex outside marriage was "always wrong," compared with 68 percent of Canadians and 36 percent of Russians (Widmer, Treas, & Newcomb, 1998). And yet, years, or perhaps only months, later many of us will find ourselves behaving differently. We will violate those vows which signaled the beginning of "happily ever after." So clearly, we believe and hope for one marital scenario, but all too often find ourselves confronted with another.

If your spouse has been unfaithful, and you learn of it, one thing is certain. Your life will never be the same. Depending on how secure or insecure you tend to feel in intimate relationships to begin with, trust may be very hard for you to come by in the future. If you decide to try to repair your marriage, this will be especially true. If you're either unwilling or unable to do that, and you "start clean" with a new relationship, you may find yourself more susceptible to doubt or jealousy than before the affair. This is the legacy of infidelity. It not only changes relationships, it changes individual lives. It changes our futures.

But there is hope. In many cases, couples who are determined to salvage a marriage can, with much hard work and patience, do so. Regardless of whether partners devote themselves to rebuilding a marriage or determine that they must move forward separately, individuals can use the pain and confusion of an affair to begin to better understand themselves and what they are like as intimate partners. They can develop more realistic expectations about marriage. With sufficient time, introspection, and self-nurturing, they are able to turn the tragedy of betrayal into personal transformation.

A note about language: Throughout this book, I alternate (although not precisely) between the pronouns *he* and *she*. This is to reflect the fact that both men and women engage in affairs, and both men and women are devastated by their partner's affair. I alternate between *husband* and *wife* for the same reason. I use both *spouse* and *partner* for the sake of variety, as well as to indicate that nonmarried individuals in committed relationships also suffer at the hands of an unfaithful partner.

How This Book Is Organized

I've conveniently broken this book into four sections:

Part 1, Infidelity and Marriage Today, looks at challenges to today's marriages and how prevalent infidelity is in our culture. It also examines different types of affairs and the factors that may contribute to them, including the Internet.

Part 2, The Experience of Betrayal, takes you into the discovery of a spouse's infidelity, your emotional reactions to an affair, and confronting a cheating spouse.

Part 3, Five Steps to Recovery, takes you through a series of steps for rebuilding your marriage. These involve remorse on the part of the cheating spouse, recommitment to the marriage by both partners, restoration of trust, rewriting the story or narrative of your marriage, and renewing your vision for your marriage.

Part 4, Your Marriage After Infidelity, is where we look at what it's like to try again after a spouse's affair and how your marriage needs to become different. Sometimes, however, a couple realizes too much damage has been done and they will be better off moving on separately. In this case, the goal is to use divorce as a vehicle for personal growth and transformation.

Essential Extras

Throughout the book, you'll find several different types of sidebars, or additional material. The purpose of these sidebars is to further illustrate what's being presented in the text or to give you a bit more information on the topic. The sidebars fall into the following categories.

These are tips on how to deal with infidelity and other relationship issues.

These include information on the trauma of infidelity.

These include various facts and perspectives on the experience of infidelity and related matters.

These sidebars contain the meaning of specific or technical terms that shed further light on the subject of infidelity.

You'll also see a fifth, name-changing sidebar that presents anecdotes, interesting facts, case histories, or other extended background information you should know.

Acknowledgments

I wish to gratefully acknowledge my editors at Alpha Books, Brook Farling, Ginny Munroe, Kayla Dugger, and Cate Schwenk, for their guidance and support during this project. They have been a pleasure to work with and to get to know.

Paul Dinas, my first senior acquisitions editor, introduced me to the world of writing for publication. Before undertaking this project, I often wondered at the glowing praise that authors are wont to heap upon their editors. I now completely understand it. His guidance, wisdom, support, and encouragement inspired and buoyed me during the early phases of this project.

My colleagues at Atlanta Area Psychological Associates, P.C., have been enthusiastic and supportive, and for that I am most appreciative.

Finally, I wish to gratefully acknowledge the role my patients have played in this work. More than they know, they continue to educate me about the mysteries of the human heart. They have also been a constant source of encouragement and have cheered me on. As always, I appreciate their gracious willingness to invite me into the most private areas of their lives. I wish each of them the very best.

Trademarks

All terms mentioned in this book that are known to be or are suspected of being trademarks or service marks have been appropriately capitalized. Alpha Books and Penguin Group (USA) Inc. cannot attest to the accuracy of this information. Use of a term in this book should not be regarded as affecting the validity of any trademark or service mark.

Part 1

Infidelity and Marriage Today

In this part, I look at how widespread infidelity is today. I examine the various types of infidelity—sexual, emotional, financial, and cyber infidelity, and different combinations thereof. I look at certain factors in our culture today that have contributed to the increase in infidelity, including the tremendous increase of women in the workplace over the past half-century. I also look at the state of contemporary marriage, our expectations, and factors that place additional stresses on busy married couples. Another key factor in the increase in infidelity is the Internet, which, with its vast amount of adult material and dating sites, has made it ever easier to cheat on one's spouse. Even apparently innocent social networking sites are leading more and more to infidelity.

I examine the anatomy of different types of affairs. While having an affair is always voluntary, there is a variety of factors that may put you at greater risk. Some have to do with environmental circumstances, such as people around you having affairs. Another factor is personality characteristics, such as narcissism. And while an unsatisfying marriage is never to blame for an affair, couples recovering from infidelity can often look back and identify ways in which they were vulnerable. I also look at the Other Person in an affair—who they are and what motivates them.

chapter 1

The Epidemic of Infidelity

Defining infidelity

Identifying the different kinds of infidelity

Identifying social and cultural factors that contribute to infidelity

Learning how other cultures deal with nonmonogamy

Infidelity is a silent epidemic in our society. It's hard to know for sure how many marriages are affected by it. After all, most extramarital activity tends to be conducted in secret. But it's probably safe to say that, even if it hasn't impacted our own marriage, we all know someone whose life has been traumatized by a partner's unfaithfulness. It may be a friend or neighbor, a co-worker, or even a family member.

In this chapter, I examine what the term infidelity means, and different types of infidelity. As you'll see, over time, the idea of infidelity has been expanded to beyond sexual and emotional affairs to include behaviors related to money and technology. I also look at some of the cultural factors that contribute to the prevalence of infidelity in our society.

Infidelity Is Broken Trust

What does it mean to talk about *infidelity?* Well, it's a broad term that refers to behaviors ranging from religious belief to the management of money. In some religious contexts, for example, an infidel is a nonbeliever, someone who doesn't subscribe to a particular theology or set of religious practices. When talking about our intimate relationships, like marriage or a long-term committed partnership, however, infidelity involves betraying a sacred personal trust.

Definition

Infidelity can refer to a wide range of behaviors. The common denominator in these behaviors is that expectations about a relationship have been violated. For this reason, feelings of emotional safety in the relationship and trust in one's partner have been damaged or even destroyed.

When we take marital vows, although the precise wording of our vows may differ, most of us pledge to love and honor our spouse and to forsake all others. While not everyone agrees on the precise definition of terms like infidelity or affair, the vast majority of us expect fidelity or faithfulness to include monogamy. But few of us actually discuss with our partner ahead of time what this means. Exactly what are the limits when it comes to interacting and socializing with members of the opposite sex? Which behaviors are appropriate and acceptable, and which are not?

And so we enter into marriage trusting that the individual we've decided to spend the rest of our life with will be faithful. We trust that he or she will treat us with respect and consideration. We trust that he or she will reserve physical and emotional intimacy for us and not share those special experiences with someone outside the marriage.

When the vow to forsake all others is violated, the emotional well-being we've entrusted our partner with is damaged, if not outright destroyed. Later, you can see that the capacity for trust in general can also be affected. Personal, social, and professional relationships may all suffer when trust has been broken.

Types of Infidelity

For many years, when people spoke of infidelity, they were generally referring to a sexual relationship with someone other than one's husband or wife. This could be the stereotypical affair with one's secretary or one's boss. It could involve a neighbor or a family friend. The identity of the affair partner was of less concern than the fact that the relationship was primarily sexual in nature.

Of course, emotions often entered into these relationships as well. In fact, research shows that we tend to develop positive, intimate feelings for people we have sex with, even if the relationship starts out as merely a sexual one. Not surprisingly, there's a lot of chemistry involved in our sexual responses. Orgasm releases hormones such as oxytocin and prolactin. These chemicals tend to make us feel closer and more emotionally connected with a sexual partner, as well as more contented and satisfied in general.

So it's not always easy to separate sexual from emotional infidelity. A relationship may start out as primarily sexual, but the participants find that they have developed strong caring feelings for each other. And, of course, a relationship that begins with sharing intimate thoughts and desires, but without sex, may easily become a physical relationship over time.

The bottom line here is that feelings and behaviors that should be reserved for one's spouse have been shared with a third party. The promise to forsake all others has been broken. In fact, that one special person with whom you decided to spend the rest of your life has diverted sexual and emotional energy from your marriage into another relationship.

Sexual Infidelity

This category may seem to be the most straightforward and uncomplicated of all the types of infidelity. After all, sex is sex, right? Well, most people would probably agree that intercourse (vaginal penetration) constitutes sex. But when it comes to alternative sexual practices, there is less consensus.

Remember Bill Clinton's famous line, "I did not have sex with that woman"? While we can't read his mind, he could apparently face both his wife and the nation and deny a sexual relationship with a young White House intern because it did not involve traditional intercourse.

Defining certain acts out of the category of sexual infidelity—or even "having sex"—has become increasingly common in recent years. For instance, there is a disturbing trend among middle schoolers to engage in oral sex but to identify themselves as abstinent because they're not engaging in vaginal sex. As the example of President Clinton reveals, adults, too, engage in this sort of denial about their sexual behavior.

Not all mental health professionals agree on the definition of sexual infidelity, either. A number of years ago, a well-known radio psychologist declared that "If no body fluids are exchanged, there is no infidelity." While this comment may strike most of us as an extreme boundary for defining sexual infidelity, it underscores that there is a wide range of opinion on this subject.

Some couples may even find a spouse's mild flirtatiousness with someone at a social gathering to be threatening to their relationship. For others, if no body fluids are exchanged, why be concerned? For most of us, what constitutes sexual infidelity probably lies somewhere in between. As Supreme Court Justice Stewart famously said in 1964 regarding the debate over pornography, "I know it when I see it."

So while there's no clear consensus as to what constitutes sexual infidelity, it's probably safe to say that, at a minimum, it involves some physical contact. This could range from kissing to fondling to actual contact with the genitals of another person. Over time, most of us develop an internal barometer that guides what we're comfortable with in our marriage.

Tried and True

The best time to have a discussion with your partner about what constitutes sexual infidelity is before you're married, or even engaged. If the two of you can't agree on which behaviors are acceptable and which aren't, you could be setting yourself up for heartache and conflict in your relationship. You can avoid misunderstanding by clarifying appropriate boundaries before making a lifetime commitment.

Self-Assessment: How Would I Feel?

Use the following questions to assess whether what you're seeing may be sexual infidelity. Fill in the blanks with a word that best describes your reaction.

- If I saw my spouse warmly hugging someone of the opposite sex, I would feel _____.

- If I saw my spouse kissing another man/woman on the lips, I would feel _____.

- If I saw my spouse with his/her arm around another person's waist at a party, I would feel _____.

Hint: Stick with your emotional reactions. Use words like *worried*, *angry*, *scared*, *unconcerned*, *betrayed*, *excited*, or whatever comes to your mind. As you look at your responses, the stronger the negative emotion (for instance, angry), the more likely it is that you're feeling sexually betrayed.

What behaviors are you comfortable with in your marriage? What feels like crossing the line into sexual infidelity? Use your answers to these questions as a springboard for discussion with your spouse. How would he or she answer these questions? Are the two of you in agreement about what's appropriate and what isn't?

Finally, a word about the impact of sexual infidelity on a marriage. Men and women tend to respond differently to this. Men are more likely to experience sexual infidelity as a "deal breaker" in the marriage. The idea that their wife has been physical with another man is a tremendous blow to the ego. It's more difficult for men to get past this than it is for women, who struggle more with the effects of emotional infidelity.

Emotional Infidelity

As we've seen, even something as seemingly straightforward as sexual infidelity can be open to debate. Emotional infidelity can be even harder to define and identify. But let's start with the premise that emotional infidelity involves sharing intimate concerns and information with someone outside your marriage, for instance, a co-worker.

Emotional infidelity generally starts innocently enough. Let's look at a case study. Eileen, for example, has to travel out of town to help her mother during a time of illness. She asks Suzanne, her neighbor and good friend, to help out with things like carpooling, the kids' afterschool activities, and some meals while she's gone. Suzanne is more than happy to give her a hand. After all, Eileen has helped her out plenty of times in the past.

As Suzanne stops by the house to pick up the kids or drop off a casserole, she and Phil, Eileen's husband, spend time talking. Before long, the conversations become more personal. There's nothing physical, mind you, but Suzanne finds she's looking forward to these conversations more and more and thinking about Phil more frequently. She's never really noticed before, but Phil's actually fairly good-looking. And he's always willing to listen to her. Suzanne and her husband have been having a few problems lately, and Phil really seems to care.

Does this constitute emotional infidelity? The answer is probably yes. Phil occupies more and more of Suzanne's thoughts, and she eagerly anticipates their personal conversations. Also, she's sharing intimate aspects of her married life with him. How would she feel if her husband could overhear their conversations?

That last question is a critical one. If you're confused about whether you're crossing the line, so to speak, in a relationship with a third party, just imagine your spouse being present when you interact with this person. Ask yourself some key questions. How would you feel? Would you feel extremely self-conscious? Anxious? Guilty? If you answer yes to any of these questions, you may be on the verge of emotional infidelity.

Emotional infidelity usually begins fairly innocently. In the workplace, for example, people may express a genuine interest in each others' lives and problems outside the office. They feel they're simply being friendly. But this interest may suggest that one is open to a more intimate relationship. Before they know it, they're involved in an emotional affair.

One of the hallmarks of emotional infidelity is that you share excessive amounts of information about intimate topics with a third party. You're even more open to this person than you are to your spouse. You eagerly anticipate your next opportunity to interact with this person. You may not be entirely conscious of this, but, on some level, you're thinking, "Finally, there's someone who understands me and what I'm going through."

Let's take the case of Maria and Joel. They've worked together in their company's IT department for the past two years. They get along well and spend a fair amount of time talking about their personal lives, as well as what's going on at work.

Their chat on Fridays and Mondays is particularly personal. They both share their plans and concerns about the upcoming weekend, or their disappointments and frustrations about the weekend that just passed. They relate to each other incidents that illustrate how they've felt ignored, disrespected, or misunderstood. Did Maria's husband sit on the couch and watch sports all weekend? Did Joel's wife turn him down for sex yet again?

Over time, Maria and Joel develop a deep emotional bond through their repeated sharing of information, feelings, and frustrations about their marriages. In many ways, they feel closer to each other than to their spouses. They've actually considered that, if they weren't already married to other people, they might be together.

Are you or your spouse getting emotionally involved with someone else? Here are a few questions to ask yourself if you are concerned about emotional infidelity:

- Are you or your spouse sharing more and more information about your marriage, your family, or your frustrations with someone of the opposite sex?

- Would you feel anxious or guilty if your spouse were to walk in on a non-work-related conversation you're having with this person?

- Does this person seem to occupy your thoughts a lot? Would you say you're even obsessed with him or her?

- Do you arrange to meet for coffee, lunch, or dinner without others present?

If you answered yes to any of these questions, you may be at risk for emotional infidelity.

Financial Infidelity

Another type of infidelity has been labeled as such only recently, but it has undoubtedly been around since men and women began pairing up and pooling their material resources. This is financial infidelity. According to some experts, it affects as many as one third of all marriages.

What does financial infidelity mean? It includes such behaviors as failing to disclose significant debt before or after marriage, incurring major debt after marriage without a spouse's knowledge or approval, or engaging in spending habits that could jeopardize a family's financial well-being.

The list of ways in which financial infidelity can put a marriage at risk is virtually endless, but it includes activities like gambling, excessive retail spending, and loaning money to family or friends. Clearly, an individual or a couple can be financially irresponsible without infidelity being involved. For instance, a couple may spend money on expensive vacations, a home or car they can't really afford, or private schools that are beyond their budget.

The key concepts in financial infidelity are secrecy, betrayal, and jeopardy. Jeopardy refers to endangering your family's financial stability and future. Secrecy reflects the hidden nature of these behaviors. They're done without a spouse's consent or knowledge. And betrayal, as with other forms of infidelity, indicates that someone is violating a sacred trust. In marriage, there is the expectation that both partners will act in ways that protect both the present and the future of the relationship. When financial resources are used unwisely, marital stability is threatened.

Tried and True

Did you know that most couples find it harder to talk about money than about sex? But if either you or your spouse has accumulated major debt, it's important to disclose that before you get married and to develop a plan for paying it down. Transparency in financial matters is a key part of a strong and healthy marriage.

Cyber Infidelity

In Chapter 5, we look closely at the role of the Internet in infidelity. For now, I'll just say a brief word about this and about the connection between technology and infidelity in general.

It goes without saying that, throughout history, people have used whatever means they had at their disposal to conduct affairs. In ancient times, that might have been a spoken message sent to a lover via a trusted servant or a traveler. Centuries later, the sentiment might have been written in a letter and delivered through the mail. In modern times, lovers might have waited for each other's phone calls, hovering near the phone to avoid an unsuspecting spouse picking up.

Of course, the phone—in particular, the cell phone—continues to play a central role in illicit communication. Before the advent of cordless and cell phones, you were pretty much tethered to the phone's location. Sometimes an extra-long extension cord afforded a little added privacy. Or there was always talking in a hushed voice, but that was sure to arouse suspicion.

The cell phone clearly circumvents many of these problems. It's portable, so calls to a lover can be made while driving to or from work, shopping, at the gym, or during a child's soccer game. The possibilities are vast and are utilized by cheating spouses the world over. In fact, cell phones and text messages are probably the vehicle by which most extramarital contact is made. (We look at the role of e-mail in Chapter 5.)

So a bit further on, we take a more in-depth look at technology and infidelity, in particular, the role of the Internet. It's not an exaggeration to say that the Internet has revolutionized and contributed to infidelity.

The Social Context of Infidelity

Like all forms of behavior, infidelity is a product of its time and environment. While this may come as a bit of a surprise, the concept of infidelity is not written in stone. Behaviors that strike us in twenty-first-century America as betrayal have been considered acceptable and commonplace in other times and places. And even in contemporary times, cultures and societies have vastly differently standards for what's appropriate in intimate relationships.

> **Bet you Didn't Know**
>
> Attitudes toward women and sexuality have fluctuated throughout history. Women in the Old Testament and during the period of early Church history were seen as highly sexual. They were temptresses, capable of bringing righteous men to ruin, like in the story of Sampson and Delilah. And the Church Fathers viewed women and their sexuality as the downfall of saintly men.

The other part of this scenario is that having multiple wives was not at all uncommon in ancient history. King Solomon of Israel, for example, was said to have had approximately 700 wives and 300 concubines!

Nonmonogamy in America

Throughout history, there have been precedents for nonmonogamy, such as with King Solomon. Even today, strict monogamy is the norm in only about 14 percent of the world's societies. Elsewhere, polygamy (the practice of having multiple wives) is permitted, but generally only if a man is able to provide for all his wives and children. And in a very few societies, polyandry (the practice of having more than one husband) is permitted.

Nonmonogamy has a long history in America as well. Over the centuries, American religious communities have espoused the practice of multiple marriages. One of the best known of these groups is the Latter Day Saints, more commonly known as Mormons. In spite of legal restrictions, certain factions of this group still insist on their right to practice polygamy.

Other groups have embraced nonmonagamy as a means of making a political statement. The Kerista commune in San Francisco, for example, instituted a "rotational sleeping schedule" as a means of overcoming jealousy, which its members viewed as politically incorrect. The founders argued that, if all members slept with each other on a regular and equal basis, there was little chance of favored relationships developing.

Why Infidelity Is a Growing Problem

Opportunities for infidelity have always existed. While we accept monogamy as the gold standard for marriage, the rate of infidelity has increased during the past decades, among both men and women. A note of caution, however, is that data on sexual behavior, particularly something as sensitive as infidelity, are inexact. People are understandably often reluctant to be completely honest about their sexual behaviors, especially when those behaviors violate social norms such as monogamy.

With that in mind, some of the best estimates place the rate of male infidelity at 40 to 60 percent and the rate of female infidelity at about 40 percent. Depending on your sources, these rates either underestimate or overestimate affairs among married people. For instance, some sources estimate the rate of male infidelity to be as high as 75 percent.

One of the major factors in the increase in infidelity in this country has been the infiltration of women into the workforce during the past century. Women have, of course, always labored alongside men and contributed to their family's maintenance. Over time, however, as more and more economic opportunities began to be concentrated in cities, young women and men were increasingly brought together in places of employment.

With growing opportunities for employment, women also found increasing financial independence. They were no longer totally reliant upon a spouse for economic support for themselves and their children. Offices and factories gave women more and more opportunities, including opportunities for interaction with members of the opposite sex.

The co-mingling of men and women in the workplace has been a major contributor to the rise in infidelity in this country. It allows for long periods of time spent together, as well as emotional interaction connected with job projects and worker relationships. In fact, studies suggest that most affairs begin in the workplace.

For decades, then, women have participated in the workforce at very high rates, even when they are also raising children. For this reason, they enjoy increased financial independence and mobility. This has brought them into more sustained contact with men other than their husbands. The result is that there are ever-increasing opportunities for affairs to develop.

Do We Practice What We Preach?

Are some societies more "infidelity-prone" than others? Very possibly. Americans have traditionally thought of Europeans as being more sexually liberated and open-minded with regard to infidelity. And yet most of Europe has historically been staunchly religious, much of it Catholic.

It's difficult to know how to reconcile these trends, other than to acknowledge the fact that there's often a glaring discrepancy between what we profess and what we actually do. Think of France, for instance, traditionally a devout Catholic country. And yet, when President François Mitterand died in 1996, his wife, his mistress, and his illegitimate daughter were in attendance at the funeral.

Americans were scandalized by such behavior, and yet Europeans seemed remarkably unfazed by it. As has been noted by more than one cultural observer, Europeans seem to spend less time critiquing sexual norms and more time simply enjoying sex.

When it comes to attitudes, Americans are among the most conservative in the world with regard to infidelity. Approximately 80 percent of Americans believe that sex outside of marriage is always wrong, as compared with 36 percent of Russians. And yet our behavior doesn't always match up with our attitudes. Our rate of infidelity is on the rise.

Essential Takeaways

- Infidelity is a general term that includes both sexual and emotional affairs, as well as financial infidelity and cyber cheating.
- Even psychologists and other professionals may disagree about what constitutes infidelity.
- Nonmonagamy has been extensively practiced in other cultures and other times, even in America.
- We often display a significant gap between what we believe and what we actually do when it comes to monogamy and fidelity.

chapter 2

The Tie That Binds

Today's marriage challenges

Making sure expectations are reasonable

New roles for husbands and wives and
the dangers of parallel lives

Does biology trump monogamy?

In this chapter, I take a look at the roles of men and
women in contemporary marriage, especially dual-
career marriages. You'll see that our current lifestyles
may be placing a strain on monogamous relationships.
I examine what we expect both from our marriages
and our partners and whether these expectations
are realistic. Finally, I look at what some behavioral
scientists have to say about human biology and the role
that it may play in infidelity.

The Challenges of Modern Marriage

Marriage is a time-honored social institution. It has
existed since the dawn of human history. Much has
been written about the purposes of marriage. It has
been described as an arrangement to ensure physical
survival, to pass along personal property, and as a stable
environment for raising children.

To this day, marriage continues to be a social and legal structure within which husband and wife pool their resources and build a shared, secure life. And in spite of the ever-increasing of number of children raised in single-parent homes, researchers and mental health professionals argue that an intact two-parent home is generally the best environment for rearing children.

But marriage faces many social and legal challenges today. Cohabitation, or living together without benefit of marriage, is no longer disapproved of by most members of society. More and more companies are offering benefits, such as medical insurance, to domestic partners. While the divorce rate has gone down slightly in recent years, divorce is still so commonplace that almost half of us who marry will eventually experience it. And bearing children out of wedlock is no longer the disgrace it was once considered to be.

In 2007, nearly 40 percent of the babies born in the United States were born to unwed mothers. This represents about a 25 percent increase in only five years.

The Changing Marital Landscape

For most of us, marriage has become a personal lifestyle choice, rather than the primary socially approved path into adulthood that it was for eons. In past decades, when post-secondary educational choices and career options for women were severely limited, marriage and motherhood were the primary options for adult women. This situation has radically changed, with more women than men graduating from college and with virtually unlimited career choices for women.

Whether or not to have children has also largely become a matter of choice. Men and women who were teenagers or adults in the 1960s and 1970s remember how advances in birth control technology revolutionized sexual relationships. The pill, in particular, allowed women to engage freely in sex with little fear of pregnancy. The increasing availability of safe, legal abortion also added to the perception that there was little or no downside to indiscriminate sex.

Childless by Choice

In the 1970s, roughly 10 percent of women aged 40 to 44 were childless. Thirty years later, that figure had almost doubled. And the more educated the woman, the less likely she is to have children.

The Gap Between Attitudes and Behaviors

When it comes to certain beliefs about marriage, the United States has traditionally been among the most conservative countries on Earth. For example, in a survey of attitudes toward nonmarital sex (for example, premarital sex and extramarital sex), 80 percent of Americans say that extramarital sex is always wrong. Only 36 percent of Russians surveyed, however, feel it is always wrong.

Within our own culture, attitudes have changed over time as well. This includes attitudes toward behaviors such as casual sex, the sexual double standard, divorce, cohabitation, and having children out of wedlock. And the subject of infidelity is finally "coming out of the closet," in the sense that it is receiving more and more attention in the mainstream media.

But our behavior tells a different story. While we may condemn infidelity and other forms of sex outside marriage, we regularly act in ways that contradict our beliefs. For example, a recent Centers for Disease Control study indicates that approximately 85 percent of women and 91 percent of men have engaged in premarital sex.

We're clearly conflicted about sex and fidelity. While it's very difficult to obtain accurate data on the occurrence of infidelity, all things considered, some experts estimate that approximately half of us cheat on our spouses. The rate is higher for men than for women, but, as in other areas, women are closing the "infidelity gap."

Have We Become Cynical About Marriage?

So is marriage even necessary anymore? Our attitudes toward it are complicated. For countless years, it was taken for granted that marriage was one of the major goals of adulthood. A recent study, however, revealed that 40 percent of young adults now think that marriage is becoming obsolete.

Many of us no longer need the economic security of marriage, as we have separate sources of income. We can have children out of wedlock without the shame that we would once have felt. And we can lead perfectly satisfying lives without tying ourselves legally and emotionally to one individual.

And yet we continue to marry in large numbers. Approximately 75 percent of us marry once, 20 percent marry twice, and 5 percent will marry three or more times. Clearly, we still have faith in the institution of marriage. How do we make sense of this?

In spite of economic and social changes that make marriage less necessary for maintaining a household, we still believe that a shared future with someone is the preferred life path. Many of us continue to believe in the existence of a "soul mate," that one special person with whom we share a deep spiritual bond and with whom we are destined to spend our life.

Heartaches

According to a recent poll, 98 percent of us believe that it's important to marry our soul mate, yet only about 30 percent of us believe we ever find that unique person.

While we don't necessarily feel we need marriage for a successful and fulfilling life, it's as if our culture is in love with being in love. Take a look at the wedding industry, for instance. And make no mistake, it's an industry, all romance aside. It's an industry that draws in $71 billion per year.

Consider that, in 2009, the average wedding budget was over $28,000, with actual wedding costs tending to run about $10,000 over the projected amount. Throw in the average $5,000 for a one-week honeymoon in Hawaii, for example, and you're looking at about $40,000 to put on a one-day shindig for family and friends.

It's entirely possible to get married with much less expense, drama, and wear and tear on one's nerves, of course. But every year, couples sign on to stage the spectacle of a lifetime. They pour endless time and energy into planning the most minute details of what they hope will be a fairy-tale event. For brides, in particular, it's often a day they've dreamed of since they were little girls.

So while times have most definitely changed in terms of marriage being almost a necessary way of life, we continue to embrace the vision of finding our soul mate and creating something lasting and satisfying. We know we have lifestyle options, but, at heart, many of us are diehard romantics.

For the Record

MISC.

Linda Lou Taylor Wolfe of Indiana is in the *Guinness Book of World Records* for the most number of marriages—23. She also holds the record for most number of vow renewals. Her shortest marriage lasted 36 hours, her longest seven years.

The case of Ms. Wolfe in the sidebar illustrates what I often hear from my clients when discussing marriage. A primary motivation is to avoid loneliness, especially in their older years. Many people envision themselves aging and becoming physically frail. They dread being alone or dependent on their adult children. Marriage can seem like a guarantee against emotional isolation and dependence.

Do We Expect Too Much?

Many of us put months, even years, into planning for our "big day." But do we devote equal time and attention to what's actually the most important day of our married life? That's the day when we return from the honeymoon and our "real life" begins. That's the day we start functioning as a married couple.

How do we prepare for married life? Probably our most powerful source of information is the role model our parents have provided. Even if we had miserable parents and we swear we'll never be anything like them, they exert a powerful influence over us, in terms of shaping our behavior in our own marriages.

We're also influenced by what we see in the media, including how marriage is portrayed on TV and in the movies. The stereotype of marriage has changed dramatically over the past few decades. Programs depicting intact families have been replaced by ones portraying divorce and frequently infidelity as the norm.

Remember that what you watch on TV and in the movies is fiction. In general, it's based on a Hollywood script and is not necessarily a reflection of the way real people live. Don't let the entertainment industry dictate choices you make for your own life and relationships.

We have expectations about every relationship we enter into, whether it's a new job, a new friendship, or a marriage. When we take a new job, those expectations are often spelled out in a contract detailing our obligations to our employer (for example, our work duties) and our employer's obligations to us (salary and benefits, for example). Although expectations about friendships aren't written out in a contract, we generally expect that our friends will be loyal, understanding, and have our best interests at heart.

Our expectations about marriage have changed over the years. They have typically included protecting the legal rights of children and ensuring that our property will stay within our family. They have also included more informal expectations about which partner is responsible for a particular set of duties that keep the family functioning smoothly.

For example, in the middle of the twentieth century, before women entered the workforce in large numbers, a common marital arrangement was for the father to earn the family's income and for the mother to manage the household and care for the children. This particular arrangement wasn't recorded on paper, but it was an expectation that was held and generally honored by both husband and wife.

These days, we expect much more than financial support from our spouse. We expect partnership in the fullest sense of the word, as well as the deep emotional fulfillment of sharing life with our soul mate. And this can be a tall order for a marriage to fill.

It's not uncommon for spouses to have been high school or college friends before they began dating. They may even have supported and consoled each other during relationships with others before they themselves became romantically involved. They may share recreational interests. Going into marriage, they understandably assume that they will continue to be best friends.

So after marriage, we may have a fairly extensive "job description" for our spouse. This may include not only financial partnership, but partnership in caring for children and in managing household tasks as well. It may also include being a primary source of recreational, social, and intellectual stimulation.

Some couples have relied so heavily on each other before marriage for recreational and social companionship that they may be setting themselves up for trouble. While it's important to share hobbies and other interests with your spouse, it's also healthy to be involved with other groups and people. To rely completely on your spouse for emotional fulfillment places an unduly heavy burden on your marriage.

Changing Roles for Spouses

As society has changed, our ideas about men's and women's roles have changed, and this has strongly influenced our ideas about marriage. Not long ago, it would have been unusual for a husband to have changed diapers, done laundry, and cooked dinner. In dual-career couples, sharing those duties is frequently the norm today. And when the wife has a more demanding job than her husband, some husbands may even take over primary responsibility for running the household and helping the children with homework and extracurricular activities, such as sports.

Heartaches

Even though societal roles for men and women are changing, many women continue to feel unduly pressured by the demands of home and children. In general, working mothers handle twice as many household chores as their husbands do. This imbalance in responsibility is a major source of marital strain for many couples.

These days, many dads routinely drive their children to and from school and other activities. They help with homework. They make dinner and clean up. They do laundry and housework. And on weekends, there are soccer games, the lawn to be mowed, and projects around the house. So while many women continue to report that they bear the brunt of household chores, husbands have, over time, redefined their role. They are no longer simply breadwinners.

Busy Parallel Lives

In some ways, spouses have led parallel lives ever since husbands went off to work as the primary breadwinners, while moms stayed home to raise the children and run the household. But families commonly reconnected at the end of the day. Dinner was a time for catching up on the day's happenings. And parents likely spent time together watching TV or reading the newspaper or a magazine after getting the kids in bed.

Some families still maintain similar routines. But the reality for many dual-career couples is different. One or both of them may bring work home at night. And one or both of them may travel on business. The impact on family and marital life can be considerable. Among other things, it can increase the chances of an extramarital relationship.

Let's look at the case of a dual-career couple who, in essence, lead parallel lives. Tom is a software executive who often travels to his company's headquarters in the United Kingdom. Elaine sells high-end medical equipment and is frequently on the road, too, visiting hospitals and doctors' offices. They do their best to avoid traveling at the same time, so that they can avoid disruption in their children's schedules and activities.

Tom is extremely outgoing and actually enjoys his business travels. He takes his seat on the plane and easily strikes up a conversation with those around him. On his last trip, he met a woman with whom he immediately began to flirt. She responded in kind. When the flight ended, they exchanged a kiss. She gave him her e-mail address.

Tom contacted her while on his trip. They began a steamy online correspondence. While in the United Kingdom, he also arranged to have dinner with a former co-worker now living abroad. After dinner, they went to her room for more drinks. And while they didn't have sex, they engaged in prolonged kissing and petting.

Meanwhile, Elaine is managing things at home, unaware of Tom's activities. Tom has his own suspicions about Elaine. He has noted that she has recently added some more provocative items to her wardrobe, has changed her hairstyle, and rushes off to work earlier than usual in the morning. And she is less and less interested in having sex with him.

Between their careers and their children's school and extracurricular activities, Tom and Elaine have very limited time together on a daily basis. And on weekends, they're equally busy running errands and tending to household chores. In therapy sessions, Tom states that Elaine has become a virtual stranger to him and that he has actually lost almost all desire for her, especially when compared to his escapades with other women.

Tried and True	Your spouse's business travel can provide the perfect cover for an affair with a co-worker. Be alert for discrepancies in how long a business trip lasts, where your spouse is supposedly staying, and objections to your meeting him or her at the airport. All of the above could signal that your spouse is meeting or traveling with a partner he or she doesn't want you to know about.

Forsaking All Others

When we wed, we vow to "forsake all others." In doing so, we are proclaiming to the world that we are ready to put past romantic relationships behind us and to forgo developing new ones. We are pledging sexual and emotional fidelity to one person until death claims one of us.

Monogamy is the foundation of the marital relationship. It symbolizes our trustworthiness in all aspects of marriage, not just the sexual part. If a partner can't be trusted in the physical aspect of the marriage, can he or she be trusted in the emotional and the financial areas of the relationship? In other words, if your spouse is unfaithful in one area of life, it's hard to compartmentalize the relationship and trust that he or she will be faithful in other areas. A partner's willingness to compromise fidelity in one area suggests he or she could do the same in other important areas of the marriage—for example, your family's finances.

One issue that often arises for couples is how to handle past relationships. These may involve former friends or lovers, or even ex-spouses with whom you're on good terms. Cross-sex friendships are more common today than in past years, due in no small part to women attending college and working outside the home.

Because of vastly increased opportunities to develop cross-sex friendships in today's culture, these relationships face special challenges. Men and women are socialized to view each other as potential romantic partners. And men, in particular, tend to consider their female friends as potential sexual partners. A third issue is how cross-sex friendships are perceived by others. Many people have a hard time believing that men and women can be "just friends." They tend to see a sexual motivation where there may be none.

While these relationships can enrich your life, they can also be a source of trouble if not managed properly. When you become romantically involved with a third party, it may be necessary to have a very frank conversation with your opposite-sex friend about the nature of your relationship. Such a conversation can help dispel any hopes that the friendship would have, in time, become sexual.

Heartaches

Research shows that there may be a reason to be concerned about your spouse's friendships with members of the opposite sex. In a study of cross-sex friendships among young adults, half of the subjects said they have had sex with someone they considered just a friend and not a romantic partner.

A relationship with an ex-spouse can be especially tricky. If you and your ex don't have children together, the situation is fairly simple. There's no compelling reason to stay in contact with each other. That's not to say that relations between you can't be cordial and respectful, simply that there's nothing that forces you to interact with each other.

On the other hand, when children are involved, there are critical issues to be negotiated and managed. These include custody and visitation arrangements, as well as financial responsibility for the children. In such cases, you'll need to find a way to handle these day-to-day details that's comfortable for both you and your husband or wife. For instance, when your ex stops by to pick up the kids for the weekend, do you invite him in to chat while the kids grab their overnight bags? Or do you have him wait in the car?

Even when your children are adults, there will likely be occasions when you'll be face-to-face with an ex-spouse. A child's graduation from college, a wedding, and the birth of a grandchild are examples of happy occasions when you'll need to be prepared to interact with an ex-spouse. Family crises can also force you into the company of a former husband or wife. Some examples would be a serious illness, an accident, or an adult child's unemployment, forcing him or her to return home for a time. In this case, you and your ex-spouse may need to cooperate and collaborate on plans for medical care or financial assistance.

 Seventy-five percent of men have discussed having sex with their ex-wives, either during or after the divorce process. Thirty percent of men have actually had sex with an ex-wife. However, only 34 percent of men say they are friends with their ex-wives.

Does Biology Play a Role in Infidelity?

I see it all the time in my psychology practice. People come in with their stories of infidelity and the havoc it wreaked in their lives. And without fail, they bring with them a rationale, an excuse, for the infidelity. They're misunderstood or mistreated at home; they're not getting enough sex at home; they're not getting the right kind of sex at home; they're married to the wrong person.

You get the picture. For every story of infidelity and its disastrous aftermath, there's an excuse. And now scientists and mental health professionals have joined the chorus. We are now using human biology as an underlying explanation for infidelity. The logic is that we just aren't meant to be monogamous.

Evolutionary psychology seeks to explain human behavior in terms of traits or actions that increase the likelihood that a person's genes will be passed on to future generations. It looks at the challenges posed by our human ancestors' environments and the behaviors they adopted to meet those challenges. Behaviors and traits that were successful in helping humans adapt to their environment were most likely to be repeated in future generations.

The Biological Argument Against Monogamy

Evolutionary psychology's argument against monogamy goes something like this. The main concern of human beings is survival, and not just survival as an individual, but survival as a species. How can we, as a species, best ensure this?

It turns out that the answer is different for men and women, but, in both cases, it involves infidelity. It's pretty simple for men. The more women a man can impregnate, the more of his genetic material he passes along to the next generation. So, according to evolutionary psychology, men are biologically driven to have sex with as many women as possible.

Women are much more limited, of course, in their ability to reproduce. During their childbearing years, they can give birth to approximately one child per year, not counting multiple births. So women's concerns are less related to the number of children they bear, and more with ensuring that their children survive to an age when they themselves become fertile and are able to procreate.

The most children born to a single couple was 69, born to Feodor and Valentina Vassileya of Russia, between the years 1725 and 1765. In the seventeenth century, the Emperor of Morocco is reported to have had 867 children. He is said to have eventually had at least 700 male descendants alone.

So how do women ensure the continuation of their genetic line? The answer is that they obtain sufficient resources, such as food, to ensure their children's survival. And they do this, according to evolutionary psychology theory, by recruiting men who are willing to support their children.

Of course, men don't simply volunteer to support a woman's child. There needs to be a compelling reason to do so. And this reason is that they need to believe that the child is theirs. And they will only believe this if they have had sex with the mother.

The Proof Is in the DNA

The advent of DNA testing may force evolutionary psychologists to revisit this part of their theory. Paternity tests have taken the mystery out of establishing fatherhood. But suffice it to say that, for countless centuries, men have been willing to devote substantial material resources to children they believed they fathered. By having sex with multiple men, women could increase the chances that they and their children would be provided for.

Based on hospital blood tests, it has been estimated that 1 in 10 babies is actually the product of an extramarital affair.

While evolutionary psychology is considered cutting edge by many, it's easy to see how it could be used as an excuse for infidelity. After all, by having sex with multiple partners, we're simply following our "genetic imperative."

Essential Takeaways

- Contemporary marriage presents a range of challenges to husbands and wives, including balancing dual careers, childrearing, and household responsibilities.

- Dual-career marriages, with long hours and frequent travel requirements, present increased opportunities for extramarital relationships.

- We have extremely high expectations of our spouses and our marriages, including a high level of companionship and emotional and social stimulation. It's probably wise to seek this from a variety of sources, such as friends and special interest groups.

- Without monogamy, it's difficult to establish trust in any area of your marriage.

- Evolutionary psychology argues that we engage in infidelity for biological reasons—that is, to maximize the chances of our survival on the genetic versus the individual level.

chapter 3

Affairs

The broad spectrum of infidelity

Factors that contribute to affairs

How long do affairs last?

Defining what an affair is can be a very subjective process. This depends to a large extent on you and your spouse, your individual histories, and your expectations for your marriage.

While there's no excuse for an affair, and your spouse must take responsibility for his or her behavior, there are numerous factors that can increase the likelihood that someone will engage in an affair. I take a look at these factors in this chapter.

Finally, you'll see that some affairs are very brief, while others last for months, even years. And while it can be very easy to get caught up in an affair, ending one can be very difficult.

What Is an Affair?

Affair is a very broad term that covers a whole range of unfaithful behaviors. In the past, it has been used as a synonym for adultery. Adultery, however, has specific legal and religious connotations. That term is now generally used in divorce proceedings.

Some people define terms like *affair* and *infidelity* more broadly than others. This can be a source of contention for you if one of you defines infidelity very broadly, while your spouse sees the same behavior as innocent.

Do you and your spouse agree on the types of friendships with members of the opposite sex that are acceptable—for example, college friends, friends from work, or members of office sports teams? If you don't, you may be setting yourself up for trouble down the road. It's important to have open and honest discussions about what's okay to both of you and what feels threatening.

Even psychologists and other mental health professionals may disagree on what behaviors constitute infidelity or an affair. Most of us would probably agree that a sexual relationship with someone other than our spouse is an affair. But what if it's just emotional? What if it's a one-night stand? What if you pay someone for sex? Or what if it's online? Are all of these affairs, or are some of these just innocent outlets for sexual energy?

I generally use *affair* to refer to a relationship between two people, at least one of whom is married or committed to someone else. The relationship is often sexual, but can also be emotional. The typical affair is frequently a combination of both.

When your spouse has an affair, it violates your expectations about faithfulness in marriage. It also involves diverting emotional energy from your marriage into an illicit intimate relationship. And when that happens, the strength of your marriage is greatly diminished.

The Anatomy of an Affair

Every affair has a certain anatomy, or structure. Just like a three-act play, it has a beginning, a middle, and an end. Sometimes it's easier for us to identify these stages in retrospect. For instance, two individuals may vehemently insist that they're "just friends." Looking back on their relationship, however, they realize they were in the initial stages of an affair.

I'll identify various types of affairs, but, for the moment, let's consider an "average" affair between two people, both married to other people. The initial stage of the affair is likely to be warmth and positive feelings. If the individuals are co-workers, the feelings may involve mutual respect and a high level of helpfulness with work tasks. Sometimes the affair simply begins with outright physical attraction, or some combination of the above.

While almost all affairs become cloaked in secrecy, most affair partners deny intending to stray at the outset. When working with them in therapy, it's very common to hear, "It just happened." The truth is that not much in our intimate relationships "just happens." We make small choices all throughout the day, day after day, that can eventually add up to major turning points in our lives.

For instance, going to lunch with a co-worker certainly seems innocent enough. After all, you have plenty to discuss—projects and deadlines, your boss and the cast of characters you work with. And getting out of the office for an hour is a welcome relief from the demands and the hectic pace of the workday.

Over lunch, you talk a bit about work, but the conversation eventually shifts to more personal topics—your spouse and his or her job, the latest on what your kids are up to, your plans for the upcoming holiday. Over time, these conversational shifts become a habit, and the tone of the relationship changes. It becomes more and more intimate and the two of you begin to regard each other increasingly as friends and confidants.

Many people do develop deep and lasting friendships in the workplace without disruption to their lives. Their families may participate in social activities together, such as cookouts, cultural or sporting activities, or camping trips. But when the co-workers are of the opposite sex, the bonds of friendship can intensify into something potentially threatening to their marriages.

> **Tried and True**
>
> Some infidelity experts recommend being cautious about how much personal information you share at work and how much time you spend in non-work-related conversation. For example, the late Shirley Glass noted that, in 25 years of working with the same co-therapist and researcher, they never discussed personal issues about their marriages. A good rule of thumb seems to be "friendly, but not familiar" in the workplace.

What Factors Give Rise to Affairs?

For years, the prevailing thought was that affairs developed largely when someone was dissatisfied in his or her marriage. And while this can certainly be a factor, researchers have learned that there may be other circumstances involved in having an affair.

Some of the most common contributing factors are opportunity; the prevailing norms in someone's group of family, friends, and co-workers; his or her personality traits; and the strength of his or her marriage. I take a look at each of these factors and how they can influence whether an affair happens or not.

>
> **Heartaches**
>
> While there are numerous factors that give rise to affairs, it's critical to remember that personal responsibility is key here. There's never a good explanation or a justification for an affair. Don't accept your spouse's rationalization for cheating.

Short-Term Affairs

Infidelity and affairs are as old as marriage itself, but modern lifestyles make it relatively easy to have a brief sexual encounter with someone other than your spouse. Many of us travel frequently on business. This can present opportunities for relatively anonymous, one-time encounters.

Some of the circumstances surrounding these "one-night stands" include being away from home, where your spouse's unfaithful behavior is harder to detect. Some business travelers report almost a sense of exhilaration at being in a new environment and meeting new people. The excitement of interacting with strangers and brief acquaintances may contribute to some one-time affairs.

These are affairs that arise primarily out of opportunity. They are not planned in advance and they tend to involve strangers or a co-worker participating in the same meeting or event. For example, someone attending a convention or a conference may encounter an opportunity for casual sex with a fellow attendee from his or her office.

News headlines are replete with stories of athletes, entertainers, and politicians engaging in extramarital affairs. Their lifestyle—frequent travel, meeting new and attractive people wherever they go, as well as their high personal profiles—certainly set up situations in which it's easy to conduct a very brief affair.

MISC.

"Addicted" to Affairs?

Tiger Woods supposedly confessed to engaging in 120 affairs occurring over the five-year period of his marriage, including an affair with one young woman he had known when she was a child. This means he averaged 24 affairs per year, or 2 per month.

Opportunistic affairs are similar to a hookup or a one-night stand in the sense that there is no expectation of a future for the relationship. There is a mutual understanding that "what happens in Vegas, stays in Vegas." Away from home and family, your spouse may feel a sense of freedom and lack of consequences for his or her behavior.

Even the traditional holiday office party can be a breeding ground for trouble. A number of surveys have shown that many office affairs actually begin at events like these. The combination of alcohol and an atmosphere of revelry can contribute to a lack of restraint among employees.

> **Tried and True**
>
> If you suspect your spouse is cheating at the office, be sure to attend all office social functions. His or her behavior toward a particular co-worker may well reveal who the other guilty party is. Look for unusual body language, eye contact, private conversations, or avoiding someone your spouse would normally be expected to talk casually with.

A word of warning is in order here. Even opportunistic affairs, however, can morph into something else. If someone you have even a single casual encounter with knows your identity, you are at risk. The partner may decide to contact you or your spouse after the fact. Clearly, pregnancy and contracting an STD are risks. Or the affair partner may express interest in developing a relationship. A casual sexual encounter is no guarantee of anonymity or keeping your marriage intact.

Long-Term Affairs

While short-term affairs can range from a casual hookup to several encounters, they are generally about the sex. They serve the purpose of physical gratification and the thrill of engaging in a secret and forbidden activity. There is little or no expectation of a serious emotional involvement developing.

Longer-term affairs are another matter, however. They, too, may begin as sexual or as an infatuation. But over time, other factors gain in importance. Companionship, emotional support, and comfort may become increasingly important. If you're thinking this is what a marriage is supposed to offer, you're right.

A long-term affair that provides the emotional benefits one normally associates with marriage might be considered a "shadow marriage." That is, it's not a legally recognized relationship. However, it operates alongside the marriage and provides many of the same benefits as marriage—for example, sex and companionship.

History is full of examples of long-term affairs. In recent times, one of the best-known is the relationship between Prince Charles of England and Camilla Parker-Bowles. Charles and Camilla's romance began approximately a decade before Charles married Diana Spencer.

During Charles and Diana's marriage, the tabloids were full of stories about the illicit relationship between the future King of England and his mistress. The feeling among many was that Camilla was more mature than Diana and that she understood Charles and the never-ending demands on the royal family.

Camilla appeared willing to remain in the background, allowing Charles to carry out his royal duties. He maintained the façade of a marriage for a number of years. His affair with Camilla, however, was an open secret. Charles and Camilla were eventually married in 2005, after confessing their "manifold sins and wickedness" before the congregation in attendance. It is noteworthy that Charles' parents did not attend the wedding ceremony, but did attend the service of blessing and the reception afterward. According to news reports, Charles and Camilla lead essentially parallel lives now; they were actually better suited to each other as lovers than as spouses.

These "shadow marriages" can arise when an individual is already married, but later meets someone who seems to be a much better match. Or, as in the case of Prince Charles, there may be strong pressure to marry within a certain class or for political reasons. But one may have already fallen in love with someone with whom marriage isn't an option. In such cases, a parallel emotional and sexual relationship may be maintained for years.

Most of us don't live under such public scrutiny. There's not the pressure to marry for political reasons. We have the luxury of marrying for love. And yet a staggering number of us end up in extramarital relationships that linger on for months, or even years.

The average affair lasts about two years. This number includes one-night stands, as well as affairs that last for many years.

The Role of Environment

Can your environment influence whether you have an affair or not? Possibly. While scientists continue to debate the role of nature (biology) versus nurture (environment), there seems to be some support for the idea that what goes on around us strongly influences how we behave.

Let's take the example of Lily, an attractive young immigrant to the United States. Highly educated, she found a job in the research and development department of a large manufacturing firm. She was new to the country and to her company as well.

Lily soon discovered that her workplace was a hotbed of infidelity. Office affairs were rampant, and they seemed to be a common means of advancing in one's career. Eager to get ahead in her profession, Lily made it known in some not-so-subtle ways that she might be interested in a relationship with her superior, Rob, a married man with three children. Soon they were involved in a full-blown affair. Rob made sure Lily's reports were impeccably written and that she was considered for new opportunities in the department.

In addition to the "sexual culture" in your workplace, think about your family and your friends. Is there a history of infidelity in your family? Did either of your parents have affairs? What about your brothers and sisters? If there's a pattern of infidelity in your family, there may be a tendency to accept an affair as a part of life.

What about your friends? Are any of them having affairs? If so, do they talk openly about their extramarital activities or even joke about them when you get together? Do you and your buddies go to strip clubs, buy lap dances, or even hire prostitutes? And what about ladies' night out at the Chippendales' show? What about bachelorette parties which feature "suck for a buck," in which random men are invited to suck Lifesavers candies off a t-shirt which the bride-to-be wears? Many people view these activities as innocent, but it's important to ask whether they actually dishonor the marriage. All these behaviors may subtly encourage you along the road toward infidelity.

The bachelor party has become, for many fiancés, an excuse for a last "fling." This can range from hiring a stripper, to going to a strip club, to oral sex or intercourse with a professional or a stranger picked up in a bar. You and your fiancé need to be very clear on what the limits are.

I refer to this as the "Tony Soprano syndrome." If you're familiar with the TV series *The Sopranos,* you know that Tony and his associates have girlfriends as well as wives. It's a given that Tony and his group all have *gumars,* or mistresses, whom they see one night of the weekend, while the other night is reserved for wives. The gumars engage in sexual acts that the men don't feel comfortable performing with their wives, the mothers of their children. As part of this arrangement, the wives also know about the mistresses. They may not like it, but it's an integral part of the culture.

When you have a family history of infidelity, or your close friends and associates engage in affairs and speak openly about it, you're more likely to accept an affair as a routine part of life. You know it may not be the right thing to do, but, hey, after all, everybody's doing it.

The Role of Personality Traits

Can your personality play a part in whether or not you engage in an affair? The answer again, just like the question about environment, is very possibly. Some personality types may be more likely to either feel entitled to a relationship outside their marriage or to seek emotional reassurance from an outsider.

Narcissists may feel entitled to a certain type of sexual or emotional experience. They feel that their marriages aren't providing what they want so they may look for it elsewhere. While they don't necessarily think this way consciously, at a very basic level, other people exist as interpersonal "objects" to meet their emotional needs.

The Rules Don't Apply to Me

Politicians, athletes, and entertainers may begin to believe their own press. They may believe that, because of their talents or accomplishments, they are entitled to whatever they want, sexually and otherwise. Just think of Bill Clinton, Mark Sanford, John Edwards, Eliot Spitzer, Anthony Weiner, Kobe Bryant, Tiger Woods, Tori Spelling, Leanne Rimes, and Jennifer Lopez. For a variety of reasons, the number of female politicians exposed as having had affairs is quite small as compared to their male cohorts, but some examples that come to mind are former Rep. Helen Chenoweth of Idaho and former Mayor of Charlotte, North Carolina, Sue Myrick.

Narcissistic individuals are mainly concerned with how others bolster their self-image and feelings of importance. Their relationships are driven by the need to feel important, special, and superior. Narcissists have very little concern for the needs and feelings of others. So given their craving for approval and adoration, an affair provides a ready means of bolstering their shaky self-esteem.

Another type of individual who may be prone to affairs is someone who is extremely insecure. If a woman feels ignored, undervalued, or disrespected by her husband, she may seek reassurance about herself from someone outside the marriage. An affair may initially provide feelings of self-worth that the marriage is not providing. If a husband has doubts about his physical and sexual desirability, for example, or if he feels that his interests and life goals don't matter to his wife, he may be more vulnerable to an affair. Ironically, though, the long-term consequence may be that a man feels worse about himself because of the affair.

Individuals who feel a strong need to be the center of attention may also look for love and validation outside the marriage. If a husband spends long hours at work or in recreational activities, his wife may feel he's ignoring her. She may then seek extra attention from a third party who is willing to devote time to her and make her feel special.

Bet You Didn't Know

Madame Bovary is a fictional character from a nineteenth-century French novel. She has come to symbolize someone who compulsively seeks reassurance and validation of her self-worth through her adulterous relationships.

Finally, researchers have recently identified a traitlike personality disposition that they call "sociosexuality." This refers to how willing someone is to engage in sex outside the context of a committed emotional relationship. People whose sociosexuality is restricted need the boundaries of an emotional relationship in order to engage in sex, while people with unrestricted sociosexuality are much more comfortable engaging in casual, uncommitted sex.

Tried and True	The Sociosexuality Orientation Inventory measures a person's level of comfort with casual sex. It's based upon sexual history, attitudes toward casual sex, and sexual desire for others outside a committed relationship. In general, men are more comfortable with uncommitted sex than women.

How Is Your Marriage?

It's important to emphasize that an unfulfilling marriage is never an excuse for an affair. But, like environmental and personality factors, it may be associated with increased risk of an affair. Sadly, couples often realize this only after an affair has occurred. They then must do the difficult work of trying to identify the risk factors in their relationship that may have made an affair more likely.

A couple's lifestyle may inadvertently contribute to the development of an affair. Both spouses may have demanding jobs, perhaps requiring frequent travel or working late at the office. And then there are children, with school and extracurricular activities. There's not much time for conversation, sharing what's on your mind, or activities that promote togetherness. It's easy for couples to gradually drift apart. And when that happens, a spouse may become more vulnerable to the interest and the attentions of an outsider.

All couples have issues communicating with each other. We come from different family backgrounds and have different role models for resolving problems in relationships. When couples don't find effective ways to communicate their needs and concerns within the marriage, they tend to have the same arguments repeatedly. And this creates emotional distance between them.

Make your marriage a priority. Set aside some time each day to connect with your spouse, to listen to his or her concerns and to share yours as well. This small investment of time and energy can keep your marriage strong and secure.

Over time, couples may develop toxic relationship patterns as well. As they become increasingly familiar with each other and their unique habits, they may develop intolerance, or even contempt, for their spouse. And when this happens, it is often the kiss of death for a marriage. A lack of respect for one's spouse can contribute to him or her emotionally checking out and seeking the respect and validation of his or her personal worth from someone else.

Is It "Purely Platonic"?

Friendships between men and women are much more common these days than in the past. Decades ago, people married shortly after high school and women typically remained in the home to raise children. There was far less contact between women and men other than their husbands. Over time, however, women entered college and the workforce in ever-increasing numbers.

With this social change, men and women interacted with each other more frequently and developed friendships. This interaction also contributed to increased opportunity for affairs. Men and women work closely together and may actually spend more waking hours with co-workers than with their spouses. Without a strong commitment to one's marriage and a sense of appropriate relationship boundaries, it's easy for friendship to intensify and lead to a romantic involvement.

While there can certainly be innocent friendships between men and women, people may also be in denial about feelings that go beyond friendship. Or if they recognize that the feelings are inappropriate, they believe that they can control and manage them. Often, it's only after an affair that they realize the extent of their denial.

A husband or wife who hears that a spouse is just friends with someone else needs to be concerned. The office has become the new breeding ground for affairs, with almost three quarters of people reporting they regularly have sexual thoughts about co-workers.

In addition to the workplace, the gym is another meeting place where the potential for sexual and romantic involvement is high. The atmosphere is casual, clothing tends to be scant, and men and women are free to mingle and socialize. It's common for people to run into some of the same members and to chat with them, creating opportunities for friendships and other types of relationships to develop.

Let's take the case of Janet. She was, to all appearances, happily married. She met Ray at her gym. They engaged in light, casual conversation and started spending time at the pool after their workouts, chatting about their jobs and their families. Before long, they were making plans to meet for lunch at the local mall's food court.

While there was no physical contact, there was sexual innuendo in their conversations, as well as veiled references to how things might be if they weren't obligated to others.

Ray's wife learned about this relationship when she overheard him on the phone with Janet. He denied there was anything inappropriate in the relationship. When his wife called Janet and confronted her, Janet, too, insisted that the relationship was just friendship. Ray's wife, however, demanded that he end the relationship and go into marital therapy with her, or else she would consult a divorce attorney.

Is It Love or Lust?

While it's difficult to speak of an average or typical affair, most affairs—except for one-night stands—probably contain both sexual and emotional feelings. We usually think in terms of having sex with those for whom we have strong feelings. But research studies have shown that the act of having sex with someone can actually give rise to positive feelings. Sexual activity releases brain chemicals that promote feelings of closeness and well-being.

Affairs generally develop out of infatuation with a new person. Novelty and discovery in a new relationship are very potent experiences. For men especially, the desire for sexual novelty is very strong. Women, on the other hand, relish the experience of being appreciated and desired emotionally. Infatuation combines both the thrill of discovery about the partner and the promise of sexual novelty.

Depending on the impact of the affair on one's marriage, the spouse who cheated may rationalize his or her behavior. For example, if a man has an affair and he and his wife decide to work on the marriage, he may minimize the strong positive feelings he had for his affair partner, claiming it was just sex. On the other hand, if he and his wife separate or divorce, he may justify his affair on the grounds that he really was in love with the partner. The truth may well lie somewhere in between.

Affairs Are Easy to Start, Hard to End

When we think about our romantic relationships, lust and infatuation are the easy parts. They're fairly automatic reactions. Being strongly attracted to someone feels out of our control. And being intrigued and captivated by someone is a natural phase in the development of an intimate relationship.

So it's not hard to see that opportunities for attraction exist all around us. Most of us encounter numerous people in the course of a day, whether co-workers, friends and acquaintances, or people with whom we interact in other contexts, such as shopping, doctor's appointments, and community volunteering. It's likely that we could feel an attraction to one or more of these people.

Another factor that contributes to the ease with which affairs begin is that we tend to be on our best behavior in public. Regardless of the stresses and tensions at home, we put on our best face and our most pleasant manner when we go out into the world. This illusion of pleasantness, however, can have devastating consequences.

In the workplace, for example, our co-workers tend to be pleasant and considerate. This can create a dangerous basis of comparison with a spouse, however. A co-worker may refrain from venting her frustrations and hostilities in the office, which can give the impression that she is calmer, sweeter, more thoughtful and considerate than one's spouse.

Of course, the unseen part of this drama is that, in the privacy and confines of her own home, the secretary who goes out of her way to be helpful and appears able to read her boss's mind, may come home and spew out her irritation and frustrations from work. So her husband sees her at her most frazzled, while her boss and co-workers see her at her best. Her boss may therefore begin to think, "I wish my wife could be as sweet and understanding as my secretary."

The start of an affair is filled with exhilaration. The secrecy, the forbidden sex, the idea that someone really gets us and is willing and eager to fulfill our fantasies is a very potent and dangerous emotional cocktail. An affair can be almost as intoxicating as a drug. But, just like marriages, extramarital affairs change over time—and not always in pleasant ways.

The movie *Fatal Attraction,* starring Glenn Close and Michael Douglas, graphically illustrates the ways in which an initially explosive, no-strings-attached sexual encounter can turn potentially dangerous, even deadly. Much to Dan Gallagher's (Douglas) horror, Alex Forrest (Close's character) is unwilling to leave their relationship at a one-night stand. She demands ongoing attention, and when Dan balks at the idea, her behavior becomes dangerous, including a suicide attempt, killing a pet rabbit (the origin of the term "bunny boiler"), the kidnapping of their child, and the attempted murder of Dan's wife.

While most affairs don't end in circumstances as extreme as *Fatal Attraction,* they are often difficult to end, nonetheless. One party may be ready for it to be over, but the other is not, and objects or threatens his or her affair partner. The other partner may be emotionally exhausted from all the secret-keeping and the planning that goes into engaging in an affair.

If one affair partner decides to end or slow down the affair and work at his or her marriage, the affair partner may become upset, even enraged, and engage in fantasies of revenge. These include calling the partner's spouse, showing up unannounced at his or her house or place of business, or damaging property, such as an automobile or clothing.

For most affair partners—those who aren't seriously emotionally disturbed—the end of the affair does not involve danger or destruction, but it may bring with it a variety of emotions. These include sadness, a feeling of emptiness or hopelessness, anger, relief, or emotional exhaustion. But one thing is certain, the negative feelings that accompany the end of an affair are very different from the anticipation and exhilaration that are part of the beginnings of an affair.

> **Tried and True**
>
> When ending an affair, you must be absolutely clear that the relationship is over. Involve your spouse, allowing him or her to listen in on your phone call or to draft your e-mail with you. Do not try to remain just friends with a former affair partner. This sends a mixed message and will undermine your spouse's trust.

Essential Takeaways

- An affair is a type of extramarital relationship that violates what we believe and hold dear about marriage.
- Affairs can be very short term, such as a one-night stand, or they can last for years and closely resemble a marriage.
- While there is no justification for an affair, there are several factors that increase the likelihood of a spouse cheating.
- The beginning stage of an affair is marked by sexual and emotional exhilaration. Over time, however, affairs become more complicated and difficult to end.

chapter 4

The Affair Partner

The portrayal of the Other Person—the other woman, in particular

High-profile infidelity scandals involving politicians, athletes, and entertainers

The various types of Other Person

The life of the Other Person

Jealousy regarding your spouse's affair

In this chapter, I take a look at that shadowy third party in your marriage, the affair partner. When your spouse engages in an affair, your relationship has effectively become a threesome. That third party greatly affects what goes on in your home and family life, even if you don't yet know he or she exists.

Research has shown that people vary considerably in their attitudes about engaging in sex. Some are quite comfortable with casual, uncommitted sex, while others need to be in a stable, long-term relationship in order to enjoy it. "Mate poaching" refers to sexually or romantically targeting someone who is already in a relationship.

The life of the Other Person, especially a single woman involved with a married man, is often misunderstood. It is generally not glamorous, as it has frequently been portrayed by Hollywood. While it may be exciting and thrilling at first, it soon becomes a life of waiting for a phone call or text message that may never come, and of repeated disappointments because the married lover must spend time with his family instead of with her.

An affair is always an extremely selfish act. Occasionally, however, the unmarried partner actually develops some empathy for the betrayed spouse. In this case, guilt may lead him or her to break off the extramarital relationship.

The Other Person

Every marriage in which there is an affair is, in truth, a threesome. The marriage is no longer simply a holy union between husband and wife. A third party has been invited in. In all likelihood, however, one of the spouses is unaware of this arrangement, at least for the time being. This secrecy creates a serious power imbalance in the marriage. The cheating spouse has important information—that is, that a third party has been invited into the marriage—that the betrayed spouse does not have access to.

While it clearly takes two people to engage in an affair—generally a man and a woman—media attention has traditionally focused on the woman in the affair. Various terms—some more judgmental than others—have been used to describe this woman. "Other woman" and "homewrecker" are some of the more common expressions used, particularly in the popular media of the twentieth century, such as *Ladies' Home Journal* and *Redbook.*

What the Popular Media Shows Us

The popular media—movies, television, books, and magazines—have devoted much attention to affairs and to the Other Person, especially the other woman. The exaggerated emphasis on the other woman, versus the other man, may simply reflect a widespread belief that men are more apt to stray in their intimate lives. Women, on the other hand, have traditionally been seen as the upholders of morals and family values. In theory, they should be less likely than men to engage in affairs.

Hollywood has historically either glamorized or vilified the other woman. She has frequently been portrayed as unmarried, and therefore sexually available. She may be part of the world of commerce and business, employed, perhaps as a secretary to a powerful—and married—man.

Or perhaps she is a member of the upper echelon of society and becomes romantically involved with a member of the tennis or polo set. In the 1940 stylish film noir classic *The Letter,* Bette Davis plays the upper-crust wife of a rubber plantation owner. Her elegant lifestyle and the virtually invisible cadre of servants who cater to her and others in her privileged British circle eventually clash horrifically with the local populace.

When the manager of the plantation is murdered, it is discovered that she had been carrying on an affair with him. She must eventually confront and humble herself before the Asian woman to whom he had been secretly married. The apparent glamour and ease of Davis' life in this film stand in stark contrast to her eventual fate. The ultimate justice is eventually exacted upon her by the shadowy, invisible locals. But her story stands as a stark morality tale.

Attitudes toward the other woman have changed over time. Adultery and "coveting another's wife," of course, have specifically been forbidden in the Ten Commandments of the Old Testament since time immemorial. And this is the mind-set and one of the principles upon which this nation was founded.

As we have seen, though, greater intermingling of men and women in the workplace and greater economic independence for women have certainly increased opportunities for adulterous relationships. And, as with most behaviors, the more we are exposed to them, the more they become part of our cultural baseline. In other words, while once we might have been shocked to learn of an extramarital affair between co-workers, we may now be saddened, disappointed, and troubled, but we're not shocked by workplace adultery.

In the Massachusetts colony during the seventeenth century, adultery was actually punishable by death. Eighteen-year-old Mary Latham and one of her many lovers were executed for their crime. Nathaniel Hawthorne's 1850 novel *The Scarlet Letter* was one of the earliest and most powerful explorations of the theme of adultery in American literature. The extreme cost of Hester Prynne's illicit relationship during the Puritan era and its impact on those around her dominate the book.

Contemporary Affair Partners

There has been a recent spate of sex scandals and affairs by politicians, entertainers, and athletes. While affairs have existed in all segments of society, they tend to be much more publicized than heretofore. And the more they are discussed in the media, the less our capacity to be shocked by them.

President Bill Clinton's affair with White House intern Monica Lewinsky, of course, stands in a category by itself. It rocked the nation and diverted our leaders' attention away from serious government matters. Investigation into Clinton's scandalous behavior also uncovered a history of coercive sexual advances to other women.

More recently, New York Governor Eliot Spitzer, a zealous crusader for moral rectitude in public life, was found to have been involved with a very high-priced 18-year-old call girl. David Paterson, who succeeded Spitzer as governor, almost immediately admitted to having had affairs, as did his wife.

Governor Mark Sanford of South Carolina shocked the nation with his bizarre story of walking the Appalachian Trail in order to gain some mental clarity. In fact, Sanford was in Buenos Aires with his Argentinian lover. Sanford's behavior shocked the nation as much for his abdication of responsibility—he failed to formally put his second in command in charge of running the state—as for the affair itself.

Vice Presidential candidate John Edwards' affair with videographer Rielle Hunter, and the daughter born of that affair, was noteworthy for Edwards' cowardice in denying both the affair and his paternity. That the affair took place while his late wife, Elizabeth, was struggling with breast cancer brought Edwards even harsher condemnation.

Of course, Tiger Woods' spectacular media meltdown has recently called attention to the sometimes glaring discrepancy between our public perceptions and the reality which underlies them. For years, Woods was the ultimate icon of sportsmanship and talent. This was particularly true for a man of mixed racial heritage playing in an historically white man's sport. It was eventually revealed that Woods had conducted affairs with approximately 120 women over a five-year period!

Sandra Bullock garnered much public sympathy when the media publicized her husband, Jesse James', affair with a tattoo model. Photos of a grim and tearful Bullock graced the covers of popular magazines for months. The revelation of the affair immediately after Bullock was awarded an Oscar contributed to even sharper criticism of James.

Categories of Affair Partners

As we've seen, not all affairs are the same. Some are one-time encounters, while others last for years. And the forces that drive affairs can vary as well. It's also impossible to paint the personality and the motivations of the Other Person with a single brush. While affairs are never justified, they can be complicated, as are the people who engage in them.

The Other Person could be anyone. She could be your husband's co-worker, a friend or neighbor, an acquaintance from the gym, someone who shares one of his hobbies, a fellow churchgoer, or even your sister. You may see her at company functions, or you may even interact with her on a routine basis, perhaps at PTA fundraisers.

On the other hand, she may be someone you've never met. Perhaps your husband met her in an online chat room, or even an adult dating website. They may have met on a "married but cheating" website, in which individuals claim they are looking for sex without complications (see Chapter 5). Or perhaps they met at a hotel bar, while your husband was relaxing after a day of meetings on a grueling business trip.

Websites utilize a wide range of acronyms or abbreviations to describe categories of people seeing others. One of the most common is m4w, or man seeking a woman. The list goes on from there to describe almost any combination of people of a range of sexual orientations and what they are looking for. "DD-free" means "drug and disease free" (no STDs), while "NSA" means "no strings attached." The person who places an NSA ad is looking for casual sex and is not interested in or not available for a relationship.

As you see, the Other Person can be anyone. The Other Person's motivations can vary, as well as the way they come into contact with your spouse. Affairs can start out when people have legitimate connections with each other. They may be co-workers, for instance, but they're careless about establishing boundaries in relationships. So a mixed male and female group of co-workers who routinely go out for drinks after work, or even just play on a coed sports team, could be setting themselves up for trouble in their marriages.

Is the Other Person Casual or Committed About Sex?

As you can see, people who engage in an affair with someone else's spouse can be almost anyone. Some people may be more likely than others, however, to do this. In Chapter 3, I talked about a traitlike characteristic called "sociosexuality." This refers to someone's willingness and comfort level with engaging in sex with someone they're not emotionally committed to. Someone who is "unrestricted" on the sociosexuality scale is much more likely to have casual, uncommitted sex without experiencing moral scruples or emotional distress about it.

At the other end of that spectrum, "restricted" people are those who truly can't imagine having sex with someone to whom they aren't firmly committed emotionally, and perhaps even married. It's not that they would never have a fleeting sexual fantasy about someone other than their spouse, for example, but they feel strongly that it's wrong and they make every attempt to banish such thoughts from their mind. Sexual and emotional fidelity tends to be a core value for these people.

Apparently there is a new trend in intimate relationships for some career-minded young women. A number of them are actually choosing to date married men because that arrangement fits better with their career aspirations. A married man is much less likely to have expectations that an extramarital relationship will lead to marriage. And a married man has a great deal to lose if his affair is discovered—for example, daily access to his children.

Kenneth was a prominent physician and medical researcher affiliated with a prestigious hospital. His work provided him with frequent opportunities to travel to conferences and meetings with other researchers. He thrived on interaction with other researchers in his field and meeting new people.

Kenneth described his sex life with his wife as "adequate, but nothing special." Over the years, he had had affairs with postdoctoral fellows who had worked with him on his research. In the lab, he had developed a reputation as a "player." He often engaged in casual liaisons when traveling on business, and even carried on steamy e-mail correspondence with women he met on planes and trains, sometimes making plans to meet them for sexual assignations. He had also had brief affairs with mothers of some of his children's friends.

When Kenneth came into therapy, I administered the revised Sociosexual Orientation Inventory. He received the highest score possible, indicating that he was indeed very unrestricted in his sociosexuality. The implications of this for his marriage and his work and personal relationships became a focal part of his therapy.

Does the Other Person Respect the Institution of Marriage?

The portrayal of affairs in the popular media in the past often centered on a man, his cold and rejecting wife, and a woman who was understanding and sympathetic. This relational "Bermuda Triangle" always spelled disaster, but the other woman might be portrayed either as filling an emotional and often sexual void in the man's life that his wife did not. Alternately, the other woman might have been portrayed as cold, calculating, and out to ensnare someone else's husband.

There is a new breed of woman that is very outspoken about its disdain for the institution of marriage. Judith Brandt, author of *The Fifty-Mile Rule: Your Guide to Infidelity and Extramarital Etiquette* (Berkley, 2002), exemplifies this attitude toward matrimony. She equates marriage and family with boredom and entrapment and openly advocates affairs, as long as they are conducted by a certain set of rules.

Her "fifty-mile rule" refers to having an affair only with someone who lives more than 50 miles from your home. The purpose, of course, is to minimize the likelihood that your affair partner will cross paths with your spouse—and you—when you're not intentionally spending time together.

In addition to reducing the chances of being caught in an affair by your spouse, the 50-mile radius, Brandt argues, can also help keep your lover's expectations for the affair in check. If you live that far apart, it won't be realistic for you to stop by her house after work every evening. Brandt also recommends that you share as little information as possible with your affair partner about your personal and your professional life. The less your lover knows about you, the safer you are.

This type of arrangement, which is primarily about sexual rather than emotional satisfaction, operates by a certain set of "rules," so as not to interfere with a marriage or other primary relationship. By its very nature, however, it displays a lack of respect for the lover's partner and for the institution of marriage itself. It is designed solely for the gratification of the cheating partner and the affair partner. Assumptions that underlie this type of relationship are "What he doesn't know can't hurt him"; "It's okay to steal from someone else in order to gratify my own wants"; and "Secrets between spouses are okay."

Does the Other Person Engage in "Mate Poaching"?

This term was coined by psychologist David Buss to describe the behavior of attempting to attract someone who is already in a committed relationship. Mate poaching turns out to be alarmingly common, with over 60 percent of men and 40 percent of women admitting that they've attempted to seduce someone's significant other strictly for a short-term fling. And equally surprising is the fact that approximately one in five long-term relationships begins with poaching.

The Evolution of Mate Poaching

misc. Evolutionary psychologists view human behavior in terms of the adaptive purposes it has served over the millennia. For women, mate poaching is seen as securing a partner with resources to care for her and her off-spring. After all, he has demonstrated that he is able to attract another woman. Men, on the other hand, are attracted by physical attractiveness, which is thought to correlate roughly with fertility.

We've probably all known people who have mate poached, have been the object of a poacher's attentions, or perhaps have even poached someone ourselves. Researchers have found that certain personality characteristics tend to be associated both with poaching behavior and with receptiveness to poaching. These characteristics include openness to new experiences, sexual attractiveness, and a strong interest in sex. One of the researchers in this area notes that it is a "slippery slope" when you get two people together who are willing to discuss their sexual feelings and desires.

While the form of infidelity known as mate poaching does occasionally result in a long-term committed relationship, it more often results in other, darker consequences, sometimes even blackmail. More than one married man has been horrified when his casual romp with a young woman who approached him at a bar is followed up with a very compromising photo mailed to his office, with a price attached for not mailing a copy to his home address.

Serial mate poachers are generally not interested in a long-term relationship with the object of their seduction tactics. It is generally more about repeatedly proving one's sexual desirability. In the case where the spouse or partner of the poached individual is known, it also tends to be about rivalry. For instance, a single woman who feels competitive with a female co-worker may actually set out to seduce her husband. She may recognize him from a picture on the co-worker's desk and may poach him at a bar that he occasionally frequents on his way home from work.

Why Do They Do It?

We've seen that the Other Person can be almost anyone and that their motivation for an affair can vary widely. Some affairs do start fairly innocently, without the intention of engaging in an affair. However, it's important always to remember that the participants in an affair make a series of choices along the way that eventually culminate in the affair.

We've looked at the concepts of sociosexuality and mate poaching, which can help explain how some affairs start and why some people are more prone than others to engage in illicit relationships. But are there other personal factors that also help us understand this destructive behavior? Perhaps.

For both men and women, competitiveness may play a role in choosing to engage in an affair. When you have an affair, you are essentially stealing from someone else. You are stealing affection, time, and resources from the spouse of your lover. After all, he can't be with you and his wife at the same time. Every moment that he chooses to spend with you is a moment he (and you) are stealing from his wife and family. And, more importantly, the emotional energy he invests in an affair is love and affection that is drained from his marriage.

For some affair partners, this diversion of emotional and tangible resources from someone who is legally and morally entitled to them can feel like a victory. But the question is, a victory over whom? Occasionally, we can find at least part of the answer by looking at events in someone's childhood.

For example, a young girl who was jealous of the attention her father paid her mother or a female sibling may grow up to be a woman who takes great satisfaction in luring a man away from his wife, if only temporarily. A boy who is constantly in competition with his older brother, but never feels that he measures up, may grow up to be a man who feels a sense of victory when he entices another man's wife into infidelity.

MISC.

Casanova Complex

The "Casanova Complex" is a term coined after the life of Giacomo Girolamo Casanova de Seingalt, a Venetian who became notorious for his amorous adventures. He wrote his memoirs and discussed extensively the art of seduction. In contemporary usage, it refers to sexual compulsion in a man.

Is It Worth It?

There's no doubt that the start of an affair is filled with the rush of sexual and emotional exhilaration. There's a saying that "new sex is good sex," and novelty certainly is a powerful aphrodisiac, especially for men. If the affair has a strong emotional component, women, in particular, find the relationship rewarding.

However, if the affair goes on for any length of time, it becomes a sort of shadow marriage, but without the benefits of a legitimate marriage. Affair partners begin to disappoint each other in ways both large and small. You may discover that your lover's table manners aren't the best, for instance. It may turn out that, after the two of you have had sex, he wants to turn over and go to sleep, or he rushes out the door to head home. You desperately wish he'd spend at least a few minutes just talking with you.

Perhaps he's been promising you he's going to divorce his wife, but needs to wait until "the time is right." You try to be patient and understanding. But after months—or years—have passed and nothing has happened, your patience has worn thin. Frankly, you no longer believe he has any intention of divorcing his wife. This leaves you with an agonizing dilemma. Do you stay in the relationship, hoping he'll eventually make good on his promise? Or do you end the affair and hope to find someone who is free to commit to you?

The life of the Other Person can be quite lonely as well. There are times when your lover will be away on vacation with his family. He may not be able to contact you at all, or there may be a few very brief calls or text messages. It's a given that he'll spend holidays with his family. Sure, he may dash by your house or apartment to drop off a Christmas gift, but he won't be able to stay and enjoy the nice fire you've made or the Christmas cookies you baked for him. He'll be expected at home, and, if he lingers with you, he'll have some explaining to do.

Valentine's Day is the one holiday when a philandering spouse is likely to make at least some time for his or her affair partner. Otherwise, there will be the proverbial hell to pay. Of course, a wife is probably expecting special treatment on that day, too, so a husband is required to do his best to juggle the two. Interestingly, the days before and after Valentine's Day are also the busiest for private detectives, as they are prime time for a suspicious husband or wife to catch a cheating spouse in the act.

The Other Person lives in a state of limbo. It's hard to make plans with family or friends, because, you never know, your lover might have a few minutes to stop by. And when you make plans with him or her, you never know when some family "emergency" will arise that will cause him or her to cancel at the last moment. Your time is not your own.

Many affair couples are understandably reluctant to go out in public. So they must entertain themselves at home. The charm and coziness of this arrangement can wear off rapidly, with the unmarried affair partner soon feeling smothered and devalued personally, as if she's not worthy of being wined and dined. Resentment can quickly build to a boiling point.

In my clinical work, I have rarely encountered anyone who, looking back, said, "I'm so glad I had an affair." There is a fairly predictable life span of a typical affair, which combines both emotional and sexual elements:

- The affair begins with infatuation and exhilaration. You are obsessed with the Other Person and can't wait to be with them again.

- As the affair develops, the two of you begin establishing the routine of your affair, whether it's that you meet at predictable times and places, or you snatch a few moments together whenever you can.

- Expectations, generally unspoken, for each other and the affair develop. Examples include: "You will take me out to dinner before we go back to my apartment and have sex," "You are never to call me at home or on the weekend," "I expect this relationship to end in marriage," or "Don't expect this relationship to go anywhere; it's just an affair."

- Over a period of time, affair partners—just like spouses—begin to irritate and disappoint each other. An affair, in this sense, begins to be a "shadow marriage."

- The affair eventually stops working for at least one of the partners. It stops providing the emotional and sexual exhilaration that it did in the beginning. You may begin to think that the solution to your disappointment is to start another affair, sometimes even before ending the current one.

Guilt and Empathy for Your Lover's Spouse

Some individuals are so narcissistic that they, on an unconscious level at least, feel entitled to whatever they want, including someone else's husband or wife. They may not be interested in a committed relationship with that person, but they want the short-term excitement of an affair. Most Other People, however, have at least some mixed feelings about interfering in someone else's marriage.

Initially, they may feel that the affair is somewhat justified, because their lover's spouse doesn't understand them or doesn't treat them with sufficient love and respect. Over time, however, it's common for the Other Person to begin to wonder if the betrayed person is really so dreadful. After all, if she were, why would her husband stay with her?

This point can be brought home in particularly dramatic fashion when, for example, a spouse and an affair partner meet at a company function. Take the example of an annual holiday party. It may be impossible to keep the Other Person and one's spouse from running into each other, and some sort of introduction must be made. To the cheating spouse's dismay, they strike up what appears to be a very pleasant conversation. The next time the spouse and the Other Person are together, she says to him, "Your wife is nothing like you described her. She actually seems very nice. We had a great conversation. If I weren't sleeping with you, I think we could be good friends."

In this type of situation, the Other Person may not only become wracked with guilt over what she is taking away from this other woman, but may also begin to feel quite a bit of empathy for her. She puts herself mentally and emotionally in the place of a woman who is being deceived by her husband. It becomes more and more difficult for her to continue with the affair.

Another consequence of learning about the betrayed spouse directly is that the Other Person now has firsthand information of her. She has made her own observations and formed her own impressions, which may vary considerably from what her lover has told her about his wife. She now feels that she is unable to trust what he tells her. Either he is very misguided and doesn't even know his own wife well, or he has been misleading her for his own selfish reasons. Either way, she may again doubt whether she wants to continue the affair.

Your Reactions to the Other Person

When you discover that your spouse has had or is having an affair, it's an almost reflexive reaction to compare yourself to the Other Person. If you don't already know her, you can't help but wonder if she's more attractive, more physically fit, more understanding, or more fun to be around. In other words, you engage in some serious social comparison to determine how you stack up. There is ample anecdotal evidence that the Other Person is rarely significantly more attractive than the spouse, if at all.

Jealousy, of course, is an entirely natural reaction when you discover your spouse's affair. Someone has, in effect, stolen what is rightfully yours, both morally and legally. Social psychologists distinguish between two types of jealousy, reactive jealousy and trait or suspicious jealousy. When talking about infidelity, the distinction is important.

Reactive jealousy refers to our jealous feelings when we've actually been betrayed. Our spouse has done something that actually violated our expectations for our relationship. If your husband masturbates to online porn, but has a poor sex life with you, you might feel jealous of the women in the photos and videos that he watches. If he has a one-night fling with someone, even though he protests that it was "just sex" and it meant nothing to him, you will likely experience jealousy. He has, after all, violated your wedding vows.

A legal action in which a third party is sued by a deserted spouse for actions that brought about the end of the marriage is referred to as "alienation of affection." There does not have to be adulterous sex, or even the intention to destroy the marriage, but simply engaging in actions that the defendant should have foreseen could destroy the marriage. This legal action has been abolished in all but eight states. In March 2010, North Carolina awarded one plaintiff $9 million in her alienation of affection suit against her husband's mistress.

While reactive jealousy is about an actual behavior that you find threatening, suspicious or trait jealousy is about the person who feels it. This refers to a personality tendency to see a threat to your relationship where there probably is none. For example, if your husband is an ob-gyn by profession, and you spend significant time worrying about him seeing women's bodies all day, you are likely experiencing suspicious jealousy.

Suspicious jealousy has been linked to other personality characteristics, such as low self-esteem, insecurity, and anxiety about close relationships. While it does not cause a spouse's affair, it can be damaging to a relationship. The husband or wife of a person with suspicious jealousy may feel that there's nothing he or she can do to demonstrate that he or she is being faithful, or that there is no external threat to the marriage.

Essential Takeaways

- Hollywood and other popular media have routinely portrayed the "other woman" as either a sympathetic figure or as a scheming "homewrecker."

- The news has been filled in recent years with sensational stories of high-profile politicians, entertainers, and athletes and their mistresses.

- While affairs are motivated by a range of factors, the Other Person may have been extremely competitive for an opposite-sex parent's attention, or may have felt he had to win at all costs against an older brother or other boys.

- The life of the Other Person is often lonely and isolated, with most of her lover's attention still going to his family.

- Jealousy is a natural response to an actual threat to your marriage. If you are chronically jealous, even in the absence of evidence of such a threat, however, you may want to consider working with a mental health professional to understand the source of your fears and to overcome them.

chapter 5

The Lure of the Internet

How the Internet can have profoundly positive or negative effects on intimate relationships

How the Internet provides a convenient and private way for people to meet for adulterous activity

The staggering range of sexual sites and opportunities on the Internet

How apparently harmless social networking sites can be hazardous to your marriage

The Internet. In recent decades, we've witnessed staggering advances in the ways that technology enables us to access information and to connect with each other. Cell phones and the Internet top the list.

In this chapter, I look at the darker side of the Internet, including pornography, chat rooms, and dating sites specifically for married people. You also see that even so-called innocent sites, like social networking sites, can be damaging to your marriage.

It's a Fact of Life

There's no escaping the Internet. In this society, it's a fact of life for almost everyone. Our children have been raised with it. Older Americans are embracing the Internet and its possibilities as well. Research indicates that those 55 years of age and older account for most of the growth in Internet usage.

Computer ownership is growing worldwide, but Americans still far exceed the rest of the world. According to a recent study, more than three quarters of us own a computer. And when you take into account educational level and income, that percentage increases. Ninety-eight percent of households with an annual income of $75,000 or more own at least one computer.

Many of us rely heavily on the Internet in doing our jobs. For example, when researching a topic in the field of psychology, I often begin with an online search. I also use the Internet to access professional journals and scholarly articles. While the next step in the process may be to check my home library, order a book, or visit a university library, an online search is a good first step and puts me in touch with a vast array of resources.

Tried and True

The next time you visit your doctor's office or have to go to the hospital, pay attention to whether doctors and nurses take notes by hand or whether they type them directly into a laptop. More and more medical practitioners are bypassing handwritten notes about their patients and typing data directly into a computer. Electronic recordkeeping is the wave of the future.

The Internet Is Accessible, Affordable, and Anonymous

Aside from being so readily available, the Internet has several characteristics that make it highly appealing. As mentioned previously, computers are everywhere. The majority of American homes own at least one computer. And by 2005, almost 100 percent of public schools had Internet access, regardless of whether they were rural or urban, or in high- or low-wealth districts. The same is true for public libraries, with virtually all of them offering free access to the Internet. The bottom line, then, is that almost all Americans have ready access to the Internet these days.

The cost of accessing the Internet varies depending on whether you're using dial-up, DSL, cable, or fiber optic services. But if speed isn't critical, you can be online for as little as about $10 per month. This makes Internet services affordable for most Americans. And when that amount is not within your budget, again, you can almost certainly get online at your local public library.

One of the most compelling characteristics of the Internet is the anonymity which it appears to offer users. It's possible to pose as a 16-year-old high school boy, when in fact you're a 54-year-old married man. And while absolute anonymity is not guaranteed, there are products designed to hide or disguise your identity. But a word of warning is in order here. You should never assume that your Internet activities can't be traced back to you.

Heartaches

The newspapers are full of stories of men caught in Internet sex sting operations, including attorneys, clergy, and doctors. These people all thought they were about to meet an underage person for sex. What they learned the hard way was that they had been communicating online with an undercover detective.

There's Something for Everyone on the Internet

Anyone who has spent any time surfing the web knows that there is virtually no topic that isn't addressed. That's one of the features that makes the Internet so useful to millions of adults and students. It's a quick starting point for research on almost any topic. And it provides access to the opinions of others, to shopping, and to entertainment.

Take holiday shopping, for example. The Monday after Thanksgiving is known as "Cyber Monday," and it marks the beginning of the online holiday shopping season. Revenue from Internet sales during the holidays increases steadily year after year. Shopping online, whether during the holidays or the rest of the year, is extremely convenient and shoppers have become much more comfortable dealing with online merchants than they were just a few years ago.

Of course, one of the major offerings of the Internet is sexually oriented content. This can refer to outright pornographic sites, adult-oriented "dating" sites, or sites for married individuals looking for affairs. While attempts to put a number on Internet sex traffic are notoriously difficult, it has been estimated that sexual sites are the most popular destination on the web and that 266 new porn sites go online every day.

Misc.

Pornography in the Workplace

Securities and Exchange employees recently made the news for attempting to access pornographic websites on company computers. One employee was charged with more than 1,800 attempts to view porn during a 17-day period. A Washington, D.C., Child and Family Services worker was recently fired for logging on to porn sites at a rate of one every 2.5 seconds. Lost hours of productivity and damage to company resources (for example, computer viruses) are difficult to calculate.

The Web as an Illicit Meeting Place

So what exactly does infidelity on the Internet look like? There are a variety of categories of online behavior that can jeopardize your marriage. Just as the Internet allows us to communicate with family, friends, and co-workers, it also makes it possible for us to contact an almost unlimited number of people, all around the world, for all sorts of reasons. And finally, it allows us access to sexual images, sounds, and text in very private ways.

Tried and True

While your spouse's online communication can be a clue to infidelity, don't ignore his or her cell phone activity. Because they are so small and portable—and because spouses generally don't share a cell phone—cell phones offer a very easy way for your spouse to stay in touch with an affair partner anywhere and anytime.

One area that bears especially close scrutiny when talking about the Internet and infidelity is communication. This includes e-mail, instant messaging, and chat. In my clinical practice, I regularly see distraught husbands and wives who have discovered inappropriate e-mails between their spouses and other people, often a co-worker. Or perhaps they've become suspicious for some other reason and have then begun checking their spouse's e-mails. In either case, what they discover in those exchanges can be devastating.

Instant messaging can allow you to communicate immediately, unlike e-mail, in which you and your correspondent may be online at different times and must wait for a response. With IM, when someone is online, a message goes out either to an individual or to an approved group of users, who may then communicate with each other in real time.

In years past, these messages used to consist simply of text. Now, however, they allow people to share video and voice as well. So your spouse can now, with the aid of a webcam, be sending and receiving sexually explicit voice and video from a friend or co-worker, for example.

Tried and True	As always, changes in your spouse's behavior are something to watch for. For example, if your spouse starts staying up much later than usual to use the computer while you go to bed, or he or she's getting up early to take care of "work e-mail," you need to be alert and look into what's really going on.

Chat Rooms, Forums, and Newsgroups

Chat rooms are online sites or locations in which participants can exchange ideas in real time, generally on a specified topic, such as infidelity, for example. The messages appear to others as soon as they are typed. A forum differs from a chat room in that the messages don't necessarily appear immediately. They may also need to be approved by a moderator. In a forum, it is also possible to send a private message, or PM, to one or more other members. Similar to a forum, a newsgroup consists of a group of people interested in communicating on a single topic. Alt. newsgroups (alternative) are a large, but often controversial, group of newsgroups that are frequently unregulated by a moderator. As such, they may contain content that is highly objectionable to many people (for example, extreme *sadomasochism*).

Sadomasochism is a term that is used clinically to refer to experiencing sexual pleasure either through inflicting pain (sadism) or receiving pain (masochism). The term is also used in popular culture to advertise to potential sexual partners what someone's preferences are. While many couples enjoy engaging in mild acts of sadomasochism, extreme practices, like sexual asphyxiation, can lead to injury or even death.

As you can see, the Internet hosts a vast array of opportunities for people to connect with strangers. Some of these communications start out innocently enough, with merely a shared interest in a topic like motorcycling, or the sexual oppression of women during the Victorian era.

But as people continue to communicate with each other, it's very possible that they will begin sharing some personal information with each other. They may begin talking about their families and their spouses, for example. This can lead to sharing areas of dissatisfaction about their partners. When this happens, a connection unrelated to the topic at hand begins to form. A boundary is crossed in the relationship and the potential for infidelity increases.

Tried and True

If you and your spouse have always shared a computer and he suggests that you now have separate computers, you should be clear on what his reasons are. Or let's say you've shared a computer and never had separate passwords, but he now wants one. You should be wondering why he's now concerned about you having access to his e-mail and other online activities.

It's Not Real, It's Just Virtual

Some people question whether there's really harm in online sexual activity. Is viewing porn or engaging in suggestive chat really dangerous? A well-known radio psychologist once said that, if no body fluids are exchanged, there's no affair. I take strong exception to that position, as I daily see the disruption to a marriage that inappropriate online behavior causes.

When couples come in for help with their marriage, I have rarely seen cases in which they strongly disagree over whether the online behavior was inappropriate. The cheating spouse may downplay the emotional significance of her behavior. She may claim, in her defense, "I didn't love him, it was just sex." But both spouses generally acknowledge that something inappropriate has occurred.

When people aren't sure if their behavior—either online, in the workplace, or in a social setting—is inappropriate, I encourage them to ask themselves a few key questions. *How would I feel if my spouse were here right now? Would I feel nervous or guilty about the way I'm interacting with someone?* If the answer to those questions is yes, then they're probably violating the boundary of their marital relationship. This applies to online behavior as well. If your spouse were to "shoulder surf" when you're online, would you be embarrassed or anxious about what he or she would see and what you are doing?

The Internet's Guidelines for Cheating

Given the wealth of affair-oriented material on the Internet, it probably comes as no surprise that tips for having a successful affair are also offered on the web. "Successful," in this context, most often means "undiscovered." The following are some of the hints for conducting an affair:

- Have realistic expectations about how much time and money you have to spend on an affair.

- Expect to become disillusioned with your affair partner at some point, just as you have with your spouse.

- Don't start another affair before ending your first one.

- Have an affair with someone who is married. He or she has more to lose than a single person.

- There is a great deal of specific information on how to use your computer so that you don't get caught communicating with your affair partner.

- Be convincing when you lie to your spouse. Stick to your usual routines and behaviors, and don't offer long, convoluted explanations for being late, for example.

- Know ahead of time that the affair will end and that it will likely be uncomfortable for both you and your affair partner.

Just as the Internet offers plenty of advice for would-be cheaters, it also offers a wealth of tips to help suspicious spouses catch them. These include behavioral signs to watch for, as well as an array of technological devices you can buy to catch your spouse in the act, such as a GPS on her cell phone, software that tracks all messages sent by her computer, and online banking software.

Cheating Is Big Business

Infidelity is both profitable and costly. Humans have always been willing to spend big money on sex, and nothing has changed in that regard. I'll discuss online pornography, dating sites, and "married but cheating" dating sites, in order to assess their financial impact.

What about online porn? Does your spouse viewing it constitute infidelity? People are divided over the answer to this. Many wives choose to overlook it as relatively harmless behavior. They become concerned only if a spouse wants to engage in masturbation rather than intercourse most of the time, or if he's neglecting other areas of his home and work life.

Some wives consider online porn to be cheating after they discover how much of a family's income their husbands have spent on it. A subscription to a single porn site can run $30 or more per month. It's not uncommon to hear stories of men racking up thousands of dollars a year in credit card bills for access to multiple porn sites, thereby jeopardizing their families' financial well-being.

Online porn is definitely big business. Consider a few numbers. Research shows that, every second, 28,258 Internet users are viewing pornography. Every second, $3,075.64 is spent on online porn. And how profitable is pornography? It reportedly brings in more revenue than Google, Microsoft, Apple, Yahoo!, eBay, Amazon, and Netflix combined.

While adulterous relationships are generally conducted in private, make no mistake that there is considerable money to be made from infidelity. An affair can be very expensive. One woman poured her heart out and said that, after examining her husband's credit card and bank statements, she discovered he had spent over $60,000 for hotels, expensive restaurants, Broadway shows, rental cars, and gifts for his lover, over a two-year period.

Cheating isn't cheap. Whether it's compulsive viewing of online porn or having a physical affair, no one is giving anything away. In spite of enticements to the contrary, access to online porn will eventually cost you something. And affair partners generally expect you to take them to lunch or dinner, pay for a hotel, buy the occasional gift, and so on. Make no mistake—infidelity will hit your wallet hard.

Adult Dating Websites

Internet dating has become a major vehicle for meeting potential romantic partners. While it's not without cost—you pay a subscription fee and must devote time to reviewing your potential matches—it's an easy way to connect with people from all backgrounds and all parts of the globe. Many satisfying relationships and marriages have resulted from contacts made on these sites.

Many of my clients, however, are shocked to learn about the vast number of Internet resources available to someone who is married but interested in having an affair. A search of "married cheaters websites" will, sadly, reveal quite a few of these. Looking at these websites can make you feel like you've entered a parallel universe, one in which people aren't willing to give up their marriages, but in which they want and feel entitled to "something on the side."

The sites vary in several ways. One of these is the amount of emotional involvement a cheating partner is willing to invest in an affair. There are numerous sites that exist primarily for sexual hookups. A word of warning is in order here. Adult dating sites don't blatantly market themselves to married individuals. However, they are very frequently used by a spouse who is motivated to cheat, as marital status is impossible to verify online. They must rely on the honesty of the user when responding to questions about marital status.

These sites may boast about their membership and about the range of sexual opportunities they can provide. Generally, they emphasize that their members are "hot and horny" and that the site provides opportunities for sexual hookups with no strings attached. They may offer member "testimonials" about how easy it was to find a partner for fabulous sexual hookups. Other sites operate as a virtual "personal ad." Users can search for—and specify—what sort of sexual encounter they're looking for: male looking for female, female looking for couple, etc. One of these sites became embroiled in a scandal involving murder a few years ago and subsequently made changes to content that may be posted on the site. Its personals, however, are still a popular way to find partners for casual sex.

Sex for Financial Security Sites

There is a category of adult website that emphasizes sexual favors in return for financial favors or security. These sites are sometimes referred to as "sugar baby" and "sugar daddy" sites, depending on whether a woman or a man is placing the ad. Women offering themselves as sugar babies are generally young and attractive and must provide photographic evidence of this, or even an interview with the agency, to substantiate that the photograph is accurate.

The sugar daddy is generally a man who is financially secure or even affluent and has income to spend on a sugar baby. Some sites make a point of telling readers that they verify the sugar daddy's income, financial status, and even profession. Without a means of verifying marital status, however, the potential for using the sites to establish extramarital affairs clearly exists. It's not hard to imagine that a young attractive woman looking for financial security might utilize a sugar baby/sugar daddy site. A relationship developing out of this arrangement could potentially disrupt a husband's marriage.

Married but Cheating Websites

There is another category of adult website that specifically targets individuals who are married but looking for an affair. Some of these sites are fairly blatant in their pro-affair attitude, with billboard and TV advertising campaigns. For example, one site states that "Life is short. Have an affair." This site's advertising campaigns have also purportedly included so-called "banned" Super Bowl ads for two years in a row, as well as TV spots that harshly condemn the company. The buzz is that the company actually sponsored the critical ads, as it was yet another means of drawing attention to the website.

As you can see, married cheating sites are serious about cheating. Serious because there's lots of money to be made in hooking up two individuals who are looking for an extramarital relationship. For $249, one site will "guarantee" that you'll have an affair. But a look at the fine print of the guarantee reveals that you must adhere to a stringent set of rules, including responding to a specified set of inquiries per month, sending a certain number of "gifts" per month, and instant messaging with other service members for at least one hour per month.

The founder of a major married cheating website argues that cheating can actually help keep couples together. He contends that monogamy is unnatural—that it's a prescription for boredom and estrangement from our spouse. He says he regularly gets feedback from his customers that cheating saved their marriage.

Social Networking Sites

Social networking sites, such as Facebook and MySpace, are also a fact of modern life. Facebook has grown exponentially to over 300 million members, and MySpace is approximately half that size. Many of our children—and many of us as well—use them throughout the day and the evening and can't imagine living without them.

These sites keep us connected to family, friends, and co-workers in easy and convenient ways. They provide us with entertainment. Sometimes they introduce us to prospective employers and job opportunities. That's the good news.

With just a few clicks, you can be searching to see if your co-workers or friends are on Facebook. By typing in just a few words, such as your hometown or the name of a sports team you were on, for example, you can be on your way to locating former classmates, boyfriends, or girlfriends, or cultivating new online relationships.

The dark side of social networking is the opportunity it presents to cultivate relationships that can potentially undermine your marriage. It's rare that a week goes by that I don't hear from a patient about the damage done to their marriage by a relationship begun on Facebook or a similar site.

Heartaches

It is estimated that affairs begun on Facebook and other networking sites account for one in five divorces. One therapist wryly comments that Facebook- and MySpace-related problems account for a significant portion of his income.

Reconnection Sites

Sites like Classmates.com are targeted to people interested in locating former school acquaintances. We all leave high school with that "yearbook" image burned into our brains. Subconsciously, our classmates haven't aged. That's part of the appeal of class reunions—to see whether that blonde cheerleader is still cute and perky. But after three kids and two divorces, she may not be. And what about the guy voted "most likely to succeed"? Has he indeed gone on to become CEO of a corporation? Or has he gotten caught in a couple of corporate downsizings, and begun self-medicating with alcohol, and is a few months behind in his child-support payments?

For many of us, high school is a time of emotional intensity. We're in the process of breaking away from our parents and their household rules and regulations. It's also a time of firsts—first love, first heartache, and first sexual experience, for many.

First Experiences

Psychological research confirms the power of first experiences. In addition to the emotional intensity of these events, the sheer novelty of them can actually alter our brain chemistry. While the rest of our lives are filled with experiences good and bad, it's the "firsts" that are so compelling.

MyLife.com is the new kid on the block in reconnection sites. It launched in February 2009 as an amalgam of Reunion.com and Wink. It bills itself as the world's first single source for searching for people. It obtains your information by searching approximately 60 other social sites.

MyLife's TV ads appeal to curiosity (and perhaps a bit of vanity) by showing an attractive young brunette curled up with her laptop and musing, "I wonder who's searching for me?" Other ads show the same woman exclaiming with delight, "Seven people are searching for me!" She wonders if one of them might be an old boyfriend. MyLife emphasizes the breadth of groups of people it can put you in touch with, including religious congregations.

Common threads in these reconnection sites are nostalgia and curiosity. It's tempting to draw stark contrasts between the complexities and challenges of our lives today with what, in hindsight, feels like our carefree past. High school or college may feel like "the good old days." What is easy to lose sight of is that, for many of us, high school was in fact not all that carefree. We had serious concerns about our identity, appearance, family relationships, sexuality, and our futures.

Are These Sites Marriage-Friendly?

While the married cheating sites are clearly in favor of affairs and make their money from linking people looking for affairs with each other, the same is not true of the reconnection sites. They play strongly on our curiosity about former friends and love interests, and in some cases, co-workers, fellow church members, etc. They also bring us back to our teen years, for most of us a time of self-discovery and ever-increasing independence from our families.

By itself, this curiosity about past acquaintances should be harmless. The simple desire to know how life has turned out for people who were an important part of our past is understandable. But that desire to know may not, in fact, be all that simple. It may be tinged with the desire to know whether someone still thinks of us, or perhaps still harbors fond feelings for us.

A problem can also arise when we attempt to integrate these past relationships—or new ones—into our present lives. Making contact on a social networking site is one thing, but building a new relationship by communicating on an ongoing basis is another. Without giving it much thought, we may actually be picking up a relationship where it left off. That guy who sat next to you in geometry class and flirted with you the whole year may begin his new connection with you in a flirtatious way. If you respond, it can feel very threatening to your spouse and your marriage.

For most of us, graduating from high school or college marks a transition to a new life, including new relationships. Assimilating past significant relationships into a marriage, for example, can be tricky, if not downright destructive. For example, if a high school boyfriend locates you on Facebook, you may be curious about his life and flattered that he remembers you. You also may be interested in corresponding with him at regular intervals. But how do you think your husband is likely to feel about this renewed connection?

Heartaches

It's fine to enjoy connecting with family and friends on social networking sites. But be careful about responding to inquiries from old sweethearts. The powerful feelings generated by these youthful romances can be hazardous to your marriage. It's probably best to not respond to these communications.

So while social networking sites can be fun and entertaining and can provide easy ways to connect with friends and family, the potential for marital harm is real. Reconnecting with old flames, or cultivating new relationships that become increasingly personal in tone, can threaten your marriage. Use them with care, and be open with your spouse about who you're in touch with.

Essential Takeaways

- The Internet offers vast opportunities to explore the world around us, but it also offers unprecedented opportunities for inappropriate sexual activity.

- Certain characteristics of the Internet make it a prime means by which to conduct an affair. It's easily accessible, it's relatively inexpensive, and—depending on how careful you are—you may be able to remain anonymous.

- In addition to pornography and adult dating websites, there are multiple websites devoted to promoting affairs between married individuals.

- The Internet offers both tips for conducting an affair as well as tips for catching a cheating spouse.

- Social networking sites may be entertaining and emotionally gratifying, but it's important to establish strong boundaries between online relationships and our primary relationships.

Part 2

The Experience of Betrayal

In this part, I look at what it's like to discover that your spouse has been unfaithful. I start with some of the signs that your husband or wife may be cheating—signs that are hard to ignore. However, it's important not to jump to conclusions. Be aware that there may be another explanation for any out-of-the-ordinary behavior on your spouse's part. Be prepared to have a frank discussion about this. You may also consider hiring a professional to confirm your suspicions. I discuss the pros and cons of this alternative and encourage you to clearly think through what you would do with evidence that your spouse is having an affair.

If you feel you have sufficient evidence to confront your partner, you need to plan the meeting and prepare yourself emotionally. This part discusses how to use the evidence you've collected to confront your spouse about the affair. This will be a highly emotional event for both of you, so I also talk about how to deal with the emotional aftershocks. You will likely experience a wide range of emotions, but nearly everyone who discovers a spouse's infidelity describes their initial reaction as "devastation."

chapter 6

Is Your Spouse Cheating?

Confirming your suspicions

Recognizing the warning signs of infidelity

Acknowledging changes in habit

Being in denial about infidelity

Living a lie

In this chapter, I deal with those nagging feelings you have that your spouse might be having an affair. You learn to identify some of the telltale signs. You learn to look for changes in your spouse's typical patterns of behavior. Sometimes, however, there is an innocent explanation for changes in your spouse's behavior, and you need to consider alternative explanations.

People react differently when they suspect their spouse is involved with someone else. Some immediately confront a spouse whose behavior is suspicious. Others wait until they have accumulated sufficient evidence to present to the cheating spouse. I deal with the process of confrontation in Chapter 7.

Some people choose to act as if the affair isn't happening. They might even be able to convince themselves that everything is just fine. In other words, they're in denial about it. A variant of this is a "don't ask, don't tell" approach, which is discussed later in this chapter. In this scenario, you and your cheating spouse have an unspoken agreement to not discuss the affair, which you both know is happening.

How Do You Know Whether Your Spouse Is Cheating?

Unless your husband or wife comes to you and confesses an affair, how do you know whether he or she is involved with someone else? This is a question that, unfortunately, plagues many of us. It's not uncommon for me to hear in a therapy session, "I don't have any proof, but I think my husband is having an affair. Something just doesn't feel right. He seems different."

The answer can come in the form of undeniable evidence of an affair, or it may be much more subtle. There may simply be an accumulation of things that don't add up, that don't make sense. I work with my clients to clearly identify the behaviors that are worrisome to them and then to explore the meaning and significance of those behaviors.

There can be a whole host of things that suggest your spouse may be involved with someone else. Let's start with some of the most flagrant examples. You come home unexpectedly for lunch one day and find your wife in bed with another man. That's undeniable evidence of a sexual affair. Or you stop by your spouse's office to surprise him with lunch and find him and his secretary in the copy room, arms around each other's waist. That kind of behavior also defies any innocent explanation.

Of course, discovering your partner in a sexual act with someone else is an extreme example of indications that he or she is involved in an affair. For most of us, the signs are not so blatant. But there are more subtle cues we can pick up on, which suggest that something isn't right.

Ever hear the expression *in flagrante delicto?* Its literal meaning is "in a blazing offense." In everyday speech, it means "caught in the act." When you hear the expression today, whether in a courtroom or in the media, it usually refers to a couple caught in the act of sexual intercourse.

Admit Your Suspicions

Something doesn't feel right in your marriage. Right now, you don't have anything specific to go on, but your gut tells you that something's different in the relationship. Your spouse hasn't said anything, but he or she doesn't seem quite like his or her old self these days.

The first thing to do is to spend some time analyzing the situation. What exactly feels different or "off"? It may even help to make a list for yourself of things you observe that cause your infidelity radar to go into overdrive. This list may potentially be useful later if you must confront your spouse about his or her involvement in an affair.

Another factor you should consider is the history of your marriage. Have you been prone, over the years, to perceive threats to the relationship where they really didn't exist? If so, you'll want to take another look at your suspicions to see whether you might be overreacting to something in your environment. It's important to be honest with yourself when doing this self-assessment. If it's hard for you to objectively scrutinize yourself, then perhaps a trusted friend or a mental health professional can help you with this process.

If you generally tend to be a fairly trusting and easygoing person, you'll want to pay close attention to behaviors that suggest your spouse is having an affair. You don't want to overreact, but you do want to be alert and attentive to the danger signals. This can save you heartache down the road.

Warning Signs of Infidelity

What are some of the cues signaling your spouse may be cheating? They tend to fall into three closely related categories: artifacts, behaviors, and habits. Artifacts are items that may indicate your spouse is unfaithful. Behaviors are what you observe your spouse doing that suggests infidelity.

And habits are an accumulation of behaviors over time that form a pattern.

Artifacts include a wide variety of things. Here are some examples of things or items that might raise your suspicions:

- A receipt for dinner at an expensive restaurant on a night when your husband said he stayed late at the office
- A second cell phone, which your wife keeps in the glove compartment of her car
- Gift-wrapped lingerie, which you stumble across in your husband's closet, but which you never receive
- A Christmas or birthday gift to your spouse—for example, a watch or a sweater—from someone you don't know or have never heard of
- An earring you don't recognize in the pocket of your husband's sports jacket
- Credit card statements and cell phone bills with unexplained charges and calls to numbers you don't recognize
- A stash of condoms in the glove compartment of your spouse's car

As you can see, the list of artifacts is potentially infinite. Anything your spouse doesn't have a reasonable and innocent explanation for is a possible sign of an outside relationship.

The list of possibly suspicious behaviors, too, is vast. It includes behaviors such as the following:

- Decreased—and sometimes increased—interest in your sexual relationship
- A desire to explore sexual activities that are new or unusual for you as a couple
- Emotional withdrawal or disengagement from you and the family
- Being more argumentative and critical than usual
- Avoiding participation in family activities

- Making frequent references to another person—for example, a co-worker or someone from the gym or other outside activity (a company sports team)

- Reluctance to mention a co-worker or someone you know your spouse interacts with on a regular basis

> **Tried and True**
>
> The Internet is full of sites claiming to identify signs that your spouse is cheating. Although it may be worthwhile to look at a few of these sites and see what they have to say, remember that they are generalizations based on the experience of a range of people. Your marriage may be different. And you want to consider whether the information provided comes from a professional source.

Behaviors that surprise you, seem strangely out of context, or are out of character for your spouse can be a sign that he or she is having an affair. Don't ignore or rationalize these aberrations from your spouse's routine.

Look for Departures from the Normal

Behaviors, when repeated consistently, turn into habits. For example, you may do a 5-mile run every morning before work. Your spouse may come home from work, open a beer, and sit down in front of the TV. The two of you may be in the habit of going to brunch every Sunday after church.

When people marry and build a life together, they come to know a great deal about each other. They learn the other person's likes and dislikes. They observe how their spouse likes to structure his or her day, whether she's a "morning person" or a "night owl." They discover a spouse's preferences in the areas of food, entertainment, and sex.

Over time, we develop templates, or mental models, for how our partner behaves in a wide range of situations. This predictability is what contributes to comfort and stability in our marriage. We don't have to wonder from moment to moment what our significant other is doing. Experience has revealed to us what the range of behaviors is likely to be.

An affair changes all that. Unbeknownst to us, our spouse now has a new, secret life. Although the two of you may have spent Sunday mornings with

The New York Times for years, your husband's affair partner enjoys a long bicycle ride followed by a trip to the dog park. Suddenly, he's out of the house early on Sundays, and his explanation is that Sunday morning is the best time for him to get some serious exercise.

Your wife has worn her hair short for years, stating that it simplifies her morning routine and enables her to get out of the house and on her way to work more quickly. She suddenly starts growing her hair out. You ask her about it and she gives you a vague answer about wanting a more feminine look.

Here are some of the changes in habits that betrayed spouses most often report:

- A cheating spouse may spend significantly more time away from home, stating that he must put in extra time at work, on business-related travel, or that he has "errands" to run.

- She may stop inviting you to work-related social events, such as holiday parties and picnics.

- The cheating partner may change his cell phone habits, not answering his phone when he's around you, or going to another room to talk, or keeping his phone with him at all times.

- She may change her computer usage habits, erasing her history frequently and minimizing screens when you're around.

- He may start using cash instead of credit cards to avoid a "paper trail" of expenses.

- He may start doing his own laundry or taking his clothes to the dry cleaner to avoid you discovering perfume, lipstick, or body fluids.

- She may begin showering more often or at unexpected times, so you don't detect unfamiliar fragrances or odors.

The range of examples we can look at is vast. The bottom line here is that your spouse is behaving in a way that's noticeably different from what you're accustomed to. Over the years, couples develop their routines and their preferences. When something changes drastically, it's worth paying attention.

Don't Assume the Worst

A word of caution is in order here, though. We rely on patterns and predictability in our lives to assure us that all is well. However, a departure from the routine doesn't always signal an affair. There might be alternate explanations that we need to consider.

Major changes in behavior can also signal the onset of depression, or your spouse's attempts to fight off a full-blown depression. Be alert to circumstances that might contribute to depression, such as failure to get a desired promotion, a recent birthday, the death of a close friend, and so on. Use events such as these to have a conversation with your spouse about how he or she is feeling.

For example, your husband or wife may have recently gone to the doctor and was told in no uncertain terms that he or she needs to lose weight. The doctor prescribes a regimen of exercise, as well as a restricted-calorie diet. Your spouse is alarmed at the prospect of not being able to enjoy retirement, leaving you alone, or not seeing his or her grandchildren grow up.

In this case, a new diet and exercise routine don't mean that your spouse is getting in shape for a lover. They simply mean that your husband or wife has priorities and goals in life that aren't compatible with poor health.

So if you observe something as benign as a healthier diet or a beefed-up exercise routine, consider all the circumstances before concluding that your spouse is having an affair. Ask your spouse specifically about issues regarding health and wellness. You may be pleased to find that the motivation is to share a longer, healthier, and happier life with you and the family, and not that he or she has a secret relationship with someone else.

The important point here is that sudden and major changes in behavior can be an indication of an extramarital affair. For example, changes in style of dress or wearing aftershave should pique your curiosity. The same holds true for unexplained changes in a spouse's schedule. You want to take note of these departures from normal. They can provide the basis for an in-depth discussion with your spouse about changes you've observed.

In Denial About Infidelity: Barb and Sheryl

Sometimes our suspicions about a spouse's infidelity are strong, or even overwhelming, but we choose to ignore what's staring us right in the face. A husband may leave a message on his computer that begins, "My darling." His wife walks by, sees it, and asks him about it. He replies that it's a response to an entire special interest group, and that the woman "always starts her e-mails that way." Does that seem like a plausible explanation? Do you decide to accept it, or do you challenge it?

> **Tried and True**
>
> When your intuition tells you that your spouse may be cheating, you need to take that feeling seriously and evaluate the evidence. Ignoring the obvious will likely lead to problems and heartache later. Research and experience have shown that our intuitions about infidelity are generally correct.

Let's look at a case of two women discussing their husbands' extramarital behavior. They're having a heart-to-heart talk about their own, as well as their parents', marriages. You will see how their different backgrounds powerfully influence how they view their husbands' behavior.

Barb was raised in a strict, moralistic home. Her family attended a fundamentalist church on a weekly basis. Sex was never discussed in the home. Although she never viewed her parents as happy, Barb did think their marriage was at least solid. Imagine her shock when she learned that her father had a two-week affair with his secretary, after which the woman left the company.

Sheryl had grown up in a large Catholic family. Her mother often seemed overwhelmed by the demands of running a home and raising six children. Most Sundays, however, the family managed to get to mass. Sheryl often heard her parents arguing and, during her early teenage years, she became aware that her father had a series of girlfriends. Although her parents argued about it, her mother didn't seem to have the energy to fight. And where would she go with six children, anyway?

Over coffee, Barb and Sheryl discuss their fathers' infidelities as well as their husbands' affairs. As you see, they have strikingly different attitudes toward these behaviors. These differences may well determine whether they stay married or not.

In Barb's case, her mother issued an ultimatum. She told her husband, "You end this tonight, or I'll take the kids and you'll never see us again." She had absolute clarity about the unacceptability of his behavior and that she would never tolerate it again.

For Sheryl's mother, however, the situation was different. With six children to raise, going back to work was not a viable option. She told herself that things could be worse. As much as she hated her husband's womanizing, at least he put food on the table and kept a roof over their heads. She decided to look the other way and even managed to tell herself things weren't so bad, that this was something all men did. She was aware of affairs that other men in her extended family had over the years.

Barb became suspicious when her husband, Roy, who had always taken his lunch to work, began to say that he had lunchtime meetings most days now and that she didn't need to pack his lunch for a while. Something just didn't sound right. Barb checked Roy's cell phone and e-mail and, to her dismay, found steamy messages to and from a female co-worker. He even made reference to her being "all the lunch he needed."

Sheryl's husband, Sam, had a string of brief affairs over the years. In the early days of their marriage, they fought about it. When Sheryl threatened to leave, Sam countered with, "Go on and leave, then." She still loved Sam, but she also realized he wasn't going to change his ways. And Sam was a good provider for her and the kids. She couldn't ignore that.

For Barb, her husband's affair became a crisis in the marriage. She wasn't yet certain what she wanted to do, but she knew she couldn't live like this. If she and Roy were to stay married, he would have to end the affair in no uncertain terms and they would have to go into couples' therapy.

Sheryl grew up in an atmosphere of chronic infidelity. So when it became obvious that her husband was cheating, she sighed and thought to herself, "Mom was right, this is how men are." Although she had more economic and job choices than her mother, her husband's behavior confirmed what she believed about men, marriage, and infidelity.

Although Sheryl is sympathetic to Barb's emotional pain, she has developed a different approach to dealing with her husband's cheating. She chooses to rationalize it and to tell herself things could be worse. At least Sam is there for dinner most nights, he's involved with the kids, and he provides a good life for them. And when he's away from the home and family at unexpected times, she mentally makes excuses for him. In other words, she is in denial about Sam's infidelity.

Barb, on the other hand, simply couldn't ignore Roy's affair. She knew this was a turning point in their relationship. If Roy were unwilling to end the affair and go into couples' therapy with her, she was certain the marriage was over. She would have to build a new life for herself and their children.

As they talk about their marriages, a couple of things become clear. Their husbands have both violated their marriage vows. Roy got involved in a brief affair. Sam is a habitual cheater. Barb exposed Roy's cheating and delivered an ultimatum. Sheryl gradually made a decision to ignore Sam's extramarital activities and to focus instead on the good things he did. ("He's a good father and provider.") In other words, she went into denial about his mysterious absences, the unexplained phone calls and hang-ups, and so on.

Denial undermines your trust in yourself. When you are in denial, not only is your partner lying to you, but you begin to lie to yourself. You tell yourself that what you know to be true isn't so. You deny the evidence of your own experience. When you do this, you teach yourself to doubt your own perceptions, observations, and feelings. You say, in essence, "I can't trust myself and what I know."

"Don't Ask, Don't Tell"

This approach to dealing with an affair may, on the surface, look like denial. In actuality, it functions more like an unspoken agreement between spouses about how to handle an affair. It's an arrangement of convenience that allows both partners to save face and continue on with the marriage.

In this scenario, your spouse doesn't come right out and confess to an affair. Instead, information is "leaked" out that strongly hints at an affair. Let's look at some examples of how your spouse might be hinting at an affair:

- He speaks frequently and in positive terms of a female co-worker, how helpful he is to her, and how much she contributes.

- You're surprised at how infrequently or reluctantly your spouse mentions a man with whom she works closely.

- He receives gifts from a co-worker that seem excessive or inappropriate—for example, clothing, jewelry, or personal care products.

- She either suggests that the two of you socialize with a co-worker and his wife, or she is reluctant to spend time together with them outside the office.

- He e-mails, texts, or calls a female co-worker frequently after work.

Heartaches

Your spouse may test your limits for her involvement with another man. If you don't react to her frequent positive comments about a male co-worker or friend, she may take that as an unspoken sign that it's okay to continue her affair.

These are just a few examples, but the point is that your spouse's behavior—and perhaps that of the co-worker—suggests a personal relationship. The co-worker may begin calling him after hours, or even calling the home, in the guise of discussing a work-related matter. The co-worker may call just to hear your voice. He or she may even drop by your house to deliver some "important" papers. The real agenda is to gain information about the lover's family and home.

Your spouse's behavior may indirectly suggest an affair, but you don't confront him about it. Your suspicions have been raised, but, for whatever reason, you remain silent. On occasion, however, you may become so irritated by indirect references to the affair partner, that you lash out. For example, if your spouse complains that you don't engage in intellectual conversations with him, you may blurt out, "Well why don't you go talk politics with Nancy?"

Your spouse may spend more time than previously at the office or out of the home, supposedly running errands, at the gym, or hanging out with her girlfriends. In the past, she might have hung around the house on weekends, perhaps catching up on sleep, tending to tasks around the house, or watching TV But now she seems eager to be out of the house. Again, you don't question her, in spite of your suspicions.

Your children may even become suspicious. If your spouse has frequently mentioned a female co-worker, they may begin wondering whether the relationship is more than professional. They may make comments like, "Gee, Dad, you really like Megan, don't you? You sure talk about her a lot."

The Silent Bargain

This arrangement—in which your spouse signals that there may be an affair, but you don't confront him or her—serves as an unspoken bargain between the two of you. You don't address the hints he or she drops, so your spouse is able to continue an extramarital life.

And what do you get out of this bargain? Well, if you confront your spouse with your suspicions, your concerns are out on the table. They have to be addressed. And if she confesses that, yes, she is involved with someone else, what do you do then? There are major, life-changing decisions you have to make.

You have several choices. One is to do nothing, which probably rarely happens. That alternative involves a tremendous loss of self-esteem and damage to one's ego. You can immediately opt to divorce your husband or wife, which can mean a drastic change in lifestyle for you and your children. Or you can issue an ultimatum that your spouse end the affair and perhaps go into therapy with you.

However, if you keep silent about the affair, which you both know he or she is having, you can keep your marriage and family intact, at least for the time being. You still present a unified image to family, friends, and co-workers. Your children don't struggle with the effects of divorce. And your financial situation and lifestyle likely continue as before.

There is, of course, an emotional price to pay for the "don't ask, don't tell" approach. The nagging uncertainty about whether your spouse is actually having an affair takes a toll. After all, he hasn't come right out and admitted it, in spite of all the hints he's dropped. And you also live with the possibility that she might eventually leave you for her lover. So this arrangement might seem like the best short-term solution, but it's no guarantee that your marriage will last.

Essential Takeaways

- There are many behaviors that may suggest your spouse is having an affair, but you need to consider other explanations for his or her behavior as well.

- When behaviors and habits deviate from what's normal for your spouse, you need to pay special attention and consider addressing that with him or her.

- Even when a spouse has strong suspicions about an affair, she may choose to deny the evidence.

- "Don't ask, don't tell" may seem like a good strategy for keeping the peace and preserving your marriage, but it's no guarantee that your marriage will run smoothly or that your spouse won't leave you at some later date.

chapter 7

Exposing Infidelity

Gathering information before the confrontation

Hiring a professional to track your spouse

Confronting your spouse with evidence of his or her infidelity

Preparing emotionally for the confession

Anticipating emotional intensity as you begin dealing with the trauma in your relationship

In this chapter, I explore some additional ways in which your spouse's infidelity may come to light. This revelation may arise out of everyday interactions with friends, neighbors, or co-workers. Sometimes, however, our suspicions are strong enough that we feel the need for professional verification of a spouse's affair.

When you decide you have sufficient evidence of infidelity, you need to carefully plan how you will confront your spouse. The initial discussion of your spouse's affair is likely to be highly emotional. There are specific things you can do to prepare yourself for this discussion.

Your spouse may confess to an affair even before you have reason to be suspicious. This is a challenging situation, because you have not had time to prepare yourself emotionally and to consider your options for the future. This requires a different approach to the problem.

Discovering Your Spouse's Infidelity

Infidelity comes to light in different ways and on different timetables. An affair may be discovered shortly after it begins, or a cheating spouse may maintain an extramarital relationship for years, even decades. The duration of the affair can make a critical difference in how you and your spouse handle the aftermath and your decisions about the future.

Over time, you may begin to wonder whether your spouse is involved in an affair. Although there may not be a single event that lets you know your spouse is cheating, changes in behavior and attitude can act as red flags. Departures from habits and routines, as well as emotional withdrawal, are always worth paying attention to (see Chapter 5), because they can signal that something is different in your relationship, possibly an affair.

Evidence of infidelity can accumulate over time. You may begin to see credit card charges that you don't recognize. Your spouse may unexpectedly begin traveling more frequently "on business." He or she may begin spending more time away from the house and offer inadequate or puzzling explanations for these blocks of time. Although there may be an innocent explanation for such behaviors, when these patterns develop, you're wise to consider the possibility that your spouse is having an affair.

You Might Be the Last to Know

Sadly, sometimes it's the betrayed who is the last person to learn of his or her spouse's infidelity. Your spouse may have become very thorough and clever in hiding evidence of his or her affair. Or you may not have been paying close attention to your spouse's behavior and the overall state of your marriage.

This last situation is particularly likely to occur when spouses lead parallel lives. Perhaps both of you have become consumed with your careers.

Perhaps you've become preoccupied with your children and their activities. In either case, the marriage may have taken a backseat to other priorities.

On rare occasions, a betrayed person might hear of his or her spouse's affair through a third party, perhaps a neighbor, one of his or her spouse's co-workers, occasionally even the actual affair partner. This way of discovering an affair can be particularly devastating.

Let's look at the case of Diana and Peter, who had been married for almost 20 years. Peter was a linguistics professor and Diana was a graphic arts designer who worked out of their home. They struggled with infertility the first few years of their marriage and were thrilled when Diana finally gave birth to a daughter, Sophie.

As Peter was pursuing his academic career and working toward tenure, Diana devoted more and more energy to motherhood and Sophie's school and extracurricular activities. Although they both thoroughly enjoyed their life choices, it was clear to friends that they spent almost no time as a couple.

One day, with Peter at work and Sophie at school, Diana received a phone call from a woman who refused to identify herself, but stated that she had the family's best interests at heart. She told Diana that Peter had been having an affair with his administrative assistant for almost a year and that the entire linguistics department knew about it.

The unidentified woman claimed that she wrestled with whether or not to call Diana. She said that what finally decided the matter for her was how she would feel if she were in Diana's shoes. She would want to know, so that she could take whatever measures she needed to protect herself legally, financially, emotionally, and healthwise.

If the news of an affair comes through a friend of the betrayed spouse, the friendship is also likely to suffer. This is why friends or relatives who know of an affair might be reluctant to share that news. The betrayed individual might accuse the friend of lying about his or her spouse and spreading rumors. A friend, relative, or co-worker who knows of an affair is in a delicate position, having to balance his or her desire to maintain a friendship with the desire to protect the betrayed from a wayward spouse.

Your Resources for Exposing Infidelity

If you suspect your spouse of cheating, you have a number of resources at your disposal for obtaining information. These range from the most basic approaches, such as going through your spouse's pockets or handbag, to highly sophisticated techniques and gadgets, such as computer spyware and GPS tracking devices.

Tried and True

Your gut instincts are probably your best and easiest barometer as to whether your spouse might be involved in an affair. There's really nothing all that mysterious about our instincts in our relationships. They grow out of countless interactions with our spouse, which add up to patterns of behavior, or habits. When these patterns are violated or changed, with no explanation, it signals that we need to pay attention.

For years, the sight of a wife going through her husband's pockets or checking his collar for lipstick stains symbolized a woman who suspected her husband of infidelity. These techniques are still in use today, of course. Lipstick on a collar, or a perfume you don't recognize as your own, is almost impossible for a husband to explain.

You probably check your husband's pants or jacket pockets if you take his clothes to the dry cleaner. If you come across receipts for items such as clothing, lingerie, jewelry, hotel stays, restaurants, entertainment, which you know nothing about, it's natural to be curious, if not outright suspicious.

As the incidence of infidelity among wives has increased, husbands, too, have more and more turned to various options for checking on their spouses. These include checking her text messages and e-mails, checking her credit card statements, following her at random times throughout the day, and even installing a GPS on her car in order to track her movements.

With the advent of e-mail, instant messaging, social networking, and texting, cheating has gone high tech. This has caused some cheating spouses to think they're less likely to get caught, but for others who are ultra-cautious, this has led to taking multiple measures to conceal one's true behavior. And just as technology has opened up new avenues for adultery, it has also given concerned spouses and professionals a new set of tools for learning the truth.

Many spouses who e-mail their lovers never think to password protect their e-mail. Even if they do, cracking a password may not be as difficult as you think. The Internet offers all sorts of resources for an inquisitive spouse who's willing to invest time and energy to discover who his or her spouse has been e-mailing and what they've been saying to each other.

Texting an affair partner has become even more popular than e-mailing for many, and texts are notoriously difficult to retrieve, unless they're stored on the handset. Cell phone companies typically don't keep them, and certainly not for extended periods of time. The availability of texts in legal proceedings is uncharted territory, so it's impossible to say with any certainty that you can retrieve your cheating spouse's texts for use in a divorce case.

It's possible to purchase computer-monitoring software that enables you to track what your spouse has been doing online. You can track how much time your spouse is spending online, including log-on and sign-out times.

Keystroke monitoring software shows what your spouse has been typing. You can also use the screenshot feature of these programs to view what your spouse has been looking at, as well as any online searches. You can view your spouse's e-mails and chat messages as well. In other words, you can monitor virtually all of your spouse's online activities, if you are so inclined and willing to spend the time to review the information.

In addition to tracking your spouse's communications with an affair partner or activity on questionable websites, it's also possible to track his or her physical movements. A GPS tracker can be installed in an unobtrusive spot in or under his or her vehicle, giving you information about your spouse's destination, length of time he or she was en route, as well as amount of time spent at the destination.

Other types of devices enable you to record both incoming and outgoing cell phone calls, as well as see who your spouse is texting and receiving messages from. You can even purchase a kit to test for bodily fluids on your spouse's clothing!

If you're thinking of recording a spouse's phone calls, check the legal statutes in your area. Laws vary from state to state. Your recordings might not be admissible as evidence in court; that is up to the judge. However, these conversations might give you the answer you need if you're wondering whether your spouse is unfaithful or not.

Should You Hire a Professional?

Clients sometimes ask me whether they should hire a private investigator (PI) to find out whether or not their spouse is cheating. That is a highly personal decision, one that is determined by a number of factors. Here are some of the questions you should ask yourself when making the decision whether or not to hire a professional.

Can you afford to hire a PI? Fees can range anywhere from $40 to $100 or higher per hour, depending on the nature of the case. There are flat fee expenses, such as background checks, GPS monitoring, or sweeping your home or car of electronic bugs. You will be required to pay a retainer, which can go as high as $5,000 in an infidelity investigation. You might want to first consider what you can uncover and document yourself, such as e-mail and texting.

What types of information do you need if, for instance, you decide to pursue a divorce after you confirm your spouse's infidelity? For example, will photographs of your spouse with his or her affair partner be sufficient to prove adultery? Do you need e-mail messages as well? This an area in which an attorney should advise you. It is relevant if you plan to file for a fault divorce on the basis of adultery, rather than a no-fault divorce.

PIs refer to the days leading up to and following Valentine's Day as "cheaters' week." If a spouse is having an affair, it's likely he or she will spend some time with his or her lover during that week. For that reason, there's a high success rate of catching a cheating spouse during what's supposed to be the most romantic time of year.

Are you willing to go so far as to use a professional decoy to see whether your spouse is willing to commit adultery? This, of course, would be arranged by your PI, and can add substantially to your PI's fee. Your PI will want to do everything possible to ensure the decoy's physical safety, such as learning whether your husband is prone to violence. Some view this technique as a form of entrapment. After all, your spouse wasn't having an affair with the decoy. But how he or she responds to the decoy and if he or she tries to initiate further interaction with the decoy can, again, answer your question as to whether your spouse is willing to cheat.

Are you prepared to use the information you obtain from a private investigation in court? In many states, adultery is an "absolute bar" to alimony, meaning that a spouse who has an affair might be awarded child support, but no spousal support at all. If it's your spouse who has had the affair, you need to decide whether you're prepared to file charges of adultery, given the consequences to your spouse and what your children might learn about the divorce down the road. You need to consider whether you want them to know that your spouse committed adultery.

Confronting Your Partner

After you feel certain you have evidence of your partner's infidelity, whether based on your own research or material provided by a professional, you need to make a plan for how to proceed. The assumption is that you will either insist that both of you go into marital therapy, or you will file for divorce. In rare cases, however, a betrayed spouse might have second thoughts about confronting a partner, and choose instead to hold on to incriminating information until a future date.

Let's assume that you have managed to amass some fairly convincing evidence of your spouse's infidelity, whether e-mail and text messages, or photos of your spouse and his or her lover taken by a PI. And let's assume you have decided to confront your spouse about the affair. You need to prepare carefully for this event.

Although there is no way to completely anticipate your spouse's response, there are several things you can do in advance to maximize the likelihood that things will go your way. These have to do with choosing an appropriate time and place, mentally rehearsing how you want to approach your spouse, and anticipating how he or she might react to this confrontation.

Choose a Safe Setting

Intimate relationships, such as marriage, are, by their very nature, highly emotionally charged. When we feel threatened in these areas, tempers can flare and things can get out of hand. You need to present evidence of your spouse's infidelity in a physically secure setting, which might mean an out-of-the-way table in a restaurant or coffeehouse. Your spouse is less likely to lose control in a public place than in your home. The goal is to ensure your physical safety.

It's a good idea to let a trusted friend or family member know your whereabouts and your plan. Let them know approximately how long you expect to be with your spouse. Have your cell phone fully charged with the ringer on the loud setting, so they can call you at a pre-arranged time. If necessary, let them know you'll need another hour or so, and ask them to call back at that time.

Tried and True

Knowledge is power in relationships. Secrecy in a marriage creates an imbalance of power. Cheating spouses have had the advantage of knowledge of their affairs and their intentions regarding their marriages. Now you, too, have knowledge of the affair. Before confronting your spouse, use your knowledge of the affair to decide what you want for your future, whether it's reconciliation, separation, or divorce.

Rehearsing What You Want to Say

Preparation is vital in planning your confrontation. You obtained the information you need. Although your spouse may deny or rationalize it at first, the information and your presentation of it need to be convincing. Your next step is to plan how you will present it.

It's a good idea to keep all your physical evidence—whether e-mails you printed out, bank statements, or photographs you obtained from a PI—with you at all times. The last thing you want to do is to unwittingly give your spouse advance notice of your plans. So you might want to consider putting all of your information into a small bag, which you can easily carry with you.

Plan in advance how you want to present your evidence to your spouse. Literally rehearse what you want to say. For instance, if you have his or her e-mail correspondence with an affair partner, you can say something like "I've seen your e-mails, and I know you're having an affair with …" If you hired a PI, you can lay some photos on the table at your designated meeting place and say, "I know you've been having an affair with …. Don't bother to deny it. I have photos of the two of you together."

The point is to organize the evidence you have and to plan in advance how you want to present it. You should also anticipate your emotional reactions and—to the extent possible—your spouse's. I generally advise clients to be prepared to be surprised, and to plan for the unexpected.

Your Spouse's Confession

During the confrontation, resist the temptation to "fill in the blanks" for your spouse when he or she is responding to you. It can be extremely difficult to sit there calmly while the person you love fumbles for an explanation of his or her adulterous behavior, but let it happen. You gain more information if you simply allow your spouse to respond than if you speak for him or her.

Although you may be able to somewhat anticipate your spouse's style of response, based on your knowledge of him or her, you should prepare yourself for almost anything. It's extremely rare for a husband or wife to simply confess when presented with evidence of an affair. A more typical scenario involves denial, rationalization, or blame of the betrayed spouse.

Your Spouse's Reaction

Again, although it's difficult to know for sure how your spouse will respond when you confront her with evidence of her infidelity, it's likely that it will take one of two forms. She may express guilt, shame, and remorse. Or she may blame you, at least in part, for her affair. Your knowledge of her personality and her past behavior can help you predict this.

In the past, has your spouse typically taken responsibility for her own behavior and mistakes she has made in the relationship? For example, does she acknowledge her role in conflicts the two of you have dealt with? Or does she tend to blame others when things don't go right? When the two of you disagree over something, does she typically blame you for that? Does she blame others when there are problems at work?

Asking yourself these questions before you confront her about her infidelity can help you determine whether she is an *internalizer* or an *externalizer*. In other words, does she see and acknowledge the role of her own behavior in her life? Or does she tend to assign blame and responsibility to other people and circumstances when things go wrong?

Definition

Internalizers are people who tend to take responsibility for their own actions, while **externalizers** attribute responsibility for feelings and behaviors to other people, especially when those behaviors are considered negative or unacceptable.

Let's consider Janine and Gary, who came to therapy after Gary discovered some questionable e-mails on their home computer. In the process of investigating these, he learned that Janine had been in contact with approximately 20 men online. Although reluctant to admit her infidelity at first, Janine eventually confessed to a series of affairs. She carried on a number of cyber affairs, including sending nude photos of herself, and arranged through Craigslist to meet a number of men for sex.

In therapy, Janine remarked that she hadn't particularly enjoyed her sexual encounters. As discussion of these events progressed, she attributed her unhappiness in the marriage to Gary. She complained about his long hours at the office and his playing golf on the weekends. Although she had female friends from work and in the neighborhood, she felt lonely much of the time.

Janine's online sexual chats gave her a momentary sense of connection and being desired and cared for, but that feeling didn't last. She then felt the need to contact someone new and experience the sense of exhilaration and anticipation all over again. As she and Gary discussed her extramarital activities and their relationship in therapy, it became clear that she blamed

Gary for her infidelity. She insisted that, if he had given her more attention and affection, she would not have cheated.

Managing Your Emotions

Confronting your spouse with evidence of his or her infidelity is likely to be a highly emotional experience. Even with rehearsal, it's hard to predict how the two of you will react as the confrontation unfolds. Among other things, although you know what information and plans you are bringing to the meeting, he or she may divulge information that you don't yet have. For example, you may learn that the affair lasted much longer than you knew, or you may find out that this was not your spouse's first affair.

As well prepared as you are going into this meeting, you are likely to feel physically "revved up." You may feel your heart racing and feel short of breath, even lightheaded at times. Remind yourself to take deep, regular breaths. Try to avoid excessive caffeine or alcohol consumption before this meeting. The caffeine will likely increase feelings of anxiety, and the alcohol may interfere with your ability to stay mentally sharp and focused.

So be prepared to be surprised by the range of emotions you may experience during the confrontation. You may start out feeling angry, but in control. Your feelings can easily progress, however, to rage, shock, confusion, and even emotional numbness, all within a single discussion. If need be, have a friend pick you up and drive you home. If you need to have your spouse spend the night elsewhere, whether in a separate room or a hotel, by all means make that clear. And hold off making major decisions until the two of you have further opportunities to talk and begin to sort out what you want for your future.

Although you want to do your best to prepare for confronting your spouse about his or her infidelity, be realistic in your expectations. This is one of the most highly emotionally charged tasks you'll ever have to undertake. Know ahead of time what your goals for the confrontation are. Do you simply want an admission of infidelity? Do you want your spouse to end the affair immediately, if he or she is still involved with an affair partner? Do you want a commitment from your spouse to attend therapy with you?

If You Had the Affair

If you are the spouse who had the affair, you may decide to confess it to your husband or wife. This scenario is less common than an affair discovered by your spouse, but cheating spouses do sometimes confess, for a number of reasons.

Unless the affair was a one-night stand, guilt alone generally doesn't result in a confession. After all, someone who is willing to betray and deceive his or her spouse for an extended period of time is probably not experiencing severe pangs of guilt. Interestingly, some cheating spouses are more motivated by what their children would think and feel than by the reaction they anticipate from their husband or wife.

But guilt does take its toll over time, and some cheating spouses are actually relieved when they are confronted with their adultery. They may also use confession to a husband or wife as a way to help end an affair that has gotten "messy" or that the affair partner doesn't want to end. They are essentially enlisting their spouse's help in the process.

You may also decide to confess if it appears your affair is about to be revealed by a third party. You may reluctantly decide your spouse should get the news from you, rather than the affair partner, co-worker, friend, neighbor, or relative. In either case, you need to do some serious soul searching as to how you feel about your marriage and your spouse, and whether you're willing to do the hard work of rebuilding your relationship, if your spouse will still have you.

Tried and True

If you have hope for the future of your marriage, it is critical that you do not blame your spouse during your confession of infidelity. Regardless of whether you wish your spouse had been more attentive, more sexual, or more attractive, you and you alone chose to go outside your marriage to get personal needs met. Your first step in working on your marriage is to admit this and to experience sincere remorse for it.

What About Your Emotions?

Revelation of adultery is almost always a highly emotional situation. You need to be prepared to feel emotionally volatile during that interaction, and for your spouse to feel the same way. Even with advance planning, you are likely to experience a range of emotions, including the following:

- Anxiety regarding your spouse's response to your infidelity

- Sadness over the loss of the affair and your secret life

- Anger toward your spouse both for his or her emotions and whatever you think his or her role was in your affair

- Fear and uncertainty over what the future holds for you and your family

Emotions are, by definition, irrational. They are feeling states. The initial conversation with your spouse about your infidelity is not the venue for sorting out all of those feelings. That process takes plenty of time and, most likely, good professional help as well. This is true whether the two of you decide to restore your marriage or you go your separate ways. That is a journey of self-discovery, and all journeys are accomplished step by step, not in a single leap.

Essential Takeaways

- Before confronting your spouse with suspicions of infidelity, you will want to gather as much evidence as possible.

- Although you can obtain some evidence on your own, you may want to consider hiring a professional to assist you, depending on your finances.

- Invest some time into planning how you want to present your spouse with evidence of his or her infidelity.

- Anticipate that the confrontation may be a highly emotional experience and plan to meet in a safe setting.

- If you had the affair, understand ahead of time whether your goal is to seek forgiveness and try to repair your marriage, or whether your affair was an exit strategy and you want to go forward alone.

- If you decide to confess to your spouse that you had an affair, accept sole responsibility and do not blame your spouse.

chapter 8

Emotional Aftershocks

The devastation of discovering an affair

The wide range of emotions after learning of the affair

Calling into question everything you believed about your marriage, your spouse, and yourself

In this chapter, I look at the emotional aftermath of an affair. I examine your initial response, as well as how your feelings are likely to change over time. Although everyone is different, there are certain emotional patterns that betrayed spouses tend to experience.

I also investigate some of the thoughts you're likely to have after learning of your spouse's infidelity. You may find yourself questioning what was real and what wasn't in your relationship. Your spouse may seem like a total stranger at times. And you may begin to question your worth as a partner.

Finally, I touch on what happens after discovery of an affair. Although you may feel temporarily paralyzed by the emotional impact of your spouse's infidelity, you need to begin planning for your future, both short-term and long-term, and for your personal healing.

Infidelity Is Devastating

Without a doubt, the word I hear most often when a new client comes to me with the story of a spouse's infidelity is devastation. The definition of the word tells the tale. *Devastation* means to lay waste, to ruin or utterly destroy. It also means to confound or overwhelm.

Both of these definitions point to important aspects of the experience of devastation. There is an emotional impact, and there is also the effect that infidelity has on your beliefs about your marriage, your life, the world in general, as well as your sense of self-worth.

When a spouse's affair is discovered, the trauma can be overwhelming. Everything you took for granted about your marriage is destroyed. Beyond that, the way you look at yourself and others may be forever changed. Trust will never come easily for you again, whether in your marriage or a future relationship.

Can a spouse's infidelity cause posttraumatic stress? The answer is possibly, if your reaction to learning of the affair goes beyond what might be considered normal or if it persists for an unusually long time. People usually associate *Posttraumatic Stress Disorder (PTSD)* with horrific events such as combat in war, natural and manmade disasters (for example, terrorist attacks), or personal assaults such as rape and robbery. But the reality is that other emotionally devastating events can have a similar effect. And whether or not you qualify for a formal diagnosis of PTSD, infidelity is traumatizing.

Posttraumatic Stress Disorder (PTSD) is classified by mental health professionals as an anxiety disorder. Symptoms include flashbacks, or a feeling of reliving the trauma; nightmares about the traumatic incident, and uncontrollable memories of it; uncomfortable physical sensations caused by the traumatic event, such as increased jumpiness; and attempts to avoid people and places associated with the trauma, as well as a general tendency to withdraw from others and from your usual activities.

Imagine the following scenario. You and your husband share a home computer. You check your e-mail and discover that your husband has inadvertently left his open. Curiosity gets the better of you and you start reading. To your horror, you discover a long string of e-mails to and from a co-worker of his whom you vaguely recall having met a couple of times. The messages leave no doubt that they're having a serious long-term affair.

That moment of discovery will not only be forever burned into your memory, but it will also haunt you in ways you may not be able to anticipate and that may resemble posttraumatic stress. Let's take a look at some of these emotional triggers.

Let's say the home computer is located in a small office, which you and your husband share. After reading the e-mails, you find it almost impossible to enter that room for some time, because it is closely associated with the discovery of your husband's infidelity. You may also have a strong desire to avoid his workplace and his co-workers, even if they know nothing of the affair. Again, it's about the emotional association between the affair, your discovery of it, and the people, places, and things that remind you of it.

Heartaches

"Flashbulb memory" refers to an extremely vivid memory of an event, which is of great importance to you and which elicits strong emotion. With flashbulb memories, you generally have a strong memory of where you were and what you were doing when the event occurred. For example, most of us have very strong, specific recollection of where we were and what we were doing when the terrorist attacks of September 11 occurred.

You may find yourself experiencing some uncontrollable physical sensations at times, too, such as a racing heart, dizziness or faintness, shortness of breath, nausea, and sweating. You may be plagued by insomnia for some period of time. You may feel as if you're always on alert, and you may be extremely irritable.

The Gamut of Feelings

You may feel like you're on an emotional roller coaster for some time after your spouse's affair. One day, you're devastated and absolutely certain that things will never return to normal. The next day, you see some small point of light at the end of the tunnel. Some days you again feel hope for your marriage, and on other days, you're convinced it can never work.

The course of your emotions is impossible to predict in advance. You simply need to be prepared for your feelings to change and to know that this is normal. It doesn't signal that anything is wrong or unusual about you. In fact, what psychologists call *lability*, or rapid changes in your emotions, is par for the course during the early stages of affair recovery. Although unpleasant, it generally subsides in time and doesn't mean you're "going crazy."

Lability is a technical term used by mental health professionals to refer to severe mood swings. In extreme cases, lability can manifest as uncontrollable crying or laughing. Lability is often associated with a marked cycling of emotions in conditions such as bipolar disorder.

Numbness

Although devastation, or that "kicked in the gut" feeling, is generally the first emotion that people report after learning about their partner's affair, a sensation of emotional numbness may set in at some later date. This can feel like the opposite of devastation, but it is actually just part of the "cocktail" of emotions you are likely to experience after your spouse's infidelity.

Emotional numbness is commonly experienced at some point after a major trauma. It can take several forms, including social withdrawal, loss of interest in activities you formerly enjoyed or cared about, as well as diminished interest in close relationships and sex. Numbness can also manifest itself in feelings of detachment from people and the world, or a sense that things around you aren't quite real.

Tried and True

Therapists who work with trauma victims recommend a number of things to help them restore a sense of order in their lives. They suggest that victms maintain a strong social support network to help them through this stressful time. They also recommend taking any sort of action that helps you regain a sense of control in your life. This can be something like volunteering in the community, or as small as reorganizing a closet. The point is to do something that gives you a feeling of being in charge of your life again.

Anxiety

Anxiety is a natural response when you discover your spouse has been involved sexually or emotionally with someone else. After all, the vow to be faithful "until the two of you death shall part" has been broken. Discovery of an affair brings everything you have taken for granted into question.

The logical follow-up to this is that you no longer know what to expect from your spouse. All of the implicit agreements between you and your partner, such as being faithful to each other, are now in question. You can't help but be flooded with anxiety about your future.

Anxiety after learning of a spouse's affair can encompass many areas. Your primary concern, of course, is your relationship status. Will you and your husband or wife work to repair your marriage? But other concerns will emerge as well, such as how you will manage financially, and whether you will need to put your children in day care so that you can return to work full time. These are just a few of the many concerns you'll face that can increase your anxiety level following infidelity.

Depression

Depression is another common emotional experience after a spouse's affair. It may set in at any time following your discovery. Although your initial emotions are likely to be intense, such as feelings of devastation and anxiety, depression may settle in after the initial shock has passed.

Depression can manifest itself in several ways. It can be feelings of sadness and loss. It can also take a more physical form, such as inability to sleep, or the desire to stay in bed and sleep all day. Some people experience severe appetite loss, whereas others comfort themselves with food. Depression can also cause loss of interest in activities you once normally found pleasurable, including sex.

Depression can also affect things like your ability to concentrate and perform some mental tasks, as well as your memory. It's not uncommon for a depressed person to even wonder whether he or she has some kind of dementia, or deterioration of mental functioning. Those with depression may feel easily confused and struggle with concentration and tasks they once performed with ease.

Both anxiety and depression can be crippling. With anxiety, you can feel so paralyzed by fear and doubt that you find it hard to carry out your daily responsibilities. With depression, too, you may find that you simply don't have the energy to handle the tasks you need to. You may just want to retreat to your bed and hide under the covers.

Do You Need Medication?

Patients struggling with anxiety or depression often want to discuss whether they need to be on medication. Although heartaches and other negative feelings are a part of life, there are circumstances when medication might be helpful for a short period of time. If you find you're so crippled by your anxiety or depression that you simply can't deal with your normal tasks, such as job and family responsibilities, then medication might be a useful short-term addition to your therapy.

Loss of Self-Esteem

Another unfortunate casualty of a spouse's affair can be self-esteem. Infidelity raises all sorts of questions about your worth as a partner, a lover, even as a person in general. When the one who pledged to love and cherish you and to forsake all others betrays that pledge by becoming involved with a third party, it's easy to feel badly about yourself.

Unfortunately, this loss of self-esteem can affect your beliefs about yourself and even your behavior. When you are convinced that your spouse's affair was somehow related to something about you, it's easy to conclude that you somehow disappointed or failed him or her. Resist falling into this trap, though, and remind yourself that your spouse chose to engage in an affair and to deceive you. You didn't force him or her into this decision.

Common Thoughts After Betrayal

Just as your emotions are in turmoil after discovering that your spouse has engaged in an affair, your thoughts may feel like a confused jumble as well. These thoughts range from questions about the true nature of your relationship and the person you married, to a multitude of concerns about yourself, to worries about your future.

Sadly, you may often discover after there's been a breach in fidelity that your partner has been deceptive about many aspects of your life together. These include secret concerns and disappointments he or she has about the marriage; dislikes about you as a person, including personality and appearance; level of attraction to other people and sexual fantasies; substance use habits; debt and financial problems; and how he or she spends time when not with you.

An affair may also take a huge toll on your self-image and self-esteem. And this can be true whether you or your spouse had the affair. As noted earlier when pointing out some of the factors that can contribute to affairs, someone who is in need of constant or excessive reassurance about his or her desirability or lovability may seek that reassurance in extramarital relationships.

Our Marriage Was a Lie

When you learn that your spouse has betrayed you, it's very easy to conclude that everything about the marriage was based on falsehood. All the things that you accepted as gospel in your relationship have now been called into question. Your spouse may vigorously protest that his or her affair only began six months ago, but you have no way of knowing for sure. If your spouse has been lying to you for six months, perhaps he or she lied to you for six years about one thing or the other.

In the past, your spouse's behaviors and statements seemed innocent. You would have accepted them at face value, but now you're skeptical. A simple declaration that "I need to run to the hardware store to pick up some of those energy-efficient bulbs," or "I need to swing by the office quickly to grab some files I'll need for my trip on Monday," now sound sinister and deceptive. You just don't know what to believe.

Heartaches

A gesture as simple and lovely as giving your wife flowers can be perceived through a negative lens. Surveys show that many women are suspicious when their husband brings them flowers. They assume that he is implicitly apologizing for some sort of bad behavior. These floral offerings are known as "guilt flowers."

The challenge you face, over time, is to separate what was real and what might have been mere appearance in your marriage. You might never know with absolute certainty when deception began to creep into your relationship, but there are a few basic questions you can ask yourself to help you get a sense of the timetable for when you and your spouse began to grow apart.

- Can I remember a time when we started doing most things separately rather than spending a lot of our free time together?

- Did we ever explicitly talk about devoting a reasonable, mutually agreed upon, amount of time to our separate interests?

- Does it seem like we have less and less to talk about with each other?

- Do we feel uncomfortable when it's just the two of us, with no kids or friends or relatives around?

- Can I remember when my spouse began to give me vague, unsatisfactory answers about his or her activities, whereabouts, and plans for the day?

Your answers to these questions may help you approximate when your marriage began to be based on half-truths, or even outright falsehoods. Although this doesn't always mean that your spouse is having an affair, it can identify when the two of you began to head down separate life paths, increasing the risk for an affair.

Heartaches

Sometimes a married couple gradually disconnects emotionally from each other, which is referred to as "marital disengagement." It generally consists of many seemingly small events that add up to a growing sense of estrangement. One example is failing to resolve apparently small disagreements as they occur. The end result is a much larger unresolved area of conflict that may feel impossible to handle.

If you and your spouse decide to separate or divorce after infidelity, wondering what was real and what was a lie can be especially troubling. Betrayal can leave you puzzled as to whether your spouse loved you as well as his or her affair partner.

There are undoubtedly special moments and memories related to just the two of you and to your family as a whole. You may wonder whether those great family vacations were an illusion. And what about the anniversaries and Valentine's Day celebrations? Were those all just a charade, or were they based on genuine love and commitment to each other? In Chapter 12, I look into the process of looking at your history and rewriting the story of your marriage.

Take Raoul and Lydia, for example, who had been married over 20 years. They had a daughter in college and one in high school. Raoul became suspicious when Lydia began spending long periods of time on the computer. He installed keystroke logging and computer surveillance software, which enabled him to track all her online activity.

Raoul discovered that Lydia had been contacted by an old boyfriend and that they were frequently e-mailing each other. Although the messages began innocently enough, they quickly became more intimate. Raoul decided to hire a private investigator, and even went so far as to set up opportunities for Lydia and the former boyfriend to meet. The investigator obtained photos, which Raoul used to demand a divorce.

Although he was adamant about pursuing a divorce, Raoul was also consumed with anxiety as to what all the years he and Lydia had spent together had been about. He began to wonder whether she ever truly loved him. He mentally revisited the passion of their earlier years, and all the fond memories of raising their daughters together. In desperation, he pleaded with Lydia to tell him that their years together had truly meant something, that they hadn't been a charade.

It Must Be Me

Another unfortunate side effect of a spouse's affair is how it makes you second-guess yourself. Prior to discovery of infidelity, you may feel strong, confident, attractive, sexy, and loved. Learning that your spouse cheated can change all that overnight.

If your spouse has been involved with someone else, whether physically, emotionally, or both, it's hard not to compare yourself to the third party, even if you've never met him or her. If your husband has cheated, you may conjure up images of a woman who is more attractive and sexual than you. If your wife was the guilty one, you may imagine her lover as more athletic, better endowed, or more successful professionally than you.

Tried and True	It's unrealistic to compare your affair partner and your spouse. Your lover doesn't have the responsibilities of home and family that your spouse does. Affair partners have a much more limited relationship, one that is focused on pleasing each other, and not on long-term commitment "for better or for worse." An affair is not a realistic experience of what life with your lover would be like.

It's almost always the case that an affair is not about finding a more attractive or sexier partner. In fact, many spouses are surprised to discover that their husband's lover is overweight or very ordinary looking, for example. Affairs are about many things, but it's rarely just about appearance or sex.

Is This Really the Person I Married?

Just as you begin to doubt your own self-worth and qualities when you learn of a spouse's affair, you may also look at your spouse with new eyes. He may suddenly seem like a stranger to you. After all, this is the person who pledged to spend his life with you and you alone, and he has violated this vow.

You undoubtedly married your spouse for what you felt were his many positive qualities. For example, he may have seemed highly trustworthy, reliable, responsible, and devoted, among other things. The betrayal of his relationship with you, as well as the deception required to begin and continue an affair, may appear to negate those qualities.

Take Brad, for example, who had recently taken a position as a pastor in another town. His wife, Rachel, homeschooled their three children and participated in leading the church's women's ministry. Together, they co-led the church's divorced singles group.

Rachel and one of the men in the group found themselves increasingly attracted to each other. Without Brad's knowledge, they began meeting for coffee to discuss his transition to being single again. Eventually, they were stealing kisses and caresses in his car.

One of the church deacons spotted Rachel and this man in the parking lot of the coffee shop one day. After some soul searching, he decided to inform Brad. Brad literally couldn't believe the news, but decided he had to discuss the matter with Rachel.

At first, Rachel said there had to be some mistake, and that the deacon must have seen someone else instead. Then, breaking down, she confessed that she and the man from the group had been meeting for coffee and exchanged some minor physical intimacies, but had not had sex. Brad said solemnly, "And I thought you were a good Christian woman." In his eyes, her life up to that point appeared to be a lie.

It's also not uncommon for the cheating spouse to question herself after an affair. She may come into therapy saying, "I don't understand this. It's just not like me at all. I've always been such an honorable, trustworthy woman." She may feel she has violated her fundamental values and sense of self, as well as the trust on which her marriage was based.

What Happens Now?

After discovering your spouse's affair, you may feel confused about what has happened and where you go from here. You're likely to struggle with a whole range of questions, including the following:

- Do you want to work together as a couple to build a better, stronger relationship?

- Do you need time to consider your future options?

- Do you now feel like your spouse is a stranger?

- What does the affair say about the spouse who cheated?

- What impact has it had on your self-esteem?

I explore these and other questions in later chapters, but this list previews some of the practical and emotional matters that you need to confront as you begin the process of recovering from your spouse's infidelity.

Essential Takeaways

- By far, the most frequent emotional experience right after learning of a spouse's affair is devastation.

- Other normal emotional reactions include anxiety, depression, and psychological numbness.

- It's common for the betrayed individual's self-esteem to plummet after discovering his or her spouse's affair.

- When your spouse has cheated, you might feel like your entire marriage was a lie and that he or she is a total stranger to you.

- It's also common to mistakenly compare yourself on all sorts of dimensions with your spouse's lover.

Part 3

Five Steps to Recovery

In this part, I look at how the process of healing from infidelity proceeds. In my clinical work, I use a five-step approach that has grown organically from my study of the topic of infidelity and my work with patients. I look at whether you and your spouse should try to heal your marriage on your own, or whether you'll do better working with a professional who specializes in this area. While the therapist clearly must work with the couple to understand what made them vulnerable to infidelity, I encourage them not to get fixated on the traumatic events of the past. My approach is to keep therapy sessions as future- and solution-oriented as possible.

The first step involves sincere remorse on the part of the cheating spouse for the hurt inflicted on his or her partner and on their marriage. Step two is a wholehearted recommitment to the marriage by both spouses. Step three requires the couple to hammer out a detailed behavioral prescription for the spouse who had the affair. These prescribed behaviors, in time, allow the betrayed spouse to begin to feel emotionally safe in the marriage again. Step four is also a challenging one, as it requires the couple to rewrite the story or narrative of their marriage in a way that accounts for the affair. Couples often struggle a great deal with the question of, "Why?" Finally, the recovering couple must craft a new vision for their future together. How do they see themselves going forward?

chapter 9

Contrition and Remorse

Beginning recovery with sincere remorse

Accepting full responsibility and not making excuses

Understanding how regret fits into this process

Deciding if you can forgive your partner

In this chapter, I look at the first step involved in the five-part affair recovery program that I cover throughout Part 3. There is frequently overlap in the steps, but each of them is critical. It begins, of course, with acknowledgment of the affair and the cheating spouse's acceptance of full responsibility for his or her infidelity. It also requires true remorse for the extramarital relationship. Can you forgive a spouse's affair? For your own sake, you may want to.

Rebuilding trust is a process unique to each couple, but it always requires behavioral "transparency" and a heavy dose of patience on the part of both spouses. You need to rewrite the story of your relationship to make sense of the affair. For some couples, this is the most difficult part of the process. A new vision for the future of your marriage—or for the two of you as individuals, should your marriage not survive—is also required.

How Are Contrition and Remorse Different?

As you read in the introduction to Part 3 of this book, there are several specific steps that couples must go through to recover from infidelity. The first of these involves the cheating spouse both feeling and expressing deep sorrow for his or her behavior and its consequences.

We hear the terms *contrition* and *remorse* frequently, but what exactly do they mean? Remorse refers to a feeling of deep anguish for a misdeed. Contrition is similar, but has slightly more theological implications. Contrition implies a desire to atone for your sins or wrongdoings. It suggests that some sort of penitence, or making amends, is in order.

What do these terms have to do with infidelity? While infidelity may not be a criminal offense, it is certainly condemned by religions like Christianity and Judaism that uphold the Ten Commandments as a behavioral code to which we should aspire. The seventh commandment explicitly states that we shall not commit adultery.

So for many people of faith, not only have they broken their marital vow of forsaking all others, but they have sinned against God. For Catholics, then, adultery would require that they confess their sin to a priest. For other Christians, this process might be a more private, direct matter, involving prayer.

Let's translate these concepts into the marital relationship. One partner has had an affair. What's the first step in the process of repairing a broken marriage? The betraying spouse must experience the deep sorrow known as remorse.

Remorse must be focused on the breaking of trust in the marriage, as well as the intense emotional pain inflicted on one's spouse. Over time, the cheating spouse must come to understand and feel and effectively demonstrate heartfelt empathy for his spouse's pain. If he is unable to "feel her pain," as the saying goes, it will be extremely challenging for him to join with her in working on the marriage.

Tried and True

As difficult as it may seem, it's always better to confess an affair than to be caught in one. And expressions of remorse must be sincere. Anything less will only damage your chances of saving your marriage.

For example, Ellie was an emergency room nurse who worked odd shifts. Her husband, Paul, was a faculty member at a local community college. He had blocks of time during the day with no meetings and no classes to teach. And when Ellie worked nights, he was alone. He often felt lonely and at a loss as to how to occupy his time.

Paul started frequenting a local bookstore/coffee shop on the evenings when Ellie worked. He made the acquaintance of a woman, Sherry, who worked in the store's customer service department. They began conversing regularly and Paul very much looked forward to his next visit to the bookstore. He even began encouraging Ellie to take on more night shifts.

Within a short time, Paul and Sherry had begun an emotional affair. They were sharing details of their intimate lives and made it clear to each other that, if they weren't already committed, they would be in a relationship. While they hadn't discussed it, Paul knew he would like to have a sexual affair with Sherry.

They began meeting for lunch at the local mall food court, as their schedules permitted. Unbeknownst to Paul, Ellie decided to run some errands at the mall one day during her lunch hour. While stopping to grab some lunch before returning to the hospital, she spotted Paul and Sherry at a table in the corner of the food court. She couldn't believe her eyes. They were deeply involved in conversation and were holding hands.

Ellie approached their table, but didn't say a word. Sherry murmured, "I'm so sorry, Paul," and hurried away. Paul announced that they'd talk about the situation that night, as he had an afternoon class to teach. Ellie called her shift supervisor and said she was ill and needed to go home. She spent the remainder of the afternoon crying and waiting for Paul to return home.

Paul wasn't sure how he got through his afternoon class, and he drove home in a fog. While he loved Sherry, he knew he didn't want his marriage to end. And he was haunted by how very badly he had wounded Ellie. He couldn't blame her if she was unwilling to give him a second chance. Ellie made no promises, but said she would consider it if Paul would go into therapy.

Within a week, Paul was in my office, fighting back tears and repeating over and over that he couldn't believe how badly he had hurt his wife and his marriage. He remained in therapy for almost a year, with Ellie joining us from time to time. In every session, he reiterated how concerned he was for her and that all he wanted was to preserve his marriage.

Saying "I'm Sorry" Isn't Enough

Of course, you have to verbally communicate to your spouse how sorry you are for your affair. You need to accept the fact that for some time to come, you will need to apologize, in words, for the damage you've done to your marriage. But words are not enough. Following are some of the other ways you'll need to communicate your remorse:

- As appropriate, tell your spouse how sorry you are for the way your affair has made him or her feel.
- Share your concerns about the impact of your affair on your marriage.
- Be willing to look into your spouse's eyes to see the pain, confusion, and hurt, even as painful as that is for you.
- Become more sensitive to changes in your spouse's moods.
- Ask your spouse how he or she is feeling, as uncomfortable as that may be for you.
- Spend time talking with your spouse, if that's what is needed.
- Find other nonverbal ways to show that you're connected emotionally and available—for example, giving a hug, holding hands, and putting your arm around his or her shoulder when you're sitting together.
- Be aware of those times when your spouse needs to be alone.

Acts of Contrition

Aside from expressing remorse and sorrow to your spouse, what else do you need to do? In Chapter 11, I examine some specific things you and your spouse need to do to start rebuilding trust. What about things like giving expensive gifts and making promises after infidelity? These have been suggested as appropriate and effective ways to preserve a marriage after an affair.

There are those who think that warning a spouse what it will "cost" them when they transgress again in the future (for example, a three-carat diamond) is an effective way to deal with infidelity. I take exception to this approach. My concern is that it sends the message that fidelity can be bought, or, that, with enough money, you can have a "get out of jail free" card in your relationship.

Promises to remain faithful after there's been an affair are also somewhat questionable. After all, you promised to be faithful when you took wedding vows. A promise by itself isn't effective. You and your spouse will need to work closely and openly with each other to develop a new way of relating and communicating.

The Cheating Ring

MISC.

When Kobe Bryant was charged with the sexual felony assault of a 19-year-old resort worker, he bought his wife, Vanessa, a $4 million, eight-carat purple diamond ring. Bryant claimed that he was disgusted with himself for having committed adultery, but insisted the sex was consensual. Rumors later circulated that Bryant was having another affair, this time with an 18-year-old LA Lakers' cheerleader, also named Vanessa.

While there is nothing wrong with giving your spouse a "gift" as a token of your remorse and your recommitment to him or her, it is not a substitute for partnering to rebuild your marriage. You must always take full responsibility for the damage you have done to your relationship. And you must be willing to do the difficult work of exploring why you felt you had the right to an affair or why an affair was a solution to the problems in your life.

Accepting Responsibility

In addition to expressing sincere remorse for an affair, one of the first things that need to happen is acceptance of responsibility. If you had the affair, this means not offering excuses for your behavior.

We live in a society of "victims" today. It seems that everyone has an excuse for why they did something wrong or inappropriate. Excuses for inadequate performance are common as well. An example of that would be your poor grades in a college course being the fault of your professor. He is unfair or too demanding or just doesn't understand your particular life circumstances.

While we've looked at some factors that may put a person at higher risk for engaging in an affair, that is exactly what those are. They are risk factors. They may make you somewhat more vulnerable, but they certainly don't cause you to have an affair. So, for instance, if you tend to have friends who are involved in extramarital affairs, you may see that behavior as more acceptable. The same is true if several of your co-workers are sleeping with each other, or if there's a history of infidelity in your family.

If any of these factors applies to you, you need to examine, very likely with the help of a mental health professional, what they are. If you and your spouse decide to work on the marriage, you also need to explore what you can do to reduce the likelihood you'll have another affair. As I noted, promising "it'll never happen again" is not an adequate safeguard.

Heartaches

Some of the top excuses for affairs are "It just happened," "It was only sex; I never loved her," "You weren't giving me what I needed," "I'm a sex addict," and "Our marriage was over long before the affair."

If you are the betrayed spouse, this will eventually mean scrutinizing your own behavior, your attitudes, and the state of your marriage around the time of your spouse's affair. It's important to remember, however, that you did not cause your husband's or wife's affair.

Nevertheless, each of us contributes to the quality and the strength of our relationship. You may find, for example, that you had become extremely involved with your career or your children and that you and your spouse weren't spending sufficient or quality time with each other.

As the betrayed spouse, you may be much too emotionally raw in the early stages of affair recovery for this kind of self-examination. But later on, whether you make a decision to remain in the marriage or to go forward on your own, it will be critical for the sake of any future relationships for you to understand what happened in your marriage. You will benefit greatly from exploring your strengths, and areas in which you need to become a better partner.

Take the case of Eddie and Pam, who relocated from a small Midwestern town to a large eastern city so that Eddie could pursue his career as an insurance executive. Pam had written for the local paper. She planned to do some freelance writing until she could find something more permanent.

Eddie worked late in an effort to get up to speed with his team. Evenings were sometimes filled with dinner meetings or with wining and dining colleagues. Pam began to feel lonely and resentful. The fact that her writing career was slow to take off didn't help matters.

Pam met a fellow jogger in their new neighborhood, a part-time pediatrician with two young children, whose wife often traveled on business. The two began jogging together and were soon sharing stories of feeling abandoned by their spouses. Before long, they became involved in an affair.

Eddie became suspicious when he observed the two talking at the mailbox for extended periods of time. He confronted Pam about the nature of the relationship. She initially denied anything inappropriate. When Eddie didn't let up, however, and threatened to go to the neighbor, she admitted their extramarital relationship.

Pam blamed Eddie, saying that if he weren't working all the time and paid more attention to her, the affair would never have happened. Initially, he argued with her, reminding Pam that he was the primary wage earner. But as Eddie thought about it, he began thinking that Pam had a point. It didn't excuse Pam's affair, but he had become so focused on his career and it was as if Pam's needs didn't matter anymore.

Regret Is Not the Same as Remorse

This may seem like a trivial distinction to many, but, when talking about affair recovery, it can be critical. Again, remorse is deep sorrow for having wounded your spouse and damaged your marriage.

In everyday parlance, we tend to use *regret* and *remorse* interchangeably. But *regret,* in this context, signifies wishing that the affair had never happened. It also suggests that the cheating spouse no longer has any fond thoughts about the affair or the affair partner.

This is where regret gets tricky. In order to rebuild his or her marriage, the cheating spouse must absolutely feel sincere sorrow and remorse. But is it completely realistic to expect that your spouse will never miss his or her old lover? Or that he or she will never relive the exciting details of the affair?

Sadly, the answers to those questions is no. We can't "unremember" something, especially something as compelling as an illicit emotional or sexual relationship. It's not uncommon for a spouse who has had an affair to confess unresolved feelings for a former affair partner to me in an individual therapy session, even as he or she is working hard to rebuild the marriage.

She might say something like, "You know, doctor, I desperately want to make my marriage work. I love my husband dearly and it tears me up that I've hurt him so badly. But I have to admit that I still think about Mark. I'm trying so hard to forget him and everything that went on, but it's not easy. Sometimes I think I'll always have a special place in my heart for him."

In this case, the wife has expressed remorse and has recommitted herself to her husband and marriage. But she has frequent and intrusive memories of the affair. She recalls how special that relationship made her feel and how exciting it was to have something all her own, in this case, a secret relationship.

Of course, as with many emotional struggles, time helps. If the cheating spouse stays away from the former lover and the things that bring the affair to mind, her sense of loss will diminish over time. But realistically, she may always retain some fond memories regarding the affair.

True regret over an extramarital relationship may be most likely to occur when the affair has become messy, difficult, or threatening to one's marriage. For example, if an affair partner threatens to go to the betrayed spouse, or refuses to accept that an affair is over. Under these circumstances, a cheating spouse may regret ever having gotten involved with his lover. She may become emotionally abusive or unbalanced at the prospect of losing her lover.

Fatal Attraction

Michael Douglas's portrayal of an unfaithful husband in *Fatal Attraction* and the dire consequences unleashed when he attempts to end his brief affair with Glenn Close vividly illustrates regret over an affair. As explosive as the sexual chemistry was between them, Douglas's character quickly comes to despise Close's character and to bitterly resent the turmoil she caused in his life.

Forgive, but Don't Forget

It's probably safe to say that no one ever forgets their spouse's affair. It is so incredibly devastating to learn that your husband or wife has been unfaithful that many couples even use a special term for the day they found out. They call it "D day," for "discovery day."

The memory of that day will be forever seared into your brain. You'll remember the wood grain of the table where you sat reading one after the other of the e-mails he wrote to his lover. You'll remember the faint drone of an airplane overhead as he says "We need to talk." You'll remember feeling physically sick as you watch him kiss his secretary and open her car door for her at the end of the work day.

If you've survived infidelity in your marriage, you have your own set of memories from D day. Depending on how long ago your discovery was, you may still be reeling from the experience. Or maybe enough time has passed that you know you'll survive. But one thing is for sure. You know you'll never forget.

Reliving D Day

Let's look at the case of Joe and Sandra, who had been married nine years and had two young boys. Joe was a pharmaceutical sales rep who occasionally had to travel to training events. Sandra had put her career as a caterer on hold until their children were in grade school.

Sandra decided to surprise Joe and meet him at the airport and treat him to lunch when he returned from one of his training seminars. She had gotten a friend to babysit and promised to return the favor. She smiled to herself as she imagined lunch with Joe and perhaps even some quick afternoon sex before she had to pick up their boys.

Sandra stood at the top of the escalator in the arrival lounge at the airport, searching the crowd for her husband. Her anticipation turned to horror when she spotted Joe on the escalator, his arm around the waist of an attractive blonde colleague.

Sandra was unsure whether to simply dash back to her car or to confront Joe. She chose confrontation and followed them to the luggage carousel. At the sight of her, Joe's smile vanished and the woman glanced nervously at Joe and said "I'll talk to you later." All Joe could say was, "It's not what it looks like."

Sandra refused to accept that statement, though, and kept pressing Joe for the truth. After a week, however—and Sandra's threats to leave him if he didn't come clean—Joe did admit that he and the woman occasionally slept together when they were traveling on business. He insisted, though, that it really was only about sex. They liked each other as colleagues and friends, but each was committed to their own marriage.

Sandra initially came to therapy by herself. She was haunted by that day and kept reliving those images. She couldn't bear for Joe to travel and she was terrified that he was talking to "that woman" whenever he was on the phone. Sandra couldn't be with him 24/7, but she worried constantly about what he was doing. She was even concerned that he might start another affair with a different colleague, "just for sex."

Joe eventually took part in the therapy. Over time, Sandra's anguish and fear began to subside and she felt some hope for the marriage. But the memory of her D day—that moment at the top of the escalator—remained vivid and painful for a very long time.

Can You Forgive Your Spouse's Affair?

While forgetting an affair is probably next to impossible, forgiving is a different matter. Forgetting is not under voluntary mental control. Forgiveness, however, is voluntary, as difficult as that may be to believe. It's what's called volitional, in the world of psychology. That means it is an act of the will, not of the heart.

Now, this doesn't mean that forgiveness is easy, by any stretch of the imagination. While it is within your power to forgive, it may feel next to impossible, especially right after learning of your spouse's affair. The timing of forgiveness is delicate.

Tried and True

If your spouse confesses an affair, or you discover it, the prospect of extending forgiveness right away may be excruciating. If you want to repair your marriage, however, you will eventually need to forgive. Without remorse on your spouse's part, and forgiveness on yours, the chances of rebuilding your relationship are slim.

In order to forgive an affair, you need to believe with all your heart that your spouse is sincerely sorrowful about the havoc he or she has wreaked in both your lives. And you need to believe that he or she is fully committed to your future together, without reservation. Only then can forgiveness feel like a possibility.

One vexing question is whether you can forgive someone for an offense if they have not asked for forgiveness. While there is no set answer to this, my inclination is that forgiveness must be requested. There are others, however, who would argue that you can simply say "I forgive you" when forgiveness has not explicitly been sought.

Like contrition, the concept of forgiveness has strong theological implications. The basis of Christianity, for example, is that we are sinful by our very natures, but that God forgives us when we ask. Christianity also makes it clear that, if we do not forgive our fellow human beings for their trespasses against us, then God will not forgive us. For someone of that faith, that's quite an incentive to forgive a cheating spouse!

The practice of forgiveness is being used more and more in psychotherapy as a tool for healing clients. And this is where forgiveness after a spouse's affair may have special relevance for you. The premise underlying this is that forgiveness benefits you as much or more than it does your spouse.

Does your spouse benefit from your forgiveness? Of course. Because true forgiveness translates into behavior, when you forgive the cheating spouse, he or she isn't subjected daily to your anger and your tirades about the affair. If your spouse is sincerely remorseful, he or she will always inwardly carry guilt about the behavior, but you won't be emotionally and verbally browbeating your spouse regularly.

One concern that a betrayed spouse often has is whether forgiving isn't equivalent to saying it's okay to go ahead and cheat again. This is absolutely not so. Part of the marital repair process is spelling out specific consequences for a future affair—for example, divorce. Forgiving does not make you a doormat.

Perhaps more important than how your spouse benefits is how you yourself benefit from forgiving. When you hold on to anger and bitterness, you suffer as much as the object of your hatred suffers. You may even suffer more. There is research evidence that links negative emotional states to physical disease. So you may be literally making yourself sick.

When you're unable to forgive, you also keep yourself "stuck" emotionally. Your energy goes into how angry and wronged you feel, rather than into personal growth and enjoyment of life. Again, it may take you some time to feel that you can forgive when your spouse asks you to, but in the end, you benefit at least as much as he or she does, if not more.

Essential Takeaways

- After an affair, the cheating spouse must both feel and express deep, sincere remorse or sorrow for the pain he has inflicted on his marital partner.

- It is critical that the spouse who had the affair accept full responsibility for her behavior and not blame her partner, deficiencies in her marriage, or other life circumstances.

- The day you learn of your spouse's affair is sometimes called D day, which stands for discovery day. You will remember the details of this day forever.

- Forgiveness is a decision you make, not a feeling you have. Understandably, you may not be able to forgive your spouse's affair immediately.

- Ultimately, forgiveness benefits both you and your spouse. It enables you to let go of bitterness and vengefulness and to begin living a full, positive life again. Forgiveness is something you do for yourself and your marriage.

Chapter 10

Recommitting to Your Marriage

> Deciding whether you want to try again
>
> Knowing if you have a future together
>
> Understanding the commitments required of each other to recover from an affair
>
> Allowing time for healing

In this chapter, I look at the second stage of affair recovery, which is recommitment. Like forgiveness, recommitment is based on a decision, not a feeling. You will learn about some of the factors that go into that decision.

And like the other stages of the process, the decision to recommit or not is complex. You need to take into account a range of factors, such as the history of your marriage and family, as well as the nature of the affair itself. You also need to assess characteristics about yourself and your spouse. And as with other stages in this journey, you need to be prepared for some emotional ups and downs mixed in with your optimism and hope.

Do You Want to Make Your Marriage Work?

The answer to this question may seem obvious to you. You're thinking, *Of course, otherwise I wouldn't be reading this book.* And you may be fully committed to holding onto your marriage.

But even for those whose lives are impacted by infidelity and who go on to rebuild their marriage, they may have required some time to reach that decision. The discovery of a spouse's affair can leave you not only emotionally devastated, but feeling completely confused and unsettled about your life, your future, and everything you took for granted before D day.

If you're the betrayed spouse, it's natural to doubt whether you can ever trust your husband or wife again. After all, they violated one of the most sacred vows an individual can ever make. So any promises they make that "It'll never happen again" may sound hollow and meaningless. And if the extramarital relationship also involved financial infidelity, such as spending family resources on an affair partner, then you may be doubly afraid. Not only has your spouse broken your heart, but he or she has been deceptive and reckless with your family's financial resources as well.

If you're the cheating spouse, you may also be unsure about the future of your relationship. This can be due to a number of things, including overwhelming feelings of shame and guilt, and doubt that your spouse can ever forgive you. Or, depending on the factors that contributed to your affair, you may experience relief that your secret is out in the open. You may even be considering a future with your affair partner. But more about that later.

Heartaches

Research shows that men tend to be more devastated by and intolerant of a wife's sexual infidelity. Wives, on the other hand, are more threatened by their husband's emotional involvement with another woman. They are more forgiving of "just sex."

Ronnie and Pat: Conflicted About Recommitting

Let's look at the case of Ronnie and Pat, who had been high school sweethearts. They had broken up a couple of times while dating, but always came back to each other. They felt they were true soul mates. They married shortly after high school. Ronnie went into the military, and Pat took a job as an administrative assistant at a local university.

Ronnie's deployments were hard on them emotionally, especially Pat. She was lonely much of the time and looked forward to the day he retired from the military and took a civilian job. Ronnie sometimes felt Pat was too needy and actually looked forward to his deployments as a temporary reprieve from her clinginess.

During his last deployment, Ronnie began an affair with a woman also on deployment. She was a single mother who often confided in Ronnie about how difficult her life was. Ronnie felt sorry for her and wished he could somehow ease her burden. He began helping with a few of her bills, unbeknownst to Pat. Ronnie shared with her his secret concern that maybe he and Pat married too soon, that they should have dated other people.

Shortly after Ronnie returned home from his last deployment, Pat received a phone call from a woman who refused to identify herself. The woman, however, made it clear that she intended to break up the marriage and show Ronnie the kind of appreciation and love he deserved.

Ronnie was genuinely stunned that the woman would call his home. He finally confessed to the affair, including the fact that he had been partially supporting her. He and Pat entered marital therapy together.

Ronnie had no interest in a future relationship with the other woman, and he felt ashamed that he had been so touched by the stories of her struggles as a single mom. Pat was conflicted. One day, she wanted desperately to preserve her marriage. The next day, she couldn't bear to look at Ronnie and felt there was no way she could ever trust him again. One of their first tasks in therapy was to wrestle with issues of forgiveness and recommitment.

Has There Been Too Much Damage?

It makes sense for a couple to take things slowly following revelation of an affair. (The exception to this would be physical violence, which calls for an immediate separation.) After all, you can always file for divorce at a later date. But if you act in haste and immediately pursue divorce, you may forever regret that you didn't take more time to consider all the options open to you and your spouse.

While many marriages do recover after an affair, occasionally too much damage has been done to rebuild the relationship. This can happen when an affair has gone on for years and the cheating spouse has essentially been leading a double life. It may be nearly impossible to recover from years and years of deception. Your spouse may feel like a stranger to you. You may realistically doubt whether you can ever trust this person again.

Another major complication arises when an affair results in a pregnancy. Some betrayed spouses are willing to accept the child into their family, or to encourage the cheating spouse to support and parent his out-of-wedlock child. Other wives can't bring themselves to welcome another woman's child into their homes and lives.

Sometimes the marriage has sustained significant damage even before the affair due to toxic communication patterns that have existed for years. These typically include major difficulties in expressing needs, conflict resolution, respect, and empathy. This type of marriage is structurally unsound, and an affair can be the final straw.

> **Tried and True**
> Renowned marital interaction researcher John Gottman warns about the "four horsemen of the apocalypse." These are negative, destructive behaviors that some couples engage in and that tend to predict that a marriage won't last. They include criticism, contempt, defensiveness, and stonewalling, or attempting to avoid conflict by withdrawing from the relationship.

Another impediment to repairing a broken relationship is a cheating spouse's thought of beginning a permanent relationship—perhaps even marrying—his affair partner. It's not uncommon for a cheating spouse to assure his partner that he plans to divorce his wife. It's just a matter of timing it right. So-called "timing" might be couched in terms of children leaving the home, or a wife finishing her education and getting a job, for example.

While these promises are notoriously hollow and unreliable, affair partners do sometimes become quite serious about leaving their own marriages and building a life together. Under these circumstances, recommitment to affair recovery is not realistic. All ties with the affair partner must be severed, and the cheating spouse must unreservedly recommit to his relationship with his wife.

Heartaches

One study reveals that only 3 percent of men having an affair divorced their wives and married their lovers. Another study reveals that three quarters of marriages between former affair partners end in divorce. So if you're counting on your affair partner's promise to divorce his wife and leave his family for you, you need to think again. The odds are definitely against you.

Are You on the Same Page?

It can't be stated too often that, following an affair, a couple needs time to process what has happened and to weigh their options. Of course, they need to make decisions about how day-to-day life will be handled in the meantime, especially when children are involved.

So there are many short-term questions to be asked and arrangements to be made. In addition to decisions about how you will manage the day-to-day details of your household, you need to sort out what information, if any, you're going to share with your children, your parents and other family members, friends, and co-workers.

Heartaches

Becoming physically intimate with your spouse after she has had an affair can be extremely awkward. You may for some time be fixated on what your wife did with her ex-lover and whether she's thinking about him during sex. Your level of sexual desire may plummet, or you may feel that your spouse doesn't "deserve" sex. Some betrayed spouses, however, are eager to resume sexual intimacy. They find it reassuring and feel that they are reclaiming their wife and their marriage by having sex with her.

If you're the betrayed spouse, you may feel intense anxiety and be willing to do almost anything to hold on to your marriage. If you had the affair, you may feel a great deal of uncertainty about your future. You may feel shame and guilt, not only for betraying your spouse, but also for not knowing whether you want to continue in the marriage.

For example, Dave and Danielle had been married for 13 years when she had a sexual encounter with a man she met at her sister's wedding. Because she occasionally traveled on business, she could arrange to meet with him for a sexual rendezvous from time to time.

Although the initial encounter was very much like anonymous sex, and Danielle never planned to see him again, over time she found that he was bright, ambitious, and a risk taker, qualities that strongly appealed to her. She began to see her lover and her husband as opposites. In time, she began to despise Dave.

Danielle was highly conflicted about the affair. It went against her moral upbringing and made her feel quite ashamed. Yet she was more and more drawn to her lover and the life he seemed to represent. She had no desire to be with him permanently, but the affair raised important questions about whether she wanted to continue in her present life.

Danielle entered into individual therapy to pursue answers to these questions. She also expressed her uncertainty to Dave. He had known something was wrong between them, but the thought of Danielle leaving him threw him into an emotional tailspin. His anxiety was almost out of control and he became very clingy with Danielle, which alienated her even more.

Dave attended several therapy sessions with Danielle. It became increasingly clear that Danielle needed time to explore her options and her thoughts and feelings about her marriage. Dave, distraught at the prospect of losing her, eventually went into individual therapy to learn to cope with the possibility of divorce.

While you will both have your own set of issues to cope with, there will need to be some consensus fairly early on after discovery of the affair. This consensus will involve practical matters regarding family functioning. The other critical question to be grappled with is whether you and your spouse will recommit to your marriage and whether you'll seek professional help in building a new relationship.

As I noted previously, you'll have many pressing decisions to make when you discover your spouse has been unfaithful. These revolve around how you and your spouse will function on a daily basis in the short term. Here is a brief checklist of some of the major concerns you'll need to address:

- Do you and your spouse need to separate for a time due to physical violence or extreme verbal abuse? If neither of these is occurring, staying in the same home makes it easier to work on marital problems. It also reduces an ex-affair partner's access to your spouse during this critical time.

- Will arrangements for child care and keeping children on schedule with school and extracurricular activities change? Children do better when disruptions to their schedules are kept to a minimum.

- Will there be changes in who pays for certain household expenses? I've worked with couples in which a husband financially "cut off" his wife after she had an affair. In cases like this, she may need to take legal action to restore reasonable support for herself and her children.

- Do you plan to share the news of the affair with family, friends, or co-workers? If so, exercise caution and divulge the information only to people you trust completely.

- Consider making an appointment with a mental health professional as soon as possible. Working with a competent, caring therapist can help you prevent further damage to your relationship, as well as lay out the tasks ahead of you, both short term and long term.

Do You Have a Future Together?

The other major question you'll have to confront is whether you and your spouse have a future together. Answering this question may take some time. It requires intense self-examination, as well as ongoing honest and open dialogue with your spouse. This is often best done with the help of a therapist who specializes in work with couples.

Sadly, numerous surveys and self-reports show that people frequently regret their decision to divorce, sometimes even before the papers are filed. The message here is that you should give yourself even more time than you think you need to make this life-altering decision. Working with a therapist for a brief period of time to explore your options can't hurt. You always have the option to file later. But once the divorce is final and your ex-spouse has moved on, that relationship is gone forever.

There are several critical factors that go into answering this question. One of these is how the process of affair recovery has gone for you and your spouse up to this point. If the cheating spouse has expressed genuine remorse for the affair, as well as a sincere desire to rebuild the marriage, those are positive signs that the two of you can have a deeply satisfying future together.

The History of Your Marriage

Other factors that go into answering this question have to do with what has already happened in your marriage. Most people look at marriage as a sort of "investment" in terms of their time, emotional energy, and even finances. For most of us, marriage is life's most significant partnership.

You and your spouse have created a home, in both the physical and emotional sense, a place of retreat from the cares of the outside world. At least, this is the case for couples early on, before they become busy and preoccupied with their own careers and lives. At some point, however, home may actually become a place we avoid, favoring instead the more sympathetic and stimulating atmosphere we find at work or in recreational activities.

Most of us have children. This changes everything when the status of a marriage is up in the air. I've heard countless times, "If it weren't for the kids, I'd leave in a heartbeat." Where children are involved, the concerns range from parental guilt over "ruining their lives," to damaging the relationship they have with their children, to financial hardship and having their children shuttle back and forth between two homes, to whether an ex-spouse will be a cooperative co-parent.

Relationships with friends and extended family are also a part of our marital investment. Divorce—or even knowledge of infidelity—will radically change many of those relationships. Some dear friends will stick by us during this trying time, while others will mysteriously vanish. Couple friends may "divide up" and side with one or the other spouse. Relatives may also take sides. In other words, our social and family life will very likely undergo some upheaval, at least temporarily.

Another intangible but important part of assessing whether to go forward together are the memories you've created as a couple. These include your wedding, first house, birth of your children, and job promotions, as well as the dark moments, such as illness, the death of a dear family member, and career failures and disappointments.

Tried and True	Any marriage can benefit from falling in love with your spouse all over again, but this is especially true for marriages scarred by infidelity. Try to vividly recall the qualities that first made you fall in love with your husband or wife. Then make it a point to remember those on a daily basis and learn to appreciate them again. Sometimes it helps to write them down, or post photos from those early days. You'll be amazed at how this simple exercise can rejuvenate your relationship.

Of course, divorce doesn't rob you of your memories, but it does mean that you won't be creating additional memories with your ex-spouse. And that is something that often doesn't hit home until after the divorce. The loneliness that it brings in its wake can be overwhelming for some. So take as much time as you need before making any irrevocable decisions.

The Future of Your Marriage

Besides the history of your years as husband and wife, you need to revisit your plans for the future. For example, you may both have had careers with retirement plans. How will divorce affect those? Will you need to keep working longer than you had planned in order to be financially self-sufficient?

I've worked with quite a few middle-aged clients who are considering divorce. One of the concerns they frequently voice is that they don't want to be alone in their later years. They want the comfort and the physical security of sharing a household with someone. They fear becoming ill and having no one to care for them. They also strongly fear loneliness.

"Gray" Divorce

Although older people tend to be more conservative in their attitudes toward divorce, the rate of divorce among Americans 65 years and older has doubled since 1980. Many of these people married early and simply want to experience a sense of freedom and independence they've never known. These divorces aren't necessarily motivated by factors such as infidelity or marital conflict, and the ex-spouses often remain good friends while they pursue separate lives.

Another question to ask is how the affair has impacted the way the two of you imagine your future together. For instance, perhaps you and your husband had planned to travel extensively after retiring. Now you are working to recover from his affair with a woman half his age. He's thinking travel is a bit too stodgy and is looking for adventure. He's thinking more along the lines of hiking the Appalachian Trail or mountain climbing. Perhaps your wife's affair with a more financially secure co-worker has you wondering if you'll be able to retire when you had planned, or if you'll need to keep working to afford the vacation home she wants. How will the two of you manage this change in vision for your future?

One simple test of whether you may be able to repair your marriage is whether the two of you can collaborate on anything, following revelation of the affair. For example, can you work together to make meaningful decisions about home repair or maintenance, or about the choice of a school for your child?

It's a positive sign if you can jointly agree on what the problem is, generate possible solutions to it and evaluate them, negotiate and compromise on a solution, and execute it as planned. These are strong couple skills that will stand the two of you in good stead during both calm and troubled times.

Allowing Yourself Time to Heal

Whether you and your spouse commit to rebuilding your marriage after an affair or decide to go your separate ways, give yourself the gift of time. After an affair comes to light, you have many decisions to make, some relatively inconsequential and some life-altering.

You'll be making decisions about the details of your daily life immediately after learning of the affair. It's best if you and your spouse can collaborate on these, regardless of how angry you're feeling at that time. This is especially true if there are children involved.

During this time, it's important to do what you can to stick to a routine with regard to matters like work and other commitments, such as social and volunteer activities. Paying attention to your physical and emotional health also helps stabilize your mood during this time. Regular exercise, good diet, and moderate use of alcohol are wise.

You may feel tremendous pressure to make major decisions shortly after discovering your spouse's affair. One or the other of you may feel you have to pursue divorce or commit to reconciliation right away. My advice to clients in this situation is to slow the process down as much as possible, as long as no physical violence is involved. I remind them that they always have the option of filing for divorce, if and when the time is right.

Let's take a look at Annemarie and Scott, who had been married for over 20 years. They had four children, one of whom was away at college. The others were twins in high school and a 9-year-old. Scott was a software executive who was occasionally able to work from home, allowing Annemarie to begin to pursue some volunteer activities.

She joined a literacy support group and after a time became involved in a brief, but intense, affair with one of the board members. Scott became suspicious when Annemarie began to have more "dinners" to attend. He started checking her e-mails and text messages, which left no doubt of her affair.

Annemarie made no attempt to deny the affair, but couldn't explain her behavior, other than to say for the first time in her life she felt like she was doing something just for herself. She wasn't in love with her affair partner and didn't want a future with him. But she felt sure she wanted a different life from the one she currently had.

Scott thought he could forgive the affair in time, but wanted her to decide immediately upon discovering her affair what her intentions were. She argued that she didn't know, but that if he kept pushing her, she would probably have to opt for divorce. Over the next few weeks, Scott went back and forth between pushing for an answer and trying to be patient as Annemarie sorted out her desires for her future.

Annemarie's initial task in therapy was to slow down the decision-making process. Her marriage and her family were at stake. She could always choose divorce at a later time, after dialoguing with her husband about what they both wanted and needed at this stage of their lives. She worked hard to resist making a decision early on, and Scott agreed to explore all possibilities with her in therapy.

Some signs that a divorce may be in order include a protracted break-down in communication, lack of trust, deception with regard to finances or outside relationships, no shared interests, and lack of respect for each other. Physical abuse and severe verbal abuse are almost always signs that a marriage is irretrievably broken.

The process of emotional healing after an affair begins with making the best decisions possible. Given the trauma inflicted by infidelity, a betrayed spouse needs to give herself as much time as she needs to explore her circumstances and her choices. It's almost always a good idea to give yourself more time than you think you need to decide for or against divorce. After all, your future is riding on it.

Essential Takeaways

- When you first learn that your spouse has had an affair, you may feel very confused and conflicted about what you want for your future.

- You will have to make decisions about how your household and your family will function in the short term. It's best for all if you and your spouse can agree and cooperate on these decisions.

- It's wise to take it slowly and deliberately when making decisions about your longer-term future. There are many stories of people regretting having decided on divorce too quickly.

- There are some circumstances, including physical abuse or a pattern of infidelity, which warrant strongly considering divorce.

- The decision to work on a marriage impacted by infidelity requires total recommitment by both spouses. A marriage can't be restored by one spouse alone if the other is uncertain or half-hearted about the relationship.

chapter 11

Restoring Trust

Working out the details

Being open and honest

Handling painful reminders

Learning how to measure your progress

Your spouse has expressed sincere remorse for having an affair. While you'll never forget the affair, you've decided to forgive him or her. After some soul searching, you both decide you want to make your marriage work. What do you do next?

In this chapter, I discuss what it is going to take to have faith in one another again. One of the first tasks a couple faces is rebuilding their trust in each other. Without this, there's little hope for the future of the marriage. This requires two things: very honest and specific conversations with your spouse, and time.

How long does this process take? Every couple is unique, and so is their path to recovery. One thing is certain. You need to be prepared for some emotional setbacks, but don't take those as a sign that your plan for recovery isn't working. It's all about communication, consistency, and patience.

Regaining Emotional Safety

Each of the five steps in this plan is critical to recovery from a partner's affair. This third step, however, is one that most couples are very concerned with early on. And with good reason. After all, if you can't trust your partner, how likely is it that you can make your marriage work?

Couples dealing with infidelity experience a whole range of emotions—shock, outrage, disappointment, anger, disgust, and fear, just to name a few. One of the biggest obstacles they face is doubt. Doubt that the betrayed spouse can ever trust again. Doubt that the spouse who's been unfaithful is truly willing to change. Doubt that they have the emotional stamina to get through this crisis. They are both desperate for reassurance and for specific tools to help them restore a sense of emotional security in the marriage.

In order to do this, a couple must be willing to share openly and honestly with each other what they need in terms of reassurance. This may actually be the first time in their marriage that they've been this straightforward with each other. But this level of honesty establishes a pattern that will serve them well in years to come. So what's needed to help the couple move along the path to restoring trust?

Creating a Plan for Restoring Trust

A critical task is establishing a plan of action for reassuring the betrayed spouse that the affair is over and that the unfaithful spouse is now recommitted to the marriage. It's not enough to simply promise that "it will never happen again." After all, your spouse promised to be faithful when he or she took wedding vows. Your spouse must now demonstrate, in both word and deed, his or her commitment to the marriage. How does this happen?

Ending the Affair

First of all, the cheating spouse must offer proof that the affair is over. How this happens depends upon the couple. Some couples decide to draft an e-mail together, with the betrayed spouse looking on while his or her partner sends it. Some couples decide to make a final phone call to the affair partner, with the betrayed spouse listening in. Some couples have even chosen to meet with the affair partner in person to end the extramarital relationship.

It is a mistake to try to maintain a relationship with the affair partner. Even an ongoing friendship or close business relationship can be awkward and lead to questions about fidelity.

The Devil's in the Details

It's common for a betrayed spouse to want to hear all the details of the affair. These details typically include the affair partner's identity, where and when they met, activities they engaged in (including sexual activities), things they said to each other, and how the affair partner compared with the betrayed spouse physically, emotionally, and even professionally.

This craving for information is understandable. It's a natural part of the betrayed spouse's attempts to come to terms with why the affair happened. What he or she is really seeking to understand is how he or she compares with the affair partner. Is the ex-lover more attractive? Is he more successful? Does she have a better personality?

Each couple, however, must determine how much information to share. Too many details may actually get in the way of recovery, as they create a vivid, indelible picture of the affair in the betrayed spouse's mind. How much information to share about an affair varies from couple to couple. Some people do better when they have more details. Most, however, probably fare better when they have the big picture of the affair without all the nitty gritty. The important point is whether sharing details of the affair will help the recovery process. Sometimes too much information can actually impede it.

The bottom line is that information about the extramarital relationship that doesn't address such key issues as why and how the affair began and the circumstances that allowed it to continue, is only likely to contribute to mental images that will be a source of distress for the injured spouse for years to come.

Accountability

Once the affair is over, the betrayed spouse needs to ask "What will it take for me to feel safe in this marriage again?" Sometimes the immediate answer to that question is "I need to know what he's doing every minute of every day." Of course, that's not a realistic option for most couples.

Given that you're not able to spend every minute of every day together, you and your spouse must arrive at some sort of workable plan for contact and reassurance. This plan will most likely include a schedule for phone calls, e-mails, and text messages. It may also include occasional breakfasts and lunches together. It may even include traveling together on business trips, when circumstances permit.

Let's look at one couple's story and see how they worked out a plan for staying in touch:

> After Lance became uneasy answering his cell phone at home, Brenda finally got him to admit that he had been communicating with a woman in the Chicago office of his company. Their personal phone calls, e-mails, and text messages were sexually explicit, and they planned to meet when Lance next traveled to Chicago. Since Lance was unable to cancel his trip or send someone else in his place, he and Brenda worked out a plan for staying in touch with each other. The first thing they did was to draft an e-mail to the woman explaining that Lance would no longer be contacting her and that she was to have no communication with him. Then, Lance agreed to change his cell phone number and e-mail address to prevent any further personal contact. In other words, their cyber affair was over.
>
> The next step consisted of planning how to stay in frequent contact with each other while Lance was away. They discussed Lance's morning, afternoon, and dinner meeting schedule. Brenda would call Lance first thing in the morning. Lance would call

Brenda before lunch and would text her during breaks in his meetings. He would make a brief call before going to dinner with his colleagues. Finally, they would have a more leisurely conversation after Lance returned from dinner and as they were both preparing for bed.

Establishing availability for contact is a key element in restoring emotional security. You and your spouse need to have a detailed conversation about the demands of your workday. You need to realistically assess how often you can call, e-mail, or text each other. Some betrayed spouses want as much contact as possible, while others are uncomfortable with that. They feel that it puts them in a parental role. They prefer more limited contact, even at the beginning of the recovery process.

Heartaches

The amount of contact that spouses decide on initially after the affair will most likely need to be renegotiated later. For most couples, as trust is restored, the need for frequent contact and reassurance will diminish.

Consistent Behavior

Affairs are often concealed by irregularities in behavior. A crisis at work may force someone to work late. Traffic jams and errands may delay getting home on time. But restoring trust requires that spouses who cheated do their best to be consistent in their behavior. For example, if your spouse normally leaves the office around 6:15 and arrives home around 7:00, it's extremely important that he or she continue this pattern.

Of course, circumstances arise that may disrupt one's schedule. Let's say you're wrapping things up at work and getting ready to head home when your boss sticks his head in the door and asks if you have a minute. It's probably not a good career move to say "no," but it's also important to give your spouse a quick call to tell him or her you'll be a few minutes late. It's also a good idea to call as you leave.

The same applies for getting stuck in traffic, remembering that you need to stop by the grocery or the pharmacy or the hardware store, or any other departure from your routine. An erratic schedule or unexplained lateness can put your spouse into a panic. Communication is key here. The minute or two that it takes to make the phone call can save both of you hours or even days of agony and unpleasantness.

While no one wants a permanent lifestyle of rigidity, the recovery phase after an affair is not a good time to make drastic changes in your behaviors, your habits, or even your appearance. Lapses in consistency in your behavior will have the same effect as lapses in transparency and honesty. If you are unpredictable in your behavior, you will sabotage the process of rebuilding trust.

The Office "Spouse"

Restoring trust can be especially challenging if your spouse works with his or her former affair partner. The "office spouse" is a term that refers to an intense, highly dependent relationship between co-workers (for example, boss and secretary). The intensity of this emotional relationship can be a precursor to a full-blown affair. Unfortunately, this situation is faced by many couples, because so many affairs begin in the workplace. Surveys show that almost 50 percent of unfaithful wives and over 60 percent of unfaithful husbands have affairs with co-workers.

Occasionally, either a spouse who has cheated or his or her former affair partner will seek employment elsewhere. But this is not an option for everyone, especially when economic times are tight and jobs are scarce. Sometimes a transfer within a company can be arranged, but this isn't always feasible, either.

When former affair partners must continue to work together, special arrangements will need to be made and monitored by both spouses. Betrayed spouses have different levels of tolerance for a partner's ongoing professional contact with an ex-lover, so the specific arrangements will need to be tailored to the couple and their circumstances.

The spouse who had the affair will need to make very clear to his wife or her husband exactly what the nature of the contact is. For example, must the former lovers interact throughout the day, or do they only attend a weekly staff meeting together? Are they required to call on clients or to entertain them together? Will they need to work closely on projects?

Business functions, too, can pose a special challenge. While some are family oriented, with both spouses attending, others are employee-only events. In this case, the partner who had the affair must be extremely professional and sensitive as to how his behavior might be perceived by the former affair partner.

Sharing Without Limits

Following the discovery of an affair, a couple committed to saving their marriage must revisit their ground rules for open and honest communication. After all, the revelation of infidelity brings everything the betrayed spouse took for granted into question. From here on, the couple must have a plan for sharing their innermost thoughts and feelings.

Transparency

We all know what the term "transparency" means when we're talking about a window or a pane of glass. It means that we can see clearly through it and that we have an unobstructed view of what's on the other side. The same idea applies in our intimate relationships. In this context, transparency means that we have a clear view of our partner's behaviors, thoughts, feelings, and motivations. There is a saying that "People who have nothing to hide, hide nothing." This nicely sums up the meaning of transparency in relationships—hiding nothing.

The late Shirley Glass, a psychologist who wrote extensively on the subject of infidelity, talks about "windows and walls" in marriage and affairs. She uses the metaphor of windows and walls for clarifying appropriate boundaries in relationships. In marriage, for instance, there should be an emotional "wall" between the couple and the outside world that protects against the danger of an extramarital relationship. There should also be a "window" between husband and wife; that is, there should be openness and transparency in terms of thoughts, feelings, and commitment in the marriage.

But when there is an affair, windows and walls become reversed. Instead of transparency in the marriage, an emotional wall is erected between spouses. And instead of a protective wall between a spouse and a potential affair partner, a window is opened in an extramarital relationship. In other words, the placement of emotional windows and walls gets switched around between the marriage and the affair.

 If you're not sure whether a relationship may be a threat to your marriage, ask yourself how you would feel if your spouse could see you interacting with the third party. Would you feel anxious or guilty? If so, it may be inappropriate. It may be more than just friendship or a work relationship.

Transparency means being open to sharing. After infidelity, the partner who had the affair may need to offer an unusual amount of detail about his or her activities. Your spouse also needs to respond openly to what may feel like intrusive questions. This is an unavoidable part of the betrayed spouse's need for reassurance about her husband's or his wife's recommitment to their marriage.

Transparency can sometimes be a struggle for the spouse who engaged in the affair. Your spouse may feel he or she is being micromanaged, treated like a child, or under house arrest. To some extent, these feelings are understandable. After all, your spouse has expressed remorse and simply wants to "move on." But the pace of recovery from infidelity is different for both partners. The betrayed spouse is in a very different place emotionally. He or she can't just move on. The couple has a great deal of emotional healing to do, and the spouse who cheated must be a full participant in that process, regardless of how long it takes.

Complete Honesty

During this phase of restoring trust, it's better to err on the side of caution with regard to honesty. So, for example, if your ex-lover is a colleague and you are assigned to work on a project together, it's far better to share this information with your wife in advance and explain to her how much collaboration will be involved. You may believe you are sparing her worry and anxiety by not telling her, but she will likely learn about this arrangement and her ability to trust you will be dealt a major setback. The restoration process will have to begin all over again, but this time with added deception.

Let's take a look at Nancy and Carlos and how her lack of honesty about the duration of her affair set back their attempts to restore trust. She had a brief affair with a man she had met at lunch one day. They visited a local motel several times over a period of three months. The affair was primarily sexual, and Nancy ended it due to feelings of guilt.

Carlos confronted Nancy when he saw a charge for a motel room on a credit card bill. She finally admitted to the affair, but said it was a one-time thing. Carlos checked Nancy's e-mail and text messages and discovered that she and her affair partner had actually communicated with each other for three months. When he confronted her about this, she tearfully explained that she had tried to protect Carlos' feelings by portraying the affair as an impulsive one-time event. Carlos angrily replied that the cheating was bad enough, but now, because of her additional lie, he didn't know if he could ever trust her again.

In the spirit of both honesty and transparency, the betrayed spouse should have access to cell phone and text messages, as well as e-mails and credit card statements, whenever he or she feels the need. For a while, this may be on a daily basis. If you're the spouse who's had the affair, you need to make this information available willingly and without resentment. It's a good idea to offer the information, but don't force it on your partner if he or she is not interested in checking at that time.

Having Patience

Another requirement for rebuilding trust after infidelity is patience. Both spouses have different timetables for recovery and there is simply no way to rush the process. The spouse who had the affair has the advantage of time and information. He or she has had full knowledge of the affair all along and has had time to determine what his or her intentions are with regard to the marriage.

The betrayed spouse is at a distinct disadvantage at this stage of the process. He or she may still be reeling from the shock of learning about his or her partner's affair. And it may be far too soon for betrayed partners to know if they have the emotional strength and determination to work on their marriage.

Let's say you are the spouse who had the affair. You're sincerely remorseful and you want desperately to save your marriage. You've expressed this to your spouse. You know what your intentions are and you're sure you'll never become involved in an extramarital relationship again. You don't understand why your spouse can't just take you at your word and go forward. But this process can't be rushed.

While the cheating spouse may feel certain of his or her intentions with regard to the marriage, it is unrealistic to expect the betrayed spouse to simply accept his or her partner's good intentions. There may be all sorts of emotional fallout such as overly aggressive questions, hurtful comments, or spontaneous bouts of crying. It is important to be patient and willing to ride out the emotional roller coaster until things settle down and trust begins to grow. The more patience and empathy you show for his or her state of mind, the more successful you'll be in restoring trust.

Heartaches

Patience can be mistaken for indifference, so the cheating partner needs to be ready to respond to his or her partner's emotional state with empathy when appropriate.

Recognizing Emotional Triggers

Part of restoring safety in the marriage is dealing with the betrayed spouse's emotional triggers. Triggers are people, places, and things that vividly bring the affair to mind. For example, reserving a room at a hotel chain where you and your lover used to meet may lead to flashbacks for your spouse. Ditto for dining at a restaurant where you used to have lunch with your affair partner. And if your spouse knows that your ex-affair partner had red hair, he or she may feel distressed at the sight of redheaded women or men for some time to come.

Movies and television programs that feature material about infidelity are also likely to make both spouses very uncomfortable. We're constantly surrounded by stories of infidelity among celebrities, sports figures, and politicians. It's almost impossible to go to the theater, turn on the TV, or open a magazine without being confronted with a story of someone cheating on his or her spouse.

Let's say the two of you are sitting on the couch, watching a movie. There's a scene in the movie that graphically portrays an adulterous relationship. Both of you are likely to feel extremely uncomfortable. If you're the betrayed spouse, how do you handle this? If you're the spouse who's had the affair, what do you do?

It's always a good idea to signal to your spouse how you're feeling. Openly acknowledging your distress at what you saw is far better than trying to ignore your reaction.

Things seemingly unrelated to the affair can also ignite strong emotional reactions in a betrayed spouse. For example, before her husband's affair, a wife may have simply thought of him as very outgoing and sociable. After learning about the affair, these qualities may seem suspect. However, asking a spouse to change his or her personality may be counterproductive and not very realistic.

It's not always easy to know what will soothe the betrayed partner when something has triggered a strong negative response in him or her. It really depends on how much information about the affair is shared. Communication is critical in dealing with emotional triggers. When in doubt about what might help your partner through a difficult moment, ask. It's fine to ask, for example, "Sweetheart, would you like me to change the channel?" or "I know you're upset; would a hug help?" or "Do you just need a little time by yourself?"

Measuring Your Progress

One of the most common questions recovering couples ask is "How long will it take for us to feel 'normal' again?" It's easy to understand why they ask that question. They are both in emotional pain and turmoil. But it's important to remember that they're at different points along the pathway to restoring trust.

There are several factors that influence the course of restoring trust. The type of affair and its duration will, in part, determine the rate of progress toward a new level of trust. For example, was the infidelity a one-night stand during a business trip? Or was it a deeply emotional affair that lasted for two years? The longer the affair and the stronger the emotional connection between the affair partners, the more difficult the path to recovery.

Another factor is whether there have been previous affairs. A history of affairs in a marriage means that deception and betrayal are more tightly woven into the fabric of the relationship. Earlier experiences with betrayal can make it more difficult for a spouse to recover from an affair. The current affair simply confirms his or her worst fears about how intimate partners treat each other.

For most couples, the path to recovery is a "two steps forward, one step back" process. Spouses must negotiate strategies for staying in closer communication and reassuring each other. When the spouse who had the affair forgets to make a phone call saying he or she will be late for dinner, or stays out a bit too late on poker night, he or she unintentionally damages the process of restoring trust with his or her spouse.

While the pain of infidelity never completely goes away, you know you're making progress when the pain begins to soften. Unwelcome thoughts and images come less frequently and are less vivid. Emotional triggers are less intense, and the betrayed spouse is able to calm him- or herself more quickly and effectively.

Progress is measured in large part by thoughts and memories of the affair occupying less of your emotional life. Other positive signs to look for are feeling more trusting of your spouse and being less anxious about what he or she is doing while away from you. Overall, you should feel more relaxed with each other and take increased pleasure in each other's company. When these things happen, you've reached a major milestone in your recovery.

Essential Takeaways

- Restoring trust in your spouse is an essential part of recovering from infidelity.
- You and your spouse will need to work out a plan that allows for honest communication.
- You will need to find ways to cope with the emotional triggers that are common after an affair.
- While there's no timetable for recovery, some positive signs are worrying less about your spouse's behavior and enjoying time with your spouse more.

chapter 12

Retelling the Story of Your Marriage

Powerful ways of thinking about our experiences and who we are in the world

Rewriting both your individual story and your couple story

Exploring your marriage through the years

Correcting unrealistic expectations you may have had about your marriage or your spouse

In this chapter, I look at the role of "story" in our lives and our intimate relationships. You learn that the stories you tell about your life, both to yourself and to others, contain a great deal of emotional power. They mold how you view yourself and your life.

Infidelity is a major event that requires both you and your spouse to rewrite your individual and your marital stories. This step in the affair recovery process can be difficult for couples. They may struggle to understand both who they were separately and as a couple around the time of the affair.

But if this step in the process is skipped or is not completed, couples leave themselves vulnerable to the threat of another affair. Without an adequate understanding of the interplay of factors that made your marriage vulnerable to infidelity, you don't have the foundation for a stronger, more resilient, more "affair-proof" relationship.

The Power of Story

Stories play an extremely important role in our lives, from the time we're young children until the time we die. Think back to the experience of a parent or teacher reading to you. For many of us, those were magical moments, when we were transported from our everyday lives to ones in which our most cherished fantasies became reality. In a fairy tale, we could, for a time, become the princess who is rescued and lives happily ever after, or the handsome knight who slays the dragon.

But stories aren't just for children. Think of the popularity of romance novels, stories in which the heroine meets someone who satisfies her both emotionally and sexually. Fiction for boys and men has traditionally featured scenarios in which they can explore their environment, experience danger, overcome hardship, and rescue or protect someone.

Of course, stories aren't only in books and magazines. These days, we are just as likely to opt for a two-hour movie as we are a book that might take us days or weeks to read. And stories of ordinary people's lives are everywhere, including online blogs, Facebook pages, and even Twitter, which purports to keep us up to date with the minutiae of someone's life in 140 words or less. These new media allow us glimpses into the lives of others just like ourselves.

MISC.

Narrative Psychotherapy

Narrative therapy focuses on questioning and challenging the implicit stories people tell about themselves. It involves looking at these stories from alternate viewpoints, in an effort to solve a problem in the client's life. It relies on the client's curiosity and willingness to collaborate with a therapist in exploring different explanations for his or her behavior.

Your Story Forms Your Identity

From childhood on, we begin to unconsciously construct the story of who we are and what our life is about. It may involve characteristics such as how good a student or athlete you are, how attractive or popular you are, your family dynamics (for example, are your parents divorced?), and your career plans.

As we grow older and accumulate new experiences, our story should ideally change to reflect these. But this doesn't always happen. We may hold on to outdated versions of our story. For example, the student who was on track to attend medical school, but who flunks out of college in his freshman year and moves back home with his parents, may find it hard to incorporate that life setback into his story. It's uncomfortable for him to allow the experience of failure into his identity. This was the case for Jim.

Jim had been his high school's valedictorian. He had a difficult time disciplining himself in college, but managed to graduate with a respectable GPA. He went into sales of chemical products after college, determined to become the top salesperson at his firm.

For a time, Jim was on track to reach his goal. At some point, however, he began to wonder whether sales was a good match for his personality, as he found himself dreading contacting his clients. His performance began to slip.

Jim neglected a couple of his major accounts, and those clients took their business elsewhere. This felt like a wake-up call to Jim, but it was too late. His manager reluctantly fired him, explaining that the company simply couldn't afford to lose more business or to have its reputation for customer service damaged.

For several days, Jim didn't even tell his wife he'd lost his job. He explained instead that he was taking a few days to work at home and catch up on paperwork. Jim struggled emotionally with having been fired. He began to drink during the day. He also began to rationalize his firing. In his mind, he began to see it as just one part of a corporate downsizing.

Your Story Is Your Public Face

The stories we tell ourselves about ourselves also combine into the way we present ourselves to the world. As the years go by, we accumulate experiences that combine to make us who we are. The sum total of these experiences—and how we react to them emotionally—form our identity.

When you're disappointed that you have not attained your major life goals, you may experience the "woulda, coulda, shoulda" phenomenon. This refers to feeling disappointment and regret, and laying blame for our failures. It can cause an individual to stay mired in self-pity, rather than taking active steps to move on with his life and move forward with appropriate goals.

We generally tend to create a public identity out of the parts of our history and experience that are the most positive—for example, our accomplishments. We understandably focus on what has gone right in our lives, rather than failures and areas of disappointment.

Some of the areas in which people typically want to highlight their successes are education, career, marriage and relationships, and their children's talents and accomplishments. People naturally feel somewhat competitive in these areas and so want to focus on their successes. It is, after all, a painful blow to the ego to be reminded of what has gone wrong in your life.

When Your Public and Private Stories Conflict

While it is natural for there to be some discrepancy between how we present ourselves to the world and what we truly believe about ourselves, many people experience a major disconnect between their public and private "faces." This can eventually become a problem in our work and social relationships. Nowhere is this more of a problem, however, than in marriage. Take the example of Carlos and Julia.

Carlos and Julia had been married for three years and had no plans for children. Julia was working hard to finish her doctorate in English literature, and Carlos held a sensitive government position that required a security clearance.

Julia became curious when Carlos started spending more and more time on the computer at night. She asked him about this and he responded that he was "just checking different things out." But as this new habit continued, her instincts told her something was not right.

Julia managed to crack his password and discovered that he had been soliciting sex from both men and women on the personals section of a major website. She was sickened and stunned when she read e-mails to and from men, describing the various acts they wanted to perform when they met in person.

The deception and betrayal were overwhelming for Julia. In particular, it was the sense that Carlos had a secret identity—in this case, a male prostitute—that devastated her. She couldn't help but feel that Carlos had been concealing some critical facts about who he was—bisexual, interested in anonymous sex, and willing to have sex for money.

While most discrepancies in our public and private stories aren't quite as dramatic as Carlos', if we take some time to examine our lives, it's not hard to find multiple areas in which we present ourselves to our spouse, our family, and the world in one way, but we privately think, feel, or behave somewhat differently, a feeling referred to as *imposter syndrome.*

Imposter syndrome refers to a sense that you really don't deserve the success and recognition you have achieved. You may feel that, if people knew the "real" you, they would know that you were a fraud and had been fooling them all along. Imposter syndrome tends to be associated with academic and career accomplishments, in particular.

So we see that major conflicts between what we present to the world, including our spouse, and what we feel to be true, in our heart of hearts, can give rise to relationship problems and to emotional discomfort. We'll continue looking at the role of story and how couples recovering from an affair must look closely at the stories they've constructed for themselves and the world.

Why Did This Happen to Us?

Aside from "How can we get past this crisis and begin trusting again?" the question "How could this have happened to us?" is the one I hear most frequently when a couple comes into therapy after one of them has had an affair. Dealing with the confusion about the reasons for an affair becomes a primary task for the couple.

It's rare that a couple has perfect clarity about the reasons for an affair at the beginning of the recovery process. They may struggle with various explanations, such as "He had lost 30 pounds and was looking for confirmation of his attractiveness," or "We had just grown apart and had nothing in common anymore." But most often they are perplexed, and the affair may likely have been fueled by a number of factors, such as personality characteristics, workplace culture, and opportunity, for example.

Remembering the Early Years

Doing an after-the-fact analysis of an affair and integrating it into your story requires going back to the beginning of your marriage. As you do so, you may find that the roots of discontent and other problems extend way back to the early history of your relationship. This was the case with Mia and Tyrone.

Mia and Tyrone met at a club when he was separated from his second wife. He made it clear that he wanted a divorce, and Mia accepted that at face value. They carried on a long-distance relationship for several months, and then decided to take a break. During this time, Tyrone got back together with his wife and three children. He and Mia continued to e-mail and occasionally talk, however.

When it looked like things weren't going to work out with his wife, Tyrone contacted Mia. They recommenced their long-distance relationship. Liza, his wife, was aware that Tyrone and his other military buddies liked to drink and go clubbing. She trusted him and wasn't particularly troubled by this until he was arrested for assault. Even then, she tended to blame others at the club that night, and made excuses for Tyrone.

Tyrone did eventually divorce Liza and he and Mia married shortly thereafter. She gave up her lucrative job in Internet advertising sales to move to the military base where Tyrone worked. She took a temporary job as an administrative assistant on the base.

Even though newly married, Tyrone expected to continue going to bars and strip clubs with his buddies. Mia tried to convince herself that there was nothing wrong with it, that she could trust Tyrone, and that her worries were "all in her mind." Two years later, after she had discovered Tyrone's affair with a dancer at one of the clubs he frequented, she wondered whether she should have acted on her instincts that something was wrong much earlier.

Tried and True	Just as with the purchase of a car, some people experience "buyer's remorse" with regard to their marriage. They second guess their choice of a partner, their timing, or even the decision to marry at all. While it may not sound very romantic, taking your time and weighing all the pros and cons of a marriage can reduce the likelihood of buyer's remorse.

A critical part of remembering the early years is getting back in touch with what it was that attracted you and your spouse to each other. Think about the circumstances under which you met. What was it that made your spouse stand out from the crowd? Try to recapture your memory of what initially attracted you to your spouse. That can go a long way in helping you regain a sense of appreciation for and attraction toward your spouse. (See Appendix A for more on how to fall in love again.)

On the other hand, many of us have a tendency to overly romanticize the first years of our marriage. But it's also important to be honest in remembering the "red flags" from that time. For example, did your spouse tend to abuse alcohol or other drugs? Did he communicate openly with you, or did he seem unresponsive to your concerns about the relationship or other life issues? How did the two of you handle conflict? Did you effectively handle disagreements, or did they go unresolved?

Those who decide to cohabit, or live together before marriage, often rationalize it as a "trial marriage" which will let them get to know each other's habits and thus make the transition to marriage easier. For years, the data showed that after these couples married, they were at higher risk for divorce. Cohabitation was associated with less commitment to each other. Some newer studies, however, have challenged this and indicate that divorce rates aren't significantly differently for couples who cohabit before marriage and those who don't.

When looking back at your marriage, you may find that the same event can have different emotional meanings for you. For example, a planned pregnancy and the birth of a child can be an occasion for unparalleled joy in your life. At the same time, the demands of a newborn and the tendency of many mothers to bond deeply with a child—often at the expense of the relationship with their husband—can mark the beginning of decreasing intimacy between them. That, in turn, can be the prelude to living parallel lives.

Understanding the Causes

For couples recovering from infidelity, this is the $64,000 question. Why did this happen to us? How could you have done this to us? Of course, everyone would like a quick and easy answer to these questions so that they can move along in the process of rebuilding their marriage. This is an area in which working with a professional who specializes in affair recovery can be particularly helpful.

In Chapter 3, we looked at different types of affairs and the factors that can contribute to them. As you saw, there is no simple answer to the question of why an affair happens. Each individual and each couple is different. For that reason, forces come together in different ways to influence the choices they make. This applies to decisions they make about their marriages and fidelity as well.

While working with a mental health professional is highly recommended, there are a number of questions that you and your spouse can ask yourselves to facilitate the process of understanding. These include:

- What information has my spouse shared with me about his or her affair?

- What questions do I still have about his or her affair?

- How did we feel about ourselves and each other around the time the affair began?

- Were there any unusual circumstances occurring during that time—for example, financial hardship, a personal setback, an adult child returning home, or an illness or death in the family?

- Were there changes I chose to ignore—for example, changes in my spouse's appearance, behavior, mood, or habits?

- What was going on in my own life at the time of the affair? Was I overly focused on career, children, or activities outside the home, such as church, volunteering in the community, or recreational pursuits?

The answers to these and other questions will need to be integrated into how you see yourself as an individual and how you see the two of you as a couple. Going forward, your couple story includes a very troubling event—infidelity. The affair and the devastation and disappointment you experienced all need to be written into the story you and your spouse share.

Listening to Each Other

As you go through this process of revisiting the early years of your marriage, it will be critical to listen closely to what your spouse has to say about what that time was like for him or for her. For many couples, those years are times when accommodations are made that can have a significant effect on the relationship. This was the case for Georgette, who met and married Frank while in college.

Tried and True	You and your spouse can prevent a great deal of misunderstanding and anguish in your marriage if you establish a pattern of expressing your concerns about the relationship when they arise. Keeping them to yourself and thinking they'll just "go away" without talking about them only leads to bigger problems.

Georgette and Frank eloped after attending the same college for one year. Frank had grown up in the area and maintained contact with many of his high school friends, including girls he had dated. After marrying, he enjoyed the shock value of mailing copies of his marriage certificate to them.

One ex-girlfriend in particular, Shauna, reacted violently to the news of Frank's marriage. She began calling his house in tears and writing highly emotional letters to him. Frank took her calls and wrote back, trying to reassure her that, even though he had married, he still cared deeply about her.

Georgette discovered some of these letters in Frank's coat pocket and was devastated. She monitored their correspondence but could not, however, bring herself to confront Frank. She became obsessed with Frank's apparently unresolved feelings for Shauna. At one point, she even considered divorce. Her parents had disapproved of the marriage, however, and pride prevented her from admitting that perhaps she had made a mistake.

Frank and Georgette came into therapy many years later after his affair with a woman he met at a rock concert. As they looked back over their history, Frank was truly stunned to learn how his continued relationship with Shauna had impacted Georgette. He said, "I had no clue. You never said a word." Georgette understood this and regretted that she had been afraid to confront Frank at the time.

> **Tried and True**
>
> A therapist who specializes in working with couples can help you learn effective techniques for communicating your feelings and your concerns to your spouse. He or she can also help you become a better listener where your spouse's feelings are concerned. These skills are crucial to a strong, healthy marriage.

Let's look at another couple. Tim and Lisa had been married for three years when they came into therapy. Both had been in long-term marriages before. Tim had gotten drunk at a party shortly after they married and had been physically inappropriate with a woman there. There was no sex, but Lisa was devastated when she discovered them. They had a volatile discussion about the incident that night and then Tim made it clear that he never wanted to talk about it again.

Lisa struggled inwardly with this episode in their relationship, but never mentioned to Tim the emotional agony and uncertainty that she lived with on an almost constant basis. Every now and then the subject of Tim's indiscretion came up, but only indirectly, and nothing was ever resolved. While Lisa didn't believe Tim would set out to have an affair, she did fear him acting inappropriately with other women again, since he seemed to have no insight into what had fueled the first incident.

Lisa felt they were stuck in a cycle of having the same argument over and over, and that was the catalyst for them coming into marital therapy. During the course of processing Tim's infidelity and its impact on their marriage, it became clear that they had other unresolved issues. In his previous marriage, Tim had been quite outspoken about what he did and didn't like. He frequently commented negatively on Lisa's cooking, her style of dress, her parenting of her adult children, and her behavior in general. Lisa found this devastating. Although he had cheated on her, her ex-husband had never been openly critical of her.

From time to time, Tim would erupt in what felt to Lisa like a barrage of criticism. After attempting to defend herself, she would simply shut down emotionally and end the conversation. Tim's response to this was to counterattack with "See, I can't say anything to you." He would then shift the argument to "You're always trying to control me. I have to ask permission to do anything. Next time I'll know to keep my mouth shut." Lisa felt confused and defeated.

Lisa was dumbfounded by Tim's comments. She had the distinct feeling that his anger and his responses had more to do with issues in his first marriage than with her. But she was at a loss as to how to tackle this problem and get them on the road to seeing clearly what their own concerns were and dealing with those in a straightforward manner.

In addition to marital therapy, Tim went into individual therapy to explore what was driving his anger and his irrational responses to Lisa. It was a lengthy process, but he could at least offer Lisa the reassurance that he was working on the problem. Lisa, too, entered individual therapy for her unresolved concerns about Tim and his infidelity.

Heartaches

A mistake couples commonly make is waiting too long to seek professional help. Understandably, they want to try to "fix" things on their own if they can. But they generally end up using the same ineffective relationship strategies they were using before, with the same results. Seeking help in a timely fashion can make all the difference.

These couples' stories illustrate the indisputable importance of honesty and openness in marital communication. Both couples suffered because one or both of the partners felt unable to share their concerns about the marriage. It was only after the level of distress in the relationship had reached a critical level that both spouses began to reveal their unspoken fears and resentments in their marriages. They could have spared themselves a great deal of heartache had they been equipped to approach these issues as they arose.

Adjusting Your Expectations

For many couples, the process of rewriting their story eventually includes revisiting what they expect from their spouse and their marriage. Upon close examination, they may find that they held unrealistic expectations for this relationship and that perhaps these expectations put them at higher risk for infidelity.

Here are some questions to ask yourself as you explore what you expect from your spouse and your marriage:

- Did you think you and your spouse should spend all your free time together?

- Did you think that love was all you needed for a good marriage?

- Did you think that your sex life would always be as good as it was in the beginning?

- Did you, at some point, begin to think you knew everything there was to know about your spouse?

- Did you think there was absolutely no chance of your spouse ever cheating on you?

If you answered "yes" to one or more of these questions, now is a good time to rethink what a healthy marriage looks like:

- Husbands and wives both need some time to themselves and time with friends or others who share a special interest, such as fishing or scrapbooking. When you spend some time apart, you come back to your marriage recharged. You're also a more interesting person to your spouse when you maintain some interests of your own.

- Ever since love became the primary factor in our choice of a mate, many couples have fallen prey to this myth. The truth is that a good marriage requires not only love, but also commitment to work through the hard times, and skills that enable you to clearly communicate, problem solve, negotiate, and compromise.

- While a couple can have a deeply satisfying sex life whether they're married 5, 25, or 50 years, that aspect of their marriage will most definitely change. The novelty will wear off, and eventually health problems may impact your sex life. But the good news is that there are plenty of things you can do to spice up your sexual relationship.

- One trap couples commonly fall into is that after a few years, they start believing they know just about everything there is to know about their husband or wife. The truth is that there is always something new to discover about our partner, and that they are constantly changing and developing as well, if only in small ways.

Of course, none of us wants to think our spouse would ever be unfaithful. But the reality is that affairs occur even in "good" marriages. There are many steps we can take to keep our marriages strong, but there are no guarantees.

Essential Takeaways

- Stories about ourselves and our relationships, including our marriage, are an important part of our lives. Our stories shape how we feel about ourselves and the world.

- We construct public stories to present to the world, but we also have private stories that contain information we generally don't share with others, such as failure to achieve important goals.

- When there has been an affair, the story of your marriage needs to be rewritten to account for it, as well as the circumstances surrounding it.

- Rewriting your couple story requires open communication between you and your spouse. When you engage each other in honest dialogue, you may be surprised at what you learn about your spouse's perspective on certain aspects of your marriage.

- As you look back over your marriage, you may find that you had some unrealistic expectations about this most intimate relationship. The good news is that it's never too late to adjust our expectations.

chapter 13

Renewing Your Vision

Growing confusion about the direction in which you are headed in life

Deciding what kind of couple you and your spouse will be going forward

Determining what becomes of your personal identity

Working with a psychologist or counselor

Allowing yourself ample time to decide what's right for you

In this chapter, I examine the process of planning for your future as a couple. If you have recommitted to your marriage, the two of you have done a considerable amount of work to repair your marriage by this time. Of course, the stages of affair recovery often overlap, but you have established a new level of trust and worked to understand factors surrounding the affair. You have rewritten the narrative of your marriage to include a "chapter" on infidelity.

You and your spouse are no longer the same people you were prior to the affair. Whatever level of comfort and security you felt in your marriage was drastically shaken. The foundation of trust on which marriage is built had to be reconstructed. And now you must revisit the dreams you had for yourselves and your future.

Many couples find this process goes more smoothly when they work with a mental health professional who specializes in relationship issues. A psychologist, for example, can help you determine your personal and marital priorities. He or she can also help you chart the course that will best help you reach your goals.

Where Do We Go from Here?

Recovering from an affair is a grueling ordeal for a couple. For many, the recommitment stage is easy. They know, beyond a shadow of a doubt, that they want to stay in their marriage. But restoring trust is a highly detail-oriented process. Couples must hash out the nitty-gritty of precisely what the cheating spouse needs to do to help the betrayed spouse begin to feel emotionally safe again.

Restoration of trust is also an open-ended process. It's not possible to precisely specify how long this stage will take. Most betrayed spouses, however, eventually reach a point where they no longer feel the need or the desire to monitor their spouse as closely as they did after discovering the affair. This may take weeks or months, depending on the circumstances and the personalities involved.

Once transparency and open communication have been established in the marriage, the couple must begin the arduous task of understanding the affair and the personal and relationship factors that may have played a part. This stage, in particular, can be painful because of the degree of self-examination required. Remember that nothing justifies an affair, and the partner who had it must accept total responsibility for his or her behavior. But understanding the affair means understanding any weaknesses in the marriage that perhaps made it more vulnerable to an outside relationship.

The question remains, then, as to what your future will look like. A couple that doesn't go through the necessary steps to reach some new level of commitment and understanding will likely not survive. Remaining in denial about the affair, or trying to "just get past it" as quickly as possible can easily lead to or inflame highly toxic patterns of communication and interaction, such as contempt and stonewalling.

Tried and True The importance of getting good professional help after your spouse has an affair can't be overemphasized. Without that, your marriage stands approximately a one in three chance of surviving. Unlike painting your house, affair recovery is not a DIY project!

Let's take a look at Enrico and Jamie, who had been married for four years. Out of guilt, Jamie confessed to Enrico that she had an affair and begged him to forgive her. Enrico was devastated, but after a time, agreed to give the marriage a second chance.

Although they had formally reconciled, the emotional climate of the marriage seemed to be steadily deteriorating. They were extremely uneasy in each other's presence, there was no humor in the relationship anymore, and they hadn't had sex in months. Jamie suggested going to see a therapist, but Enrico snapped back that he didn't want to "air their dirty laundry" to a complete stranger.

Enrico forbade Jamie to talk to family or friends about the affair. In her desperation for comfort and understanding, she divulged the affair to a male co-worker with whom she frequently had lunch. Not surprisingly, within a few months, Jamie began a second affair, this time with her co-worker. Eventually, she came to Enrico and told him she wanted a divorce.

If you and your spouse are simply unable to work through the early stages of the affair recovery process, you might conclude that divorce is your only option. If this is the case, there are still important issues to be addressed. For example, if you have minor children, co-parenting them must become your first priority. Issues of child support, custody, and visitation are determined, in part, by the court in accordance with the laws of your state. But establishing an amicable post-divorce relationship with your ex-spouse is up to the two of you.

Who Do You Want to Become?

An affair calls almost everything in your life into question. Your most intimate relationship, the one in which you probably felt most secure, was violated. For many people, even worse than the cheating is the deception itself. It can be a long struggle indeed to feel you can never take your partner at his or her word again.

Your sense of your future, both as a couple and a person in your own right, may also be casualties of the affair. Perhaps you envisioned yourself and your spouse retiring to travel around Europe or to visit the national parks in your RV. Perhaps you saw the two of you visiting your children and grandchildren several months out of the year. Perhaps you were looking forward to working only part time.

On the individual level, maybe you planned to pursue your hobbies after taking early retirement. Perhaps you hoped to take up photography or woodworking on a semi-professional level. Perhaps you even planned to go back to school, get a second degree, and start a second career. Or perhaps you hoped to devote your time to creating a show-stopping garden.

An affair can derail your dreams for the future. Some harsh realities, such as an unplanned pregnancy with an affair partner or contracting an STD, can change your life in drastic ways. A child born to an affair partner needs to be supported for approximately 18 years, perhaps consuming your retirement nest egg. And if the female affair partner is married, there can be major repercussions. You might find yourselves dealing with an irate or even dangerously jealous spouse.

As a Couple?

As you work through the steps of affair recovery, you need to redefine yourselves as a couple. A critical part of this is confronting the harsh realities that the affair has introduced into your lives. Again, this includes dealing with the consequences of the affair.

The consequences of an affair can be enormous and far-reaching. Not only have you ravaged your relationship with your spouse, but you have introduced other players into your family and work relationships and your friendships. Your affair partner is only one of a cast of characters whose lives are changed by your illicit relationship.

If you have children, their lives will be forever impacted in one way or another. If you are considering divorce and your children are minors, you need to think about how all the details of day-to-day life will be managed. You need to establish a consistent routine for them. This, and your continued expressions of your love, will eventually allow them to regain some measure of emotional safety. If you and your spouse decide to salvage the marriage, however, you also need to consider how much, if anything, your children know about the affair. This is a complicated issue that I address in Chapter 15.

How children are impacted by a parent's affair depends in great part on their developmental level. Younger children may see the affair as due to their own "bad" behavior, as perhaps even something that they caused. Teens and young adult children may become highly moralistic and respond with contempt and disgust. They may also conclude that it's impossible to trust in a relationship, so why even bother striving for intimacy and faithfulness?

Others affected by the affair may include extended family members. Understandably, they may have taken sides with the betrayed spouse. Occasionally, though—and this is especially true if it's their son or daughter who has been unfaithful—they may blame the injured spouse for letting the marriage deteriorate or not meeting his or her spouse's needs. If the extended family has become polarized over the affair, a great deal of repair work needs to be done so that everyone can gather together peaceably at holidays and other special occasions. So it's probably best not to engage in major "character assassination" if you're trying to work on your marriage.

Other stakeholders in your affair clearly include your former affair partner, assuming you have ended the relationship and are working diligently to build a new relationship with your spouse. If you ended the affair and he or she wants to continue it, your ex-lover may become extremely distraught. He or she may threaten to inform your spouse, your boss, or even to commit suicide. Although all threats of suicide must be taken seriously, and you may need to assist your ex-partner in getting appropriate psychiatric help, such threats should not deter you from your intention to recommit to your spouse and repair the damage you've done to your marriage.

If your former lover is married, you may also have to deal with his or her spouse. Men are particularly sensitive to sexual infidelity, and the thought of his wife being physically intimate with another man can send someone into a jealous rage. Again, your affair partner's husband or wife may threaten to inform your spouse, to ruin you professionally, or to harm you physically. As with threats of suicide, threats of harm must be heeded, and appropriate law enforcement personnel should be involved.

Take Audrey, for example, whose marriage and career were threatened by an irate spouse who discovered that Audrey was having a cyber affair with *her* husband. Audrey and Dennis had been married for almost 20 years. Both had done well in their careers with the same multinational banking firm, but recently Dennis was promoted to a senior executive position. He left for work earlier in the morning, brought more work home with him, traveled frequently on business, and talked about the challenges of his new position incessantly.

Although Audrey was pleased at his success, she felt somewhat abandoned. Their children had both recently left for college, they had no relatives in the area, and, because of their demanding work schedules, they put little effort into developing friendships with other couples.

Audrey attended a professional development conference in another country. While on the train, she struck up an in-depth and fairly intimate conversation with the man seated next to her. They exchanged business cards. Audrey didn't expect to hear from him, but, within a week, he e-mailed her.

As Dennis poured more of his emotional energy into his career, Audrey corresponded with the man from the train more and more frequently. Their e-mails became extremely intimate and sexual, with each of them rationalizing that their spouses emotionally checked out of their marriages some time ago. They even discussed plans to meet for a rendezvous in the near future.

Audrey's e-mail partner's wife eventually discovered her husband's highly sexual correspondence. In a rage, she e-mailed Audrey and threatened to contact Dennis with details of the cyber affair. She also threatened to expose her husband's and Audrey's infidelity to their supervisors, in an attempt to damage their careers.

Unwilling to risk her career, Audrey never contacted the man from the train again. But she also decided not to work through her unhappiness in her marriage. She entered individual therapy, but continued to feel isolated and estranged from Dennis.

In addition to the emotional turmoil of an affair, there are physical risks as well. Pregnancy and STDs are a real risk when there is an affair. A child born of an affair will obligate you to your affair partner forever. You might incur child support obligations for at least 18 years. And, of course, there is the question of how involved you will be in that child's life. Is the nonbiological father willing to raise the child as his own? Should the child know at some point that the man raising him is not his biological father? Even after the child is grown, there will be circumstances where you will have to interact with your former lover, graduations and weddings, for example. And through all of this, you will need to consider and be sensitive to your wife's feelings, while bearing in mind the best interests of your out-of-wedlock child. If you are a woman who becomes pregnant in the course of an affair, how do you deal with your husband's emotions and wishes when he learns of the pregnancy? What do you tell your other children?

Even if you are convinced you've been practicing safe sex with your affair partner, you should be tested for sexually contracted diseases at the appropriate intervals. This is important whether or not you plan to work on your marriage. You owe your spouse the certainty of whether or not his or her health has been compromised by your affair. And if you are the betrayed spouse, you, too, should be tested for STDs, regardless of what your spouse tells you about having used condoms. Your health is too important to leave in the hands of someone who was willing to lie to you in the first place.

Don't assume that the use of a condom equals safe sex. HPV (human papillomavirus), which has been linked to cervical cancer, can live on the skin of the scrotum, and some types of warts can be transmitted through oral or manual sex. The Centers for Disease Control states that one in three Americans have a sexually transmitted disease by age 35. Approximately 1 in 300 people are infected with HIV, and 25 percent of this group is unaware that they are infected.

As Individuals?

In addition to the sense of security that you took for granted in your marriage being destroyed, your sense of worth as an individual might be severely shaken by an affair. You might know, on a conscious level, that you didn't cause your spouse's affair. But at a deeper level, you involuntarily question whether there was something about you as a person, or something you did or didn't do, that drove your spouse into an extramarital relationship.

Women, in particular, seem prone to self-blame when their husband has an affair. Although they know it's not rational, they scrutinize themselves for evidence that they somehow contributed to it: they were less attractive or less interesting than the affair partner; they weren't as much fun to be around; they talked too much (or not enough); they didn't make their husband feel as appreciated as he would have liked. The list goes on.

Men, too, might also experience pangs of self-doubt when their wife has an affair. For instance, they might immediately engage in an implicit comparison with the affair partner regarding their sexual prowess or their adequacy as a provider. But they tend to move much more quickly than women into blaming their spouse. They generally don't struggle with protracted periods of doubting their worth as an individual and a partner.

So as you recover from your spouse's affair, do you find you are looking at yourself in a different light? Are you feeling less adequate, accomplished, desirable, and worthy than before? If so, take some time to think about steps you can take to recover your sense of being a worthwhile person. Here are a few ideas:

- Remind yourself that your spouse chose to have an affair. There was nothing you said or did—or didn't do—that forced him or her into it.

- Make a list of your accomplishments, such as your performance at work, your parenting skills, and your friendships. Remind yourself that you are a valuable human being.

- Take up some activity that you've always wanted to try, whether jogging, pottery, skydiving, or volunteering at a nursing home. Allow yourself to feel good about your new activity without being judgmental about your performance.

- Reconnect with your spiritual or religious foundations. Focus on teachings about unconditional love and remind yourself that you are unconditionally loved by your creator.

- Utilize available support groups, whether sponsored by your church or synagogue, or a group such as Beyond Affairs Network.

Although mental health professionals often focus on the damage to the betrayed spouse's self-esteem, the flip side of the coin is that the cheating spouse frequently has self-esteem issues as well. In fact, the affair may be an attempt to bolster a negative self-image. Concerns about aging, sexuality, lovability, and even mortality can contribute to the decision to engage in an affair.

Patrick's low self-esteem led to his affair. Patrick and Lynne had been married for almost eight years. It was a first marriage for both, but they were in their mid-30s when they met and married. Lynne was unable to conceive, and testing revealed that Patrick had an unusually low sperm count. Lynne decided she was unwilling to undergo IVF. Patrick was devastated and felt rejected.

Patrick traveled on business approximately two weeks out of the month, but when he was home, he enjoyed landscaping and home improvement projects. He often invited Lynne to join him in trips to the hardware store or in working in the yard. She consistently declined, and Patrick eventually felt that she cared little for him or his interests. He began to comfort himself with food and alcohol. Within a short period of time, he put on 35 pounds.

As he began to feel increasingly isolated and undesirable, Patrick started picking up women in bars while traveling, as well as frequenting strip clubs and buying lap dances. One of the women with whom he had casual sex while on the road e-mailed him and they began sending nude and masturbation photos. Although still sensitive about his weight, Patrick felt desirable again. He felt reassured that he was able to arouse and sexually satisfy a woman.

Lynne discovered the e-mails and the photos and threatened divorce if Patrick did not attend therapy with her. Desperate to save his marriage, he agreed. Patrick was filled with remorse and shame. In therapy, Lynne also came to understand how her repeated rejections of Patrick made him feel. He agreed to stay in close touch with Lynne while he traveled and make his e-mails and cell phone records available to her. Lynne expressed an interest in occasionally traveling with Patrick and agreed to participate in some of his around-the-house projects.

If you are the spouse who had the affair, part of your work in recovery will be to examine whether any of these concerns about yourself increased your vulnerability to becoming involved with someone outside your marriage. Individuals with a strong, secure sense of self and core values generally don't make the decision to participate in an affair, even if their marriage is far from perfect.

Can You Do This on Your Own?

Throughout the affair recovery process, you may wonder whether you should enlist professional help. Although time and finances are realistic concerns for most people, many couples choose to look at therapy as an investment in their marriage. Therapists are unable to guarantee a time frame within which you'll feel like your marriage is on more solid ground, but it's certainly reasonable to talk about a schedule for evaluating your progress. Don't hesitate to ask questions about the process and what to expect.

> **Tried and True**
>
> If you choose to work with a therapist, it's perfectly acceptable to ask questions about the process, the fee, and how the therapist plans to work with you. Although he or she may not be able to specify exactly how long you'll need to be in therapy, a reputable therapist should be willing to answer your questions and to agree to evaluate your progress and make decisions with you about further therapy.

Some couples choose not to work with a professional as they struggle to recover from an affair. This is a riskier choice, and the odds of your marriage surviving decrease considerably. However, there are numerous self-help books and online programs, as well as support groups in churches, synagogues, and the community.

It's not unusual for a couple impacted by infidelity to rely heavily on the support and advice of friends, family, and perhaps co-workers. A robust social support network is valuable for a variety of reasons—for example, help with child care or transportation, preparing meals, shopping, and companionship. But advice on whether to stay married or how to go about repairing your damaged relationship is probably best left to professionals. Although friends and family probably have your best interests at heart, they also have an implicit agenda. And you might receive contradictory advice, leaving you in an even greater state of confusion.

Therapy and Counseling Options

If you and your spouse decide to work with a professional, you have many resources from which to choose. There is a considerable range of specialties in which people can become credentialed and licensed. These include the following:

- A psychologist with a Ph.D. or a Psy.D., both of whom obtain doctoral degrees and complete a lengthy sequence of clinical training experiences. A Ph.D. will also have extensive research experience.

- A counselor with an L.P.C., who has a Master's degree and supervised clinical training.

- A clinical social worker with an M.C.S.W. or an L.C.S.W.

- A marriage and family counselor with an M.F.T.

- A psychiatric nurse with an R.N.

- A psychiatrist with an M.D.

Of these specialties, only the psychiatrist is legally allowed to prescribe medication, except in New Mexico and Louisiana, where licensed psychologists also have prescribing privileges. However, practitioners in the other disciplines regularly collaborate with psychiatrists and refer their clients to be evaluated for medication. So, for example, a couple might come into therapy after an affair and work with a psychologist. The psychologist might determine that the betrayed spouse is depressed and is a candidate for short-term medication. In that case, he or she would make a referral to a psychiatrist, who would prescribe and monitor the medication.

> **Tried and True**
>
> Trying to locate a good therapist can feel overwhelming. Word of mouth can be helpful, if you know someone who had a positive experience in therapy. The American Psychological Association and many state psychological associations also have therapist referral websites, which profile therapists in your area, giving information about their background, their theoretical orientation, and their specialties. The popular magazine *Psychology Today* also maintains a website with a therapist referral service.

A brief word on the difference between psychotherapy and counseling is in order. Counseling generally refers to advising with respect to a specific problem. Psychotherapy refers to a more in-depth process geared toward uncovering motivations and unconscious conflicts in someone's life. It is generally a lengthier process than counseling and requires a different type of training. Although psychotherapists may find themselves counseling, in many circumstances, counselors generally don't have the training required for in-depth psychotherapy. In reality, there is often significant overlap between the two, however, depending on the circumstances.

Do We Need Individual Therapy?

While working with a couple to repair their marriage after an affair, I may also work with one or both of them individually. Or I may refer them to another psychologist for individual therapy, depending on a host of factors. Many couples do not need individual therapy as they recover from infidelity, but sometimes they realize that there are significant issues that are better addressed on a one-on-one basis.

For example, during marital therapy, a spouse may make a connection between his father engaging in affairs during his childhood and his behavior as an adult. A wife who has been betrayed by her husband may recover memories of childhood sexual abuse during therapy. She may understand that her history has played a role in her inability to respond to her husband sexually. These are both issues that are appropriately dealt with in individual therapy. Of course, they have implications as well for the therapeutic work that the couple does together and will enter into the joint sessions, as warranted.

Adult Attachment Styles

One factor that is often addressed in individual sessions after an affair has to do with "attachment," or how one connects with other important people in his or her life. Attachment styles are thought to develop early in life and to reflect how safe and secure we felt in relationships with our caretakers. Attachment styles are described as secure, avoidant, ambivalent, or disorganized. Later relationships can also impact how securely attached we feel. Infidelity is likely to erode our sense of security in relationships in general.

Individual therapy can be especially useful when a couple decides that divorce is their only option. In this case, therapy can be a venue for processing what went wrong (and right) in the marriage, and what each partner contributed to the relationship. The goal is to help the individual gain perspective on that chapter of his or her life and to better understand what sort of relational partner he or she is. The decision to enter individual therapy might be made at the time of the divorce, or at some later point, when legal and financial details have been addressed and some level of day-to-day stability has been attained in your life.

Deciding What's Right for You

In working on your marriage after an affair, you and your spouse have two critical psychological tasks. One is to become a stronger, more unified couple. The other is for each of you to become stronger, more developed, and more resourceful individuals in your own right.

Clearly, the decision as to whether you are both invested in saving your marriage is the starting point for these tasks. Going forward as a couple is a different process from going forward on your own. When you and your spouse decide to rebuild your marriage after an affair, there are major issues of trust and effective communication that must be addressed.

If you have been working through the five steps of affair recovery, you've discovered what a detail-oriented process restoring trust can be for many couples. There may have been some period of time during which you needed the reassurance of knowing virtually everyone your spouse communicated with and everywhere he or she went. After a time, however—and the length of time varies from couple to couple—you no longer felt you had to be quite as vigilant. In fact, that level of vigilance might have eventually begun to feel burdensome. You made the decision to trust again and to take him or her at his or her word.

With regard to communication, the affair recovery process may have dramatically revealed how inadequate your couple communication skills are. The term *communication* covers a wide range of skills and abilities, including the following:

- Active listening

- Being able to take the perspective of the other, so that you can understand what he or she is hearing from you

- Being able to summarize and reflect back the other's message

- Problem definition

- Solution generation, including brainstorming

- Solution evaluation

- Negotiation and compromise

- Solution implementation and evaluation

So part of your affair recovery process may involve training and practice in the areas of communication that you and your spouse struggle with. Your therapist may teach you specific communication techniques, such as using *I* statements instead of *you* statements. He or she may also have you practice the techniques and perhaps even role play with you during sessions. You may be quite surprised at how honing your communication skills can improve your marriage.

The two of you will also need to look at how you were functioning as individuals before and during the affair. How did you deal with anxiety, disappointment, frustration, and loneliness, for example? Going forward after the affair, you may realize that you struggled with these feelings and that you were emotionally needy where your spouse was concerned. Or perhaps you turned away from your spouse during these times and isolated yourself, instead. In either case, recovering from the affair needs to include healthier, more balanced ways of depending on each other for emotional support.

Another key question raised during affair recovery is the degree of balance between your marriage and the other areas of your life. For instance, have one or both of you been overly involved with career or your children? Do you have sufficient outside interests that keep you connected with others and the world? If not, you might find that expanding your circle of friends and broadening your interests not only enhances your life, but makes you more exciting and appealing to your spouse as well.

Essential Takeaways

- Recommitting to your marriage and working through the earlier steps of the affair recovery program (such as restoration of trust) might leave you wondering, *Where do we go from here?*

- You will need to assess in detail what kind of couple you want to be going forward. This assessment must take into account practicalities, such as the financial impact of the affair, unintended pregnancies, or STDs.

- Whether you plan to work on your marriage or have concluded that divorce is your only recourse, you will also need to take an honest look at yourself and what kind of relational partner you are.

- You might need to work to rebuild your self-esteem after your spouse's affair.

- Psychotherapy can dramatically improve the chances of saving your marriage. It can also help you in dealing with whatever personal issues might have been highlighted by the affair.

Part 4

Your Marriage After Infidelity

In this part, I look at different scenarios after infidelity. In one scenario, you and your spouse have decided to reconcile. It's critical that you don't recreate the same marriage you had before, with its vulnerabilities to infidelity. Your "new" marriage needs to be built on a firm foundation of realistic expectations about each other and about marriage itself. After progressing through the five stages of my affair recovery program, you will be communicating more honestly with each other than at any time in your marriage.

The other scenario presupposes that, once you learned of your spouse's affair, you knew you would opt for divorce. Or perhaps you and your spouse decided to try marital therapy after the affair. Perhaps you were hopeful for a time, but your spouse became unwilling to put in the hard work of rebuilding a marriage after the devastation of infidelity. Or perhaps too much damage had been done to the marriage by the time you came to therapy. If divorce becomes inevitable, you may, however, still have to find a way to co-parent your minor children and put their interests before your negative feelings about your ex-spouse. Legal and emotional divorce don't occur at the same time, and you will have a number of important psychological tasks ahead of you, in order to convert your divorce from tragedy to personal transformation.

chapter 14

Trying Again After an Affair

Deciding to give your marriage a second chance

Maintaining open and honest communication

Being free to be who you authentically are and seeing your spouse in a new way

Keeping your marriage fresh

Protecting your marriage by establishing healthy boundaries between it and potentially threatening relationships

In this chapter, I look at what it's like to try again with your marriage after there's been an affair. As you have seen, this is an ongoing, multistage process. But the work of restoring your marriage can be a labor of love, with positive discoveries about yourself and your spouse along the way.

The goal is not to recreate your old marriage, but rather to craft a new relationship, one that is based on a deeper level of honesty than the old one. One of your tasks as a couple will be to rediscover each other and to learn how you have both changed since you first met.

The commitment of marriage is never without risk. But there are things you and your spouse can do to reduce that personal risk. And there are positive, exciting things you can do to enhance and strengthen your relationship along the way.

Deciding to Try Again

Recovery from an affair is a lengthy and complex process. It involves taking sufficient time to deal with your initial emotional responses to your spouse's infidelity. You both must recommit to your marriage, and you will need to grapple with the question of forgiveness.

Prior to your spouse's affair, you may have thought "It could never happen to us." The truth is that infidelity can happen in any marriage, even one that looks solid and happy. Infidelity is complex, and doesn't always indicate something major lacking in the marriage. It may just as likely reveal something lacking in the person who has the affair.

One national survey indicates that only about 35 percent of marriages survive an affair. Clearly, the odds are not in favor of a couple struggling to recover from a spouse's infidelity. However, there are many concrete steps that spouses can take to build a secure, happy, and lasting marriage.

As you and your spouse struggle with the impact of infidelity on your marriage, you must come to grips with the sobering awareness that no relationship is totally immune. Regardless of what you do or say, your spouse could cheat on you again. The question you must ask yourself is whether you are willing to take that risk again.

A fresh start in your marriage is not an ironclad guarantee. But does the likelihood of a more solid, realistic relationship outweigh the chance that your spouse could betray your marital vows again? You need to take your time and ponder this question before you make plans regarding your future.

Some betrayed spouses are unwilling to risk even the remote possibility that they could feel that searing pain again. Learning that their husband or wife has cheated a second time would simply be too hurtful to bear. They conclude, sadly, that they must go forward alone, and that perhaps some future relationship will offer the fulfillment and happiness they didn't find in their current marriage.

It's probably true that some marriages are irreparably damaged after an affair. An affair may have gone on for years, meaning that a spouse essentially led a "double life" for a very long time. For many betrayed spouses, the deception is more difficult to handle than the affair itself. It's the months or years of lying and secrecy that they just can't get past. And that's a very tall offense for a cheating spouse to try to mend.

Heartaches

In working with clients traumatized by a spouse's infidelity, the pain of the deception, even more than the affair, is emphasized over and over. Experts also point out that the cheating spouse has likely been deceiving himself as well in terms of his motivation for an affair. He may rationalize that a stale marriage is to blame, whereas, in reality, he's dealing with fears about aging and sexual prowess, a desire for the thrill of sexual novelty, and a general sense of boredom with himself.

A New Awareness of Each Other

If you have decided to go forward in your marriage, one of your first—and most critical—tasks will be to take a fresh look at your spouse. When we marry, or even cohabit, we tend to assume that we know pretty much what there is to know about our partner. We know his or her likes and dislikes, habits, and hopes and dreams.

While we may have the big picture in these areas, we need to constantly remind ourselves that each of us is a "work in progress." We don't stop growing and changing emotionally just because we're physically grown and have reached the age of legal majority. As with children, adults respond to changes and challenges in their environment, and their minds and bodies change as well. Such was the case for Ashley and Ted, college sweethearts.

Ashley and Ted met during their freshman year in college. They both felt relief to have escaped oppressive and controlling home environments. They lived in the same dorm and shared the same circle of friends. It was natural that they would feel drawn to each other.

Ted suggested that they move off campus and share a house with some other students. Ashley countered that her parents would never approve and would cut her off financially. Ted, in turn, proposed marriage. Once Ashley realized that he was serious, she weighed the pros and cons. In the end, she decided that she was unlikely to ever find a partner who was nicer and more considerate than Ted. She accepted his proposal.

Ashley and Ted eloped, but over time, her parents came to accept Ted. He was bright, ambitious, and became quite successful in his career as a software entrepreneur. As they saw Ted creating an affluent lifestyle for Ashley and their two young daughters, they were less and less critical of him and his working-class origins.

When Ashley became pregnant with their first daughter, they both concluded that the best thing would be for her to take a break from her career as a school guidance counselor and raise their child. A little more than a year later, their second daughter was born. With no discussion, it was assumed that Ashley would become a full-time at-home mom while Ted pursued his career.

Their lives were hectic, with the demands of Ted's career and Ashley raising their young daughters. In general, it seemed things were going well. What was missing, however, was honest discussion about their life aspirations and disappointments. They took for granted that their marriage and their lives were on course.

As Ashley concentrated on her children and volunteer activities, she and Ted began to grow silently apart. They didn't argue, but they simply began to pursue separate lives. After a few years of this, Ted began having affairs on the road. They eventually divorced after Ted started a fairly public affair with a co-worker who shared his interest in rock music and concerts.

> **Tried and True**
>
> You and your spouse should make it a point to regularly check in with each other regarding attainment of life goals and dreams. It's easy to assume we know what our partner values and wants to pursue in life. But if you really want to know your partner and stay in touch with him emotionally, have brief, regular discussions about both of your careers and outside interests. You might be surprised at what you learn!

Communication Is Key

Where so many couples get off course, so to speak, is in substituting assumption for communication. In the early stages of a romantic relationship, we can't wait to be with the object of our affections. We spend as much time with them as possible, we may spend hours on the phone, or e-mail and text throughout the day. And we're hungry to learn all we can about them.

Over time, however, we gradually come to think that we know most of what there is to know about them. We may believe we know all their personal history, their values, their likes and dislikes, as well as their life aspirations. We may even think we know how they're going to finish their next sentence.

This assumption is erroneous, though, and can be dangerous in an intimate relationship. As we saw in the case of Ted and Ashley, it's easy to get distracted by our responsibilities and the choices we make in life. When we allow this to happen, we may stop engaging in meaningful communication with each other. And when this happens, it's very easy for couples to grow apart, putting them at higher risk for an affair.

> **Misc.**
>
> **Tuning Out**
>
> In one social psychology experiment, researchers found that, after only a few minutes, subjects tended to ignore further information about their partner in the study. This finding demonstrates the need to stay open and interested in what our partner has to say and cares about. Otherwise, we may miss information that is vital to the health of our marriage.

Honesty Is the Only Policy

Part of a healthy communication style is being open and honest with our partner. While this does not mean our husband or wife needs to know every random thought that goes through our head, it does mean that you need to share information about the things that influence the health of your marriage. Here is a partial list of areas in which you and your spouse need to communicate regularly and honestly:

- Family expenses and finances
- Major decisions affecting the family, such as a desire to change jobs, retire, or stop working to raise your children
- Relationships that develop outside the family, especially with members of the opposite sex, whether at work, church, the gym, or through recreational interests
- New interests and hobbies, especially those that may require a fair amount of money or time away from the family
- Changes in your health status, whether physical or mental
- Changes in how you view yourselves as a couple, whether now or in the future

All of the topics listed here need to be discussed from time to time. Some issues, like finances, should be discussed on a regular basis. Many couples either pay their bills together, so that there is transparency where family resources are concerned, or they hold regular meetings in which they discuss the family's financial health and goals.

The Risk of Keeping Secrets

While your spouse does not need to know every random thought that crosses your mind, it is important to be open and honest about the things that might affect your marriage and your family. These include your relationships with others, your spending habits, and even your online behavior.

Anything less than total honesty can damage your relationship. If your husband asks what you did today and you say, "Well, I did the grocery shopping," and, in fact, you also went to the mall and bought a $200 pair of shoes, you're straying into the territory of financial infidelity. On some level, you probably realize that the shoe purchase was not a good idea, that it might even deplete funds set aside for the mortgage, groceries, or other family expenses. Otherwise, you would not have withheld that part of your day from your spouse. The intentional decision not to tell your spouse something, known as a "lie of omission," can be just as damaging as an outright "lie of commission," in which you misstate or misrepresent the truth.

Tried and True	If you find yourself censoring what information you share with your spouse, stop and ask yourself why. Are you concerned about how he would react? If so, think about the reaction you imagine and the role your behavior plays in that. For instance, would he become jealous because he found out you've been corresponding with an old boyfriend on a social networking site?

Freedom to Be Yourself

The old adage about women marrying men, hoping to change them, and men marrying women, hoping they'll never change, contains much truth. While we adore the person we choose to marry, there may be little quirks or traits that annoy us, even before the wedding. We think we can either overlook these, or that we'll be able to do something about them afterward.

The truth is that this rarely happens. If anything, the traits and habits you see tend to become accentuated over time. If you are fairly casual about housekeeping, you are not likely to become a "neat freak" after the wedding. If your spouse likes to sleep in on the weekends, he will probably resist getting up with you for a 6 A.M. Sunday run.

This raises the question of the expectations we hold for our spouse and our marriage. It's probably not realistic—nor is it fair—to expect our spouse to become a substantially different person after the marriage. For example, if your fiancé tends to be quiet and a bit introverted, he's not going to become the life of the party after the wedding. And he may be more content to sit beside you on the couch at night, quietly watching TV. He's probably not going to want to spend the evening talking nonstop, if that's not who he was before the wedding. Let's look at Ralph and Barbara, a couple who struggled with maintaining their individual personalities within their marriage.

Choosing to Stay Single

While marriage continues to be a highly desirable goal for most of us, the percentage of people aged 20 to 44 who never marry has increased exponentially in recent decades. For example, 10.5 percent of 25- to 29-year-old men had never married in 1970, compared with 57.6 percent of men in the same age bracket in 2008. Comparable figures for women in that age bracket are 19.1 percent in 1970 and 43.4 percent in 2008. Experts attribute this trend to a number of factors, including the increasing financial self-sufficiency of women, as well as young adults' changing perceptions of marriage, due partly to having witnessed their parents' own divorce.

Ralph had been a talented athlete in both high school and college. He had been president of his fraternity and enjoyed an active social life. He was involved in a number of other organizations and helped organize many volunteer charity events. He described himself as a "people person."

Ralph met Barbara in church during high school. He was immediately struck by her appearance and touched as well by her shy ways. She was different from some of the other girls he had known in high school, who were sexually aggressive. He found her reticence appealing.

Ralph attended a large state university, while Barbara enrolled at a small nearby Christian college. She attended church and mid-week services regularly, but otherwise tended to focus on her studies. She stayed in close touch with her parents and her younger sisters back home.

Ralph and Barbara married right after graduation. Ralph's strong inter-personal skills made him a natural for a sales position. He enjoyed his work and his opportunities for interaction with other people, but disliked that he traveled most of the week.

Barbara had grown up in a large, close-knit family and wanted to work with children. She took a job as a preschool teacher, with the intention of pursuing a Master's degree in early childhood education as soon as she and Ralph felt financially stable.

The couple came into therapy after Barbara came across some slightly racy text messages on Ralph's cell phone. She became suspicious and began checking his e-mail. She discovered suggestive e-mails and pictures from the same woman who had sent the texts.

Barbara angrily confronted Ralph with her suspicions that he was at least guilty of emotional infidelity, if not an outright sexual affair. Ralph countered that her accusations were preposterous and that the woman who had sent the texts and e-mails sent them to everyone on the sales team, men and women alike.

Barbara refused to accept Ralph's explanation and insisted that they attend marital therapy. During an individual session, Ralph expressed to me the feeling that he was "caught between a rock and a hard place." He loved Barbara without reservation, but found her suspicions troubling and hard to deal with. He explicitly denied any involvement—emotional or sexual—with the woman who sent the messages. He explained that she was a divorced woman with a "dirty mind" and that the team simply ignored her.

Ralph ended his individual session on a wistful note. Tears welled up in his eyes as he talked about feeling like he couldn't be himself around Barbara. He talked about how energized he felt around other people and that that was a plus about his work. But Barbara's suspicions about him and his co-workers took much of the joy out of his life. He ended by saying, "She knew who I was when she married me. I don't know what's changed."

Ralph and Barbara's story illustrates what can happen when we become disapproving and begin to disparage our spouse's personality characteristics after marriage. Another challenging situation arises when we begin to "forbid" a spouse to engage in activities he or she used to enjoy before we got married.

While we can look at any hobby or interest someone may have engaged in prior to marriage, let's take the example of motorcycle riding. Anyone who has been on a motorcycle knows what a thrill it is. And many couples enjoy riding together. I know countless stories about couples who rode together until they got married and started a family.

The riders I meet at scenic overlooks, gas stations, and restaurants tell similar stories. Their wives used to enjoy riding with them, or at least were impressed with the fact that they rode. But after marriage, other concerns took over. Concerns about safety, about discomfort on the back of the motorcycle, about appearance (having "helmet hair" by the end of the day), about money spent on a motorcycle and its upkeep, and ultimately about control in a relationship.

Some of these men continue riding, but without their wives. Others eventually reluctantly give it up as a way to avoid the nagging and the pressure at home. But they resent having to forego an activity that had been a source of tremendous pleasure, and one that helped to define who they are.

When this happens, regardless of whether it's the husband or the wife, or the nature of the activity, some part of that person's identity becomes suppressed. They may still silently long to engage in it, or they may find a substitute activity. But that aspect of their identity and source of pleasure in life becomes walled off from their spouse. Distance begins to form between them.

Heartaches

When couples begin denying each other the right to pursue their passions, they are on the path to resentment and to leading parallel lives. And this puts their marriage at higher risk for an affair and divorce. It's important to discuss beforehand how you feel about your and your spouse's interests and what role those will play in your married life.

Challenges to Your Marriage

There's no doubt about it. Marriage is probably the most challenging relationship we experience in our lifetime, even more so than parenthood. By the time we marry, we have well-formed personalities, established habits, likes and dislikes, and preferences for how we like to do things.

For many of us, there is almost an unspoken expectation that marriage will make our lives easier. After all, we can now give up the search for that one special person who will complete us emotionally. We have someone with whom we can grow old and share the rest of our life. And we now have someone to help shoulder the mundane tasks of daily life, such as grocery shopping and household chores.

While marriage does, without a doubt, bring joy, it can also bring trials and tribulations. Those cute little quirks our spouse has can, over time, turn into annoying habits. The sexual excitement of the early years of a marriage can fizzle. The infatuation you initially felt for each other can turn to boredom, and even temptation to look elsewhere. And the shared hopes and dreams of a young couple in love can, if not protected and nurtured, be crushed by the realities of raising children and providing for your family.

And if there has been an affair, a marriage faces even greater challenges. There are virtually endless questions you will ask yourself. Can I trust my spouse again? How did this happen? What role did I play? What did he see in her that he didn't see in me? Can I forgive her? How do we fix this? Should we just give up and move on?

The answer is that, yes, you can love and trust each other again, if you are strongly committed to your marriage. Damaged relationships can be repaired with remorse and forgiveness, with heartfelt and total recommitment, and with a willingness to look at the history of the marriage and the role both spouses played.

It's wise to avoid making major decisions as you and your spouse work to repair your marriage after an affair. For instance, it's not uncommon for a couple to think that having another child will help them feel more committed and intimate. While there are clearly many reasons to have a child, a fragile marriage is likely to be even more stressed by adding another child.

One of the special challenges that marriages face, especially after an affair, is keeping a relationship fresh, lively, and appealing. Another major challenge is looking at relationships with people outside the marriage, such as co-workers and friends, and making sure that appropriate emotional boundaries are in place in those relationships so that your marriage is protected.

Keeping Your Marriage Fresh

The covers of popular women's magazines constantly tout ideas for keeping your marriage exciting. Most of these tips and tricks have to do with spicing up your sex life. While I wholeheartedly recommend doing this in a way that feels fun and natural to you and your spouse, take what you read with a grain of salt. Much of what is offered in those periodicals is designed to attract attention to the cover and to sell the magazine and is common sense.

There is a wealth of information available on the topic of sexuality and improving your sex life. There are countless books, ranging from ones that suggest various activities and sex games, to ones that explicitly depict a whole host of sexual positions. The Internet also offers a broad spectrum of information on couples and sexuality. As with any topic you research online, you want to consider the source to determine whether it's reputable and authoritative.

Ultimately, you and your spouse need to give thought to who you are as a couple, what you have enjoyed in the past, and what your fantasies are. For example, do you enjoy acting out different roles during sex? Commonly enjoyed roles include student and teacher, patient and doctor or nurse, or total strangers having anonymous sex.

What many couples enjoy about sexual role playing is that it brings novelty back into a marriage without the complications of adding a new partner. It gives you and your spouse permission to experiment with different identities and sexual preferences. It can be like having sex with a new person, but without the risks and damage to your marriage.

But keeping a marriage lively and enjoyable certainly doesn't hinge just on sexual novelty. It's advisable to take an informal inventory of other areas of your life as a couple. For example, if you began your married life as a couple who regularly attended religious services, assess where you are now with your spiritual life. Consider committing to do some church- or synagogue-related volunteer activities together.

And what about sports and fitness activities? Were you into running or walking early in your marriage? What about bicycling, swimming, or skiing? What about golf? While there's no need to participate in every activity together, a shared passion for something is an excellent way for the two of you to stay connected.

Taking up a new activity together can also be an exciting way for a couple to reestablish a sense of emotional closeness and interest in a partner and a marriage. For example, you might take tango or ballroom dance lessons together. You might learn to play chess or bridge. You might take up photography or cooking. The options are virtually endless.

You want to strike the appropriate balance between shared activities and individual interests. Your spouse will actually find you a more exciting, appealing person if you pursue some interests individually. It will subtly remind him or her that he or she doesn't know everything there is to know about you, that there are things yet to discover about you. So, by all means, go ahead and take that class in Gaelic and surprise your spouse by planning a trip to Ireland. You may be amazed at the effect it has!

However you choose to go about it, make it a priority to bring new and different activities into your relationship. Choose ones that appeal to both of you, and be sure to maintain your own individual interests as well. You and your spouse will find each other more appealing and more exciting to be around.

Establishing Healthy Boundaries

Another critical challenge to a marriage, especially one impacted by an affair, is to establish healthy emotional boundaries between the couple and the outside world. As we have seen, the failure to have these boundaries in place can be one of the factors that leads to an affair.

What does it mean to have healthy boundaries in a marriage? It certainly means that the couple remain physically faithful to each other. It's easy to see that this applies to sexual intercourse, but there are other behaviors that might violate a couple's boundaries as well. You and your spouse may want to look at how you behave with friends and co-workers in a range of situations. Ask yourselves the following questions:

- Does it feel like hello and good-bye hugs and kisses, which are a routine part of social interaction for most of us, linger a bit too long or are a bit too intense?

- Does it feel that there is inappropriate touching going on, for instance, standing with an arm around the waist or shoulder of another man or woman?

- Is either of you excessively "touchy feely" in a way that makes your spouse uncomfortable? For example, is your wife constantly touching the arm or hand or another man when at social functions?

- Are you and your spouse respectful of the personal space of others, or do you tend to stand too close, or even make body contact, for instance, when sitting next to someone?

Of course, healthy boundaries in relationships require more than just being mindful of your physical interactions with others. At least as important—and perhaps trickier to manage sometimes—is the emotional aspect of your interactions.

Most affairs begin in the workplace these days, and it's not hard to understand why. Women are in the workplace in record numbers these days, working right alongside men in all kinds of settings. We may actually spend more time with our co-workers than we do with our spouses and families.

Working together can breed a kind of emotional intensity between people. You may spend long hours working together on projects. You may have difficult co-workers or an unreasonable, demanding boss. You may even travel together as part of your job. The high stress of the work environment can slowly but surely encourage a kind of emotional bonding.

This kind of relationship may feel like simple friendship at first, especially as co-workers share details about their home and personal lives. This kind of sharing is the norm in many work settings in our culture. And while it feels natural and can make our jobs more enjoyable, it also contains the seeds of potential danger to our marriages.

As co-workers begin to share more and more information about themselves and their lives outside the office, certain barriers are broken down. And if we're not vigilant, we may find ourselves developing fond, even romantic, feelings for a co-worker. A parallel process often occurs in which we begin to be less and less open and emotionally invested with our spouse, and more and more obsessed with the co-worker. Let's look at how Brad and Becky handled a similar scenario.

Becky and Brad were young, ambitious attorneys working at different law firms. Brad worked for a well-established conservative tax law firm, while Becky had chosen criminal law. Her co-workers tended to be aggressive and thrill-seeking. They often gathered at a local watering hole to review the events of the day, before returning home.

Brad became concerned when Becky began regularly joining her associates for happy hour. Several of the members of her firm had a reputation as womanizers. Becky spoke often and in admiring terms about one of these colleagues, and Brad was worried that their relationship was becoming too close.

He finally confronted Becky with his observations and his fears. At first she dismissed them, but, when Brad became tearful, she realized the depth of his concerns. Becky agreed to become more vigilant in her interactions with her male associates. She also agreed to join them for happy hour no more than once a week, just to "stay in the loop." She also invited Brad to stop by and join them. Brad was relieved and felt he could live with that solution.

It's a good idea to periodically assess whether "walls and windows" are where they need to be in your marriage and your relationships. It's also important to listen to your spouse's concerns about whether walls and windows have become reversed. In other words, are you becoming more emotionally intimate and accessible to a third party than you are to your husband or wife? Take your spouse's concerns seriously and see whether you and a co-worker are perhaps on your way to being more than "just friends."

Essential Takeaways

- There is always some risk in trying to repair a marriage after an affair. But with a high level of commitment from both spouses, and the willingness to work hard, it can be done.

- Become tuned in to your spouse as a person with interests, desires, and characteristics that make him who he uniquely is.

- It's important for you both to communicate honestly about your life satisfactions and dissatisfactions, without an expectation that either of you will "change" the other in fundamental ways.

- When spouses are less than honest with each other, whether about finances, outside relationships, or other important matters, secrets can develop which put your marriage at greater risk for an affair.

- You and your spouse should discuss and mutually agree on appropriate boundaries between the two of you and other people who might potentially be disruptive to your marriage.

chapter 15

If Divorce Seems Inevitable

Recognizing some marriages cannot be saved
after an affair

Distinguishing between spouses who want to make
the marriage work and those who are unwilling to try

Knowing why it's critical to understand the reasons
for the affair

Enlisting professional help as you process what
happened in your marriage and plan for your future

Tending to your children's needs and concerns
during this transitional time

In this chapter, I take a frank look at the fact that some
marriages might not be salvageable after an affair.
The pain of betrayal might simply be too great. And
there might have been unhealthy communication and
relationship patterns firmly in place before the affair,
which aren't easily reversible.

Even if you've made the difficult decision to divorce,
you need to come to grips with what happened in your
marriage and the reasons for the affair. Although a stale
marriage or a marriage in crisis never justifies an affair,
it might have made the relationship more vulnerable to
one.

If you have children, you want to be particularly attentive to them. Children react differently to the news that their parents are divorcing. Even if they appear to have no reaction, you can be sure they have unspoken fears and emotions. And depending on a number of factors, children express these concerns in different ways.

Not All Marriages Can Recover from Infidelity

It's a sad fact that not all marriages can endure the stress of an affair. Statistics indicate that only about 35 percent of marriages survive after infidelity. Studies show that almost one out of five divorces is caused by infidelity. And in an interesting sign of the times, 66 percent of matrimonial attorneys point to indiscretions on a major social networking site as evidence of infidelity in their divorce cases.

According to a recent survey, Facebook plays a role in one out of five divorces in the United States. It has even been called a "portal to infidelity" by one church leader. Facebook and other social networking sites not only offer us the opportunity to meet potential new romantic partners, but to reconnect with ex-boyfriends, ex-girlfriends, and ex-spouses. Memory can be selective when it comes to these relationships. When we are either bored or stressed in our lives, nostalgia can make us wish for "the good old days." These sites can be convenient ways to stay in touch with family and friends, but use them with discretion.

The Pain Is Too Intense

Everyone responds to the pain of betrayal differently. Some people can forgive infidelity fairly quickly and are eager to "move on" with their lives and their marriage. Other people need more time to process a spouse's affair and the impact on the marriage. They might also need to seriously contemplate whether they can recommit to someone who has violated their marriage vows in such a deep and hurtful way.

For others, reconciliation after an affair is out of the question. They are simply too wounded by their partner's betrayal of their trust. Even after time spent in trying to forgive, to understand what fueled the affair and to empathize with their spouse, they simply cannot recommit to the marriage.

You might wonder how, after 10, 20, or 30 years, someone could decide to "abandon" the marriage after learning of a spouse's infidelity. For some individuals, adultery was a deal breaker all along. Whether the affair occurred during the first, the fifth, or the twenty-fifth year of marriage was of no consequence. The same might be true if the spouse became addicted to alcohol or drugs. Some behaviors are simply not negotiable for many people.

MISC.

Psychological Resilience

Psychologists have recently become interested in a process called "resilience." This refers to an individual's capacity to withstand and resist the effects of negative events and environments in his or her life. For instance, someone born into an environment of poverty and lack of social support, but who goes on to become successful, self-sufficient, and content with his or her life, demonstrates resilience. A spouse's infidelity is a strong test of your psychological resilience.

The history of our past relationships is crucial in understanding the impact of infidelity. If someone has grown up witnessing infidelity in his or her parents' marriage, or has been through repeated relationship violations in his or her own life, the mental template of relationships might include betrayal and heartbreak.

For other individuals, however, witnessing or experiencing deception and betrayal in close relationships might have set them on a different course. Some unknown combination of personality and environmental factors might have propelled them toward a healthier life, one in which they are unwilling to tolerate relationship betrayal.

Our tolerance for "relational pain" varies from person to person and for different reasons. It is a fact, though, that for some individuals, the anguish of a spouse's affair is simply too much to recover from. They feel too fragile or don't have the emotional reserves to draw on to attempt to rebuild their marriage.

Too Much Damage Has Been Done

Sometimes a couple has engaged in unhealthy relationship patterns for a prolonged period of time. This often begins long before the affair and becomes worse after it is discovered. Or a couple might come into therapy after having tried on their own for some time to repair the damage caused by the illicit relationship. But their attempts have involved behaviors and attitudes that only damaged the relationship further.

Many couples have never had an effective means of conflict resolution. They reflect back and say things like "We just can't communicate," or "We've never known how to fight fair." They might be able to accurately identify some of the dynamics of their dysfunctional communication patterns. For example, they might point out that "When she starts in on me, I just shut down and that makes her all the more determined to get me to argue with her." But they're at a loss as to how to escape that cycle.

After years of engaging in these maladaptive ways of interacting, couples can easily become "relationally stuck." That is, they're unable to break free from old, ineffective ways of addressing conflict and other sensitive areas. They automatically resort to firmly entrenched habits. This was the case with Derek and Leila, who had a difficult time effectively communicating their feelings with each other.

 Tried and True Relationship expert John Gottman emphasizes the importance of positive communications with our spouse. He recommends that we have a ratio of approximately five positive communications to each negative one. So although we need to be able to share our cares and complaints with our spouse, we need to balance those with expressions of appreciation. This helps build a base of caring and positive interactions with our spouse.

Leila and Derek came into therapy six years into their marriage. It was the second marriage for both of them. Although Derek did not have a sexual affair, he was habitually flirtatious with other women. This was the subject of numerous arguments over the years.

Invariably, their arguments about his behavior with other women expanded to cover other aspects of their marriage, such as how much time he had to pursue his hobbies and Leila's failure to keep the house as tidy as Derek wanted. These arguments tended to spin out of control, with every grievance and complaint, particularly on Derek's part, being fair game.

In therapy, they worked on improving their communication skills, specifically, being able to pinpoint a problem and conduct a brief discussion about it. They made little headway, however, in coming to grips with Derek's behavior with other women. Derek blamed it on his tendency to drink too much in social situations. Leila refused to accept that explanation, however, pointing out that Derek tended to be overly friendly in work situations as well. After five months of therapy, they decided they needed to seriously consider whether their marriage was salvageable.

Heartaches

"Kitchen-sinking" refers to adding issue on top of issue during an argument. For example, a wife might complain about her husband's inadequate help with household chores. He might counter that, if she didn't spend so much time on the phone with her mother, she could accomplish more around the house. She might respond that he spends too much time and money on his hobbies. He might snap back that he works hard and is entitled to spend his money as he sees fit. Within the course of a single argument, this couple has covered division of labor in the household, use of time, family relations, and money. Kitchen-sinking is basically a failure to stay on topic during an argument and, when it occurs regularly, can be highly damaging to a marriage. It becomes an opportunity to attack your spouse about anything and everything.

You've Outgrown Each Other

Marriages don't always end with overt conflict and emotional fireworks. They sometimes end when, over the long course of pursuing careers and raising a family together, you realize you've become strangers to each other. Without either of you noticing, you simply grew apart.

Most couples begin their married lives with a shared vision of who they are and what they want in life. They might need to hash out the details, but the vision generally includes whether or not to have children, their career aspirations, how to manage money, family relationships, spirituality, ideas about travel, recreation, and socializing, as well as plans for retirement.

Sometimes a change in life goals can subtly pull a couple apart. For example, when a husband gets a major promotion that requires travel or frequent entertaining of clients, a spouse might feel excluded or left behind. Or when a woman who has raised her children now decides to reenter the workforce or go back to school, her husband might feel that she has a new life and wonder how much it includes him.

It's not uncommon to be attracted to someone who seems radically different, or even exotic, when compared with our own background. Sexual chemistry combined with novelty can make for an exciting relationship, but it poses its own set of challenges when we're talking about marriage. Let's look at Brynna and Seth, and how their differing priorities affect their relationship.

Brynna and Seth met when she came to him for lasik surgery. He trained at UCLA and set up his ophthalmology practice in Salt Lake City. They felt an immediate attraction and began dating after her procedure. Seth was fascinated by Brynna's Mormon background and large, close-knit family. She, in turn, was intrigued by his family's Jewish customs.

Both families expressed concerns when Brynna and Seth married. They felt that the religious and cultural differences were simply too great to be overcome. The first few years went smoothly, however, with Seth continuing to build his practice and Brynna raising their growing family. It was agreed that Brynna would home school their children.

Seth's work required him to attend medical conferences and meetings. Over time, Brynna felt that she played less and less a role in Seth's life. After nine years of marriage and five children, she was absorbed in the children's education. Seth attended professional events, taught seminars, and, when he wasn't working, played tennis and enjoyed skiing. Over time, Seth and

Brynna had little to talk about and, except for the children, seemed to have little in common.

Seth began an affair with his practice manager. He enjoyed that she had a professional life and thoroughly understood his work. She was also vitally involved in scheduling his travels and occasionally accompanied him on business trips.

Eventually, Seth confessed his affair to Brynna and asked for a divorce. He assured Brynna that she and the children would be well taken care of and would be able to maintain their lifestyle. Brynna offered little objection, feeling that she and Seth were so different in terms of their values and had grown so far apart emotionally that a divorce would make little difference to either of them.

Brynna and Seth grew apart over the course of their marriage. Seth was excited and energized by his work and wanted someone who shared his enthusiasm. Brynna became almost exclusively focused on the children and their education. Seth was a more than adequate provider, and, as long as the children had what she felt they needed, she, in truth, had little interest in Seth's field of ophthalmology and his thriving practice. They began to inhabit two different emotional worlds.

Bet You Didn't Know	People in certain jobs and professions tend to divorce at a higher rate than in others. Dancers, choreographers, bartenders, and massage therapists tend to have the highest divorce rates, whereas engineers, optometrists, and the clergy tend to have the lowest rates. It's not clear whether the demands of the job contribute to the higher divorce rates, or whether people who are more divorce-prone are drawn to those professions.

Agreeing to Disagree

One of the most distressing situations a marital therapist deals with is that of a couple in which one person wants desperately to save his or her marriage, and the other spouse is either noncommittal, or knows already that he or she wants out of the relationship. I have seen the spouse who wants to try again beg, plead, sob, bargain, and promise in an effort to hold on to his spouse. And I have seen spouses who want to end the marriage sit in stony silence, cry along with their spouse, state that they need time and can't make any promises, or state flat out that the marriage is over and nothing he or she can say or do will change that.

When a couple comes to the realization that divorce is inevitable, they have several tasks ahead of them. One of these is to process what went on in the marriage and the circumstances surrounding the affair. In other words, it's critical that both of you understand the reasons for the divorce. Remember the saying, "Those who forget history are doomed to repeat it."

Make no mistake, the two of you might never agree on the reasons for the divorce, or even what your marriage was like up to that point. If your spouse had the affair, you might contend that everything was fine until then. You might see his adultery as having destroyed what was basically a solid marriage. He, however, might continue to blame his affair on feeling that his needs were not being met in the marriage and that you stopped caring about him a long time ago.

Heartaches

It is possible to obtain a "no fault" divorce in all 50 states. In other words, you don't have to prove that your spouse did something wrong—like commit adultery—to get a divorce. You can simply cite something like "irreconcilable differences" as the basis for your request. Sadly, it is true that it takes two people to make a marriage work, but it only takes one to end it.

Of course, if you're planning on trying to rebuild your marriage, it's important that the two of you reach some consensus on what happened and what you need to do going forward. But if you see divorce as your only option, the focus will be somewhat different. Although you'll still need to process the events that led to the end of your marriage, you'll focus on your personal growth and awareness as a single individual, and not as part of a couple. Your psychological health, however, will make you a better partner in any future relationship that might develop.

Understanding the Reasons for Your Divorce

When a couple reaches the decision to divorce, there is often the impulse just to "get it over with and move on." However, it can be a mistake not to invest some time and energy in grappling with the affair and with the history of the marriage. Anything you can learn about yourself as a partner and the patterns you can identify in your relationships will benefit you as you move forward with your life. Let's look at Carlos, who needed to learn from mistakes he made in his first marriage to Elena. These mistakes were about to be repeated with his new wife, Mia.

Elena and Carlos had been married for almost three decades. They had one adult son who had been out of the house for a couple of years. Elena was a neonatal intensive care nurse and Carlos taught architecture at a local university.

Carlos complained that Elena had always put her work first and was never available to do anything with him that was unrelated to work or the home. He enjoyed a range of outdoor activities, such as bicycling, fishing, and hiking, and he repeatedly pressed Elena to join him. Most of the time, she turned him down, complaining that she was too tired, had housework to do, or had to work. Eventually, he stopped asking.

Carlos was just a few years away from retirement and was teaching a light course load. He didn't have a sense yet of how he wanted to spend his retirement. He and Elena had no common vision or dream for how they wanted to spend their later years. A sense of boredom began to set in for him.

During his spare time at work, Carlos began scouring Facebook and other social networking sites for old friends and acquaintances. He eventually made contact with Mia, who was his high school girlfriend. Over the next few months, they e-mailed regularly, began calling each other, and eventually made plans to meet.

As Carlos' affair with his ex-girlfriend heated up, he began feeling that he and Elena were fundamentally ill-matched and that he had finally found his true soul mate. Against Elena's wishes, they divorced and he married Mia. Within a few short years, however, Carlos again began to feel restless. Mia was concerned that she was seeing a reprise of how his marriage to Elena ended.

Carlos agreed to come to therapy with Mia. Over time, Carlos realized that his feelings of boredom and restlessness had less to do with his choice of a life partner and more to do with himself. He operated on the implicit assumption that, if only he could find the right partner, the right profession, the right recreational activity, he would finally be happy.

Although Carlos and Mia ended up not divorcing, they both learned that Carlos had a tendency to always look outside himself for his satisfaction in life. And Mia learned to be patient with Carlos and how important it was that they maintain interest in each other's activities and to be sure to have some shared hobbies. Finally, they both achieved recognition of how important it was to communicate their feelings and expectations to each other in clear terms.

Being Clear About the Consequences of Your Divorce

At first glance, the consequences of divorce might seem obvious. If you're the spouse seeking the divorce, all you can think of is how relieved you'll feel when this ordeal is over. But the reality can be much more complicated than that. There are, of course, important legal and financial ramifications to divorce. But there are significant mental and emotional effects as well.

When it's clear to both you and your spouse that you'll be divorcing, the first order of business is for both of you to retain competent legal counsel. You might, at first blush, think you don't need it and that it's a waste of resources. But unless you're newly married and have few assets and no children, hammering out the details of a property settlement and a custody agreement can be much more complicated than you first imagine.

Of course, there might be many outward changes in your life and your lifestyle after divorce. Depending on your financial circumstances, you might find that you are living on a much tighter budget. And if you have stayed home to raise children, most courts will take that into account and might award you spousal support, but you will be expected to seek gainful employment at some point.

Although individual circumstances vary widely, one influential study of the economic effects of divorce on families found that women tend to experience a 27 percent decline in their standard of living following divorce, whereas men experience a 10 percent increase in their post-divorce standard of living. Some scholars attribute this difference to the fact that men still on average earn more than women, and many of them fail to honor their child support obligations as well.

Your "Emotional" Divorce

As you go through the divorce process, remember that there are two aspects to your divorce. One is legal, and is in effect when the divorce decree is granted by the court. The other is emotional and has no set timetable. Your emotional divorce will likely take much longer than your legal divorce.

In all likelihood, you will always retain some emotional connection to your ex-spouse, especially if you have children. If you are co-parenting, you need to find ways to set aside your differences and your feelings about each other in order to provide the most stable and loving environment possible for your children. Although the court will have a say in establishing custody and visitation, it will be up to you and your spouse to honor those agreements and to make your children's transition from one home to the other as seamless as possible.

Tried and True

One of the biggest challenges for divorcing parents with minor children is to establish consistency in their children's lives during what is often an emotionally tumultuous time. It's not necessary that you and your spouse agree on every detail of how to handle the children, or even all the "house rules" that will be in place in mom's home and dad's home. It is critical, however, that you agree on the big picture, or themes, in your child's life—for example, academic success. You might think it's important that your child do his homework as soon as he gets home from school, whereas your ex-spouse feels the child needs some down time before hitting the books. What matters is that you both value his academic success and have rules in place for helping him achieve it.

Even after your children leave the home, there might still be circumstances and occasions that require that you and your ex-spouse interact. There will be decisions to be made about college expenses. There will be graduations and weddings to attend where you will, at the very least, be required to acknowledge each other's presence.

As time passes, you will likely feel much less raw emotion about your spouse's infidelity and other perceived wrongs. Your life will take on a new rhythm and include new people and relationships. Remember, forgiving, but not forgetting, can greatly set the stage for your emotional divorce. In the next chapter, we look at the ways in which your divorce can help you achieve personal growth and transformation.

Gradually, you will probably feel less and less emotional connection, whether positive or negative, with your ex-spouse. Your anger over his or her infidelity will diminish. Some individuals are surprised that they continue to have some positive feelings for an ex. Some miss the companionship and the life they had built with their former spouse. And some actually regret the decision to divorce. According to one study, 40 percent of those who divorced eventually regretted it. They felt that, had they and their spouse worked harder to rebuild the marriage, divorce would have been unnecessary.

Seeking Professional Help

One of the biggest mistakes I see in couples who want to try again with their marriage is waiting too long to obtain professional help. Perhaps they thought time alone would heal the pain, or that they could go it on their own. Perhaps they were concerned about the financial expense, or knew someone who had difficult experiences in therapy. Perhaps they were simply afraid to become even more emotionally vulnerable in therapy with a spouse who already wounded them.

Whatever the reason, many couples simply wait too long to make the critical call that just might help them salvage their marriage. But even couples who are fairly clear that divorce is the best solution for them need to consider working with a mental health professional during this difficult time. There are many life-changing decisions to be made, and it's easy to become overwhelmed. A psychologist or other therapist can help you prioritize the divorce-related issues and tasks you must deal with and help you develop the tools to do so.

> **Tried and True**
>
> As you go through your divorce, let your attorney handle the legal and property matters, and work through the emotional issues with your psychologist or other mental health professional. Both of these individuals are highly trained in their own fields, but not in each other's. An attorney, however, generally charges considerably more for his time than your psychologist. You don't want to pay your attorney $350 per hour for mental health consultation when that's not his expertise. Your psychologist might charge $150 per session and will have a much better grasp of the emotional impact of divorce and ways to help you through it.

The willingness of a spouse to participate in couple therapy in order to ensure the smoothest possible divorce can sometimes even put the couple on the track to relationship recovery. Take the case of Dean and Janelle, who had been married 17 years when Dean filed for divorce.

Dean came to the difficult decision to file after years of frustration with Janelle's continual promises that she would do better in the areas of housekeeping and meal preparation. Dean also felt marginalized in the family, because Janelle's every thought was of their two daughters. Janelle quit a lucrative job as a medical office manager and volunteered daily in her daughters' school. Dean felt under a great deal of financial stress and he perceived that Janelle didn't really care about his concerns.

Dean pleaded with Janelle to go to therapy with him. She found myriad reasons to refuse—she didn't like the therapist's picture on the website, the therapist probably treated gay and lesbian couples, and so on. Dean began individual therapy to get some perspective on his decision to seek a divorce and how best to move forward with his life.

During one therapy session, Dean began to review all the frustrations and disappointments in the marriage that led him to believe divorce was inevitable. He acknowledged that he played a role in the breakdown of the marriage. But at one point, he became tearful and said, "You know, if she agreed to come in here with me just once, I would have held off filing the papers. That would have told me there was some hope for us."

A competent mental health professional who specializes in relationship issues can help you first and foremost determine whether divorce is really the best route to go. Except when physical violence is involved, I encourage couples to let time be their ally in the process of recovery from infidelity. It's always possible to file for divorce later. But it's far too easy to make an impulsive decision about ending a marriage and living with regret or questions for the rest of your life.

When it's clear that divorce is inevitable, your therapist can help you sort out the issues to be dealt with and prioritize which need to be addressed first. For example, I always encourage my clients who have unequivocally decided on divorce to get the best legal help they can afford and to be an active partner with their attorney in the process. Don't just assume your attorney has your best interests at heart. Keep an ongoing list of questions and concerns, communicate with him or her regularly, and make sure you understand the process.

What About Self-Help Divorce Books?

Clients often ask about self-help books during the divorce process. There is plenty of material out there, and some of it can be useful. As you peruse your bookstore's shelves or search online, pay attention to who has published the book (is it a large, well-known publishing house?), the author's area of specialization (does he or she work extensively with relationship issues and infidelity?), and the author's slant or agenda with regard to the topic (is the author coming from a religious or exclusively pro-marriage perspective?). See Appendix B for more suggestions.

When legal and financial matters are adequately managed, other top priorities include helping the couple plan for breaking the news of their decision to divorce to their children. It's often tempting for a couple headed for divorce, but working together in therapy, to get sidetracked with accusations and recriminations. Your therapist will help you get back on track. At this stage, it's not uncommon for one or both spouses to be in both individual and couple therapy for a time.

Helping Your Children Cope with an Impending Divorce

Without question, divorce is one of the most stressful life events a child can go through. Each year, countless numbers of children must begin to try to make sense of life again and to manage strong emotions. Concern about how their children will fare after divorce is what most often prolongs or delays the decision to leave a bad marriage for many parents.

The research on children and divorce is complicated. Overall, it suggests that children whose parents divorce might be more susceptible to behavioral and emotional problems. These include academic problems, troubled interactions with their peers, low self-esteem, and poor relationships with their parents. Although these children might be more vulnerable than their peers from intact families, it's important to note that the majority of children of divorce manage relatively well and do not need any special intervention.

Much of my work with divorcing parents centers around preparing them to talk with their children about the divorce. This prospect frightens some parents so much that they delay the conversation or avoid it altogether. Doing this has the unfortunate effect of merely giving their children additional time to construct disastrous scenarios in their young minds.

I encourage parents to sit down together—and with me, if necessary—to rehearse what they want to tell their children. They need to choose a date and time and decide who will start. I generally recommend they gather all the children together.

Depending on the ages of the children, this can pose a challenge. If, for example, you have four children ranging in age from 4 to 16, you might be dealing with four distinct levels of psychosocial and intellectual development. And although you might need to share the overall message that you are divorcing, there will undoubtedly need to be further conversations—perhaps with the children individually—explaining the situation, your plans, and how their lives will be impacted.

The conversation you have with your children must convey two messages. One is that the divorce is not their fault. They did not do anything that made Mom and Dad stop loving them or each other. Mom and Dad will continue to love the children every bit as much as they always have. The second part of the message is that Mom and Dad will do their best to make sure the children stay in their same schools, see their same friends, and, if possible, stay in their old house, at least part of the time. In other words, the parents will do everything in their power to minimize the disruption to their children's routines.

> **Tried and True**
>
> Much of the difficulty children experience when their parents divorce comes from their feelings of powerlessness in the situation. In studies of the adjustment of young adults whose parents divorced, fewer than 20 percent said both parents talked to them about the divorce, and only 5 percent said their parents explained the reasons for the divorce and gave them an opportunity to ask questions. When these young adults reflected on their parents' divorce, those who were able to express concerns and ask questions had less painful memories.

So although it's critical that you reassure your children that the divorce is not because of something they did, and that you will continue to love them just as you always have, you don't need to share the gory details of the divorce, or that there has been an affair. Of course, if they are already aware of your spouse's affair, that information will need to be carefully managed as well. This is another area in which your therapist can be of help. Be alert to what your children are asking and answer only those questions for the moment.

Do Your Children Need Professional Help?

It's not uncommon for parents considering divorce to ask me whether they should line up a therapist for their children as well. Damaging their children emotionally is the number one fear of most divorcing parents. My answer typically is "It depends, but probably not right now."

I encourage and instruct parents in how to become good observers of their children's behavior. The first step in this is knowing what is developmentally appropriate for your child. The older the child, the more they can verbalize their concerns, and the more nuanced their understanding of relationships. A young child, however, is likely to have more black-and-white ideas about people and the world, and is less able to express in words what's troubling him. He might, instead, act his concerns out behaviorally, such as aggression, withdrawal, or refusing to go to school; or in physical symptoms, such as headaches, stomachaches, and insomnia.

After parents understand what is "normal" for children of different ages, they need to take stock of their child and develop a mental baseline of his typical behaviors. This becomes the standard of comparison when deciding whether to seek professional help for him. For example, if your son is normally very active, he might become a bit more so. Or if your daughter tends to be somewhat withdrawn, she might seem a bit more introspective than usual during the divorce process.

What you want to look for are significant departures from your child's normal behavioral and emotional patterns. Also be alert for prolonged periods of sleep disruption or appetite change. Certainly any overt expressions of suicidal thoughts or impulses need to be addressed immediately. But other, more subtle signs, such as giving treasured possessions away, should be considered in the same light. Never dismiss a child or adolescent's statements about wanting to die as just "wanting attention" or being dramatic.

Essential Takeaways

- Not all marriages can be repaired following an affair. The issues of broken trust might run too deep, or the couple might have such firmly entrenched negative ways of interacting with each other that they simply don't have the motivation or the energy to learn new patterns.

- In some marriages, spouses began growing apart at some point. One of you might have pursued a career or family at the expense of your marriage. Or one spouse might have remained fairly stagnant in terms of personal growth, while his or her partner decided to pursue additional educational, career, or personal development opportunities.

- Even though you won't be sharing a life together as you go forward after the affair and divorce, it's important to understand what happened in your marriage and the circumstances surrounding the affair.

- You will undergo both a legal and an emotional divorce. The emotional divorce is a much longer process. You might even find yourself missing your ex-spouse, in spite of your relief at the painful parts of your marriage finally being over.

- How you manage this transitional time is critical. There are many delicate issues to be addressed. You might want to get the help of a psychologist or other therapist. You will probably need some help with how to deal with your children during this time and how to know whether they, too, need the help of a professional.

chapter 16

The Second Time Around

Transforming divorce into an opportunity for personal growth and positive change

Healing and learning from the experience of the affair and your first marriage before entering into another intimate relationship

Feeling that it's safe to trust others again

Choosing your partner wisely

Basing a future marriage on mutual respect, shared values, and interests

Communicating in order to handle the challenges that life invariably brings

In this chapter, I look at the positive role your divorce can play in your life. You can choose to view it as a failure, or you can choose to step forward in confidence and faith that your future can be better than you imagined. This requires you to make a choice for health and happiness.

After your divorce, you need to take time before getting into another serious relationship. You need to understand the factors that drove you and your ex-spouse apart and contributed to the affair. You need to be honest in assessing what kind of partner you were and what you might have done differently.

Learn to look for relationship "red flags" as you move forward after divorce. Give yourself time to get to know someone. Understand that, if something in a new relationship feels wrong, it probably is. Be willing to back away from a situation that's not healthy for you.

Your next relationship needs to be based on a firm foundation of knowledge of yourself and your partner. Respect for each other's autonomy and individuality is critical. You also need to share core values and some interests. There must be the ability and the desire to communicate openly and honestly, as well as effective tools for handling the conflicts that all couples face at one time or another.

Divorce as Personal Transformation

It's understandable that individuals going through a divorce often refer to their marriage as "failed." After all, you took vows to love, honor, and cherish each other "'til death do you part." And it's not death that parted you. If your spouse had an affair, it's the betrayal of those vows that, at the very least, contributed to the dissolution of the marriage.

That sense of failure in marriage is partly a function of how long the marriage lasted. For instance, if a person marries young, the marriage lasts only a few months or years, and there are no children, it's almost as if the marriage "doesn't count." When asking clients about their marital histories, I find that they tend to dismiss these types of marriages as youthful mistakes or *starter marriages* and unlike their later marriages.

Starter marriage is a term coined by author Pamela Paul in her look at the trend of people in their 20s marrying, having no children, and divorcing less than five years later. She attributes this to the infatuation of young adults with weddings and the idea of marriage. She also notes that, for many of these individuals, marriage seemed like the next logical step in a relationship and was easier than breaking up, even when things were not going well.

We are a culture in love with the idea of true love. We tend to believe there is that one special person out there somewhere for whom we are destined. In addition, we love the spectacle of a wedding. It's common these days to spend a year or more planning and obsessing over the countless details of a wedding and reception, not to mention bachelorette and bachelor parties, rehearsal dinners, and honeymoons.

Getting married is the easy part. Given sufficient money, you can design the wedding of your dreams. Of course, there's no law that says you must give any amount of thought or consideration to how well suited you and your fiancé are to each other, how committed you are to your marriage, and how you will handle the inevitable conflicts and challenges to your relationship.

Add no-fault divorce to the mix, and it becomes easier to see how we have become a society in which almost half of all marriages end in divorce. There is the obsession with finding that person who "completes" us. And then there is our "15 minutes of fame," our "queen for a day" mentality. As an engaged person—this applies to women, in particular—we take on a special status that demands special attention and consideration from everyone.

Serial Monogamy

Actress Elizabeth Taylor was married eight times and was rumored (prior to her death) to have been on her way to her ninth walk down the aisle. She is reputed to have said, "I've only slept with men I've been married to. How many women can make that claim?" Although we might remain monogamous during our marriages, the new relationship pattern for many of us is sequential marriage.

But do we devote equal attention to assessing how closely our deeply held values align with those of our soon-to-be spouse? Have we experienced a major conflict with our fiancé? If so, what have we learned about our conflict resolution skills? Are we able to problem solve, negotiate, and compromise?

What Is a "Failed" Marriage?

Couples who come to me for therapy often talk about their "failed" marriages. They speak about these relationships with a mixture of emotions, including sadness, anger, frustration, despair, shame, and resignation. They have created certain narratives, or stories, which have explained to them how these relationships fit into their lives and who they are, both as individuals and as romantic partners.

As a psychologist, one of my tasks is to help these individuals and couples whose marriages have been ended by infidelity reframe their experience. Instead of focusing only on the marriage ending and the things that went wrong, I encourage them to look for and draw on the positive elements of those past relationships as well.

For example, virtually all the individuals I see in my clinical practice who have children say "they'd do it all over again," simply because of the children born of that marriage. Having children changes us, our lives, and our view of the world forever. Most of us can't imagine life without our children, and we readily concede that we'd put up with the "same old stuff" if only for them.

Some experts have argued that our extended life span makes it unrealistic to spend our entire adult lives with a single romantic partner. Some have gone so far as to say it makes sense to think in terms of a first marriage, in which we rear our children and establish ourselves professionally, and a second marriage, in which we pursue later-life tasks, such as in-depth personal goals and development. Take Liza and Ted, for example.

Throughout history, great writers have contemplated the end of love relationships. They have written eloquently about the pain that accompanies the loss of love, as well as the resilience of the human heart. The following two quotes capture the strength of spirit that carries us through relationship endings: "Some of us think holding on makes us strong; but sometimes it is letting go," (Herman Hesse) and "There is a time for departure even when there is no certain place to go." (Tennessee Williams)

Liza and Ted both had first marriages of long duration. Although trained as an attorney, Liza chose to stay home with her two children until they were in college. Ted had an older son who had been out of the marital home for almost 10 years. They met through their church's divorce care group and began dating.

Except for the joy of the children from their first marriages, they both sometimes regretted that they had not met and married earlier in life. However, they both quickly concluded that their sometimes volatile temperaments, the stresses of raising children, and establishing themselves professionally might very well have driven them apart.

With their children grown, Liza and Ted were able to fully enjoy each other and to devote themselves to new areas of professional growth. They also had their evenings free for long conversations, reading, and movies. Without family responsibilities, they traveled or entertained most weekends. Neither of them regretted the years, the energy, and the resources devoted to raising their children from their first marriages. But they thoroughly enjoyed their "adults only" lifestyle.

If your sole criterion for marital success or failure is whether you make it "'til death do you part," then, yes, divorce represents a type of relationship failure. But when viewed from the perspective of what you and your ex-spouse gained from the relationship, including your children, there is probably no such thing as a failed marriage. The critical question is the wisdom you have acquired that you are able to apply in your new life and in future relationships.

Divorce Rituals

Divorce is our legal mechanism for ending a marriage. This generally includes division of property, determination of custody, and establishing visitation schedules. But how do we mark our emotional divorce?

Our culture abounds in rites of passage to mark various milestones in our lives. We have ceremonies to acknowledge birth, death, and marriage. We hold retirement parties to signal the end of our working life. We even hold housewarming parties to celebrate moving into a new home.

Our religious traditions mark major turning points in our lives as well. For example, the Bar Mitzvah and the Bat Mitzvah acknowledge that the young Jewish person is now responsible for his or her own actions. In the Catholic faith, first communion is a critical event in the religious lives of its adherents. The Quinceañera is held to recognize the passage of a young Hispanic woman from childhood to adulthood.

But there has traditionally been no such ceremony to mark the dissolution of a marriage. The pain of divorce has been borne privately, or, at best, shared with close friends and family. In part, this was due to the stigma that accompanied divorce until relatively recently.

 It's important to take steps to mark your divorce. This can be something as simple as buying new linens for your bed, or as symbolic as giving your wedding rings to your children or having them set with a new gemstone. Some churches are even beginning to offer formal divorce ceremonies. Understandably, however, with organized religion's emphasis on marriage, many clergy are reluctant to perform these.

Learning to Love and Trust Again

Although there are many lessons to be learned from surviving your spouse's infidelity, one of the most powerful—and most difficult—is that all relationships contain some element of risk. Going into a first marriage, we're often unaware of this. We might even think we're immune from that risk, and that affairs are something that happen to other people.

Your spouse's infidelity can undermine your sense of security in a marriage, or relationships in general. People are remarkably resilient in forgiving a whole host of relational transgressions, but deception tends to be one of the most destructive. It erodes the trust, which is the foundation of our most meaningful relationships.

Bet You Didn't Know	From the moment we're born, we begin learning whether other people are trustworthy or not. Renowned psychologist Erik Erikson divided the human life span into eight stages, each with an associated developmental task. The task in Stage One is developing a sense of trust that our caretakers will meet our needs and that the world is a safe, predictable place. Failure to develop this leads to a lifelong sense of mistrust. Consistency and reliability in our relationships is critical.

So how do you begin to trust again? The first step is acknowledging that there is always some risk of betrayal in a relationship. And although you can't control your partner's behavior, there are steps you can take to increase the likelihood of having a healthy, gratifying relationship.

Second, learn to spot relationship "red flags." These are signs that something might not be quite right in a relationship. In the process of getting to know a potential romantic partner, here are some things to be aware of:

- He or she is trying to push the relationship along too quickly and isn't giving it time to develop before pressing you for a commitment.

- He or she is trying to sweep you off your feet with gifts, flowers, expensive dinners, even trips.

- He or she seems vague about work and recreational schedule.

- He or she won't give you a home phone number. Worse, you are instructed not to call him or her at home or on the weekend.

- He or she takes phone calls out of earshot from you and is vague or uncomfortable telling you who he or she was talking to.

- He or she seems uneasy talking about his or her past, or when told, the "life story" seems just a bit too rehearsed.

- You catch him or her in an outright lie.

When you find yourself in any of the previous situations, you need to confront it. Don't wait, thinking it will magically get better. And don't make excuses for him or her. If you have a strong intuition that someone is lying to you, he or she probably is. Ignoring it will not improve the situation and will lead only to heartache.

After being scarred by a spouse's infidelity, you might think you can never love again. You might feel unwilling to open yourself up to the possibility of heartache again. But in closing yourself off from intimate relationships, you also insulate yourself from the pleasure and the joy of sharing your life with another person.

What About Online Dating, Matchmaking Services, and Personal Ads?

Just as the Internet plays a role in the development of extramarital affairs and cyber cheating, it also plays an ever-increasing role in the development of healthy, long-term relationships. In fact, one of the largest online dating sites (Match.com) claims that one in five relationships now starts online.

Several well-known sites offer matching supposedly based on your personality. Of course, there is a price tag for this service and for accessing your matches. The fee can range from approximately $30 per month to $60 for a single month, with discounts for a multimonth subscription. So although not inexpensive, online dating sites point out that you're likely to spend more on a single date than you are for a monthly subscription.

Chemistry.com claims to evaluate you and potential matches not only on the basis of personality traits, values, and interests, but that mysterious factor we call "chemistry," as well. This company hired a renowned scientist who has done lab experiments on some of the things that attract us to each other. In one experiment, she had women sniff the T-shirts of several men and choose the one that smelled the "sexiest." Results were that women chose a shirt from a man whose immune system was different from, but compatible with, hers. The scientific logic behind this is that we try to maximize the diversity of our gene pool by selecting a mate who differs from us.

Another format for finding new love is the increasingly popular realm of matchmaking services. In the dating world, these services position themselves as appropriate for busy professionals whose time for a social life is limited. Matchmakers conduct an interview with you and then begin the process of searching for an appropriate match. They even arrange the first meeting, whether it's a lunch date or drinks after work. It's Just Lunch is one of the oldest of these services. It was founded in 1991 and now has offices worldwide.

There are also matchmakers who focus exclusively on identifying a potential spouse (generally a wife) for men of financial means. These services emphasize the "total package" quality of the women waiting to be matched—beauty, brains, and personality. These services are pricey for both the men searching for wives and the women hoping to be matched with them. The registration and interview fees for women can run in the $1200 range, whereas male clients might spend anywhere from $50,000 to $500,000 to be suitably matched. One matchmaking site in particular offers the opportunity—for a fee, of course—to go out with the founder of the service or one of her employees to discover the secrets of dating wealthy and successful men.

Tried and True	Awareness of the potential dangers of dating someone you meet online can't be overemphasized. Some common safety tips include not giving out your home address, not arriving at the date location by yourself, and always letting a third party know where you will be and what time you expect to leave. Caution is the name of the game with Internet dating.

Personal ads did not start with Craigslist. In fact, as far back as 300 years ago, advertisements for husbands and wives began to appear in newspapers in both Europe and the United States. These were quite common by the mid-nineteenth century, although those who placed them were frequently looked down upon. The British police, in fact, continued to arrest those who placed personal ads until the mid-1960s.

The content of personal ads shifted in the mid-twentieth century, with more and more emphasis on dating and sex, and less on finding a marriage partner. Dating sites are often broken down into demographic groups (for example, gay, Asian, men seeking women) or particular sexual practices (for example, fetish, bondage, and dominance).

Again, the buyer should beware with Internet dating. The person you're contacting is a total stranger to you and might not be what he or she seems. It has been estimated that 35 percent of individuals using single dating sites are, in fact, married. And a perusal of many of the ads on a certain website suggests that the person who placed the ad might be a prostitute. Let's look at Ken's experience with Internet dating.

Ken was a highly successful orthopedic surgeon married to Vanessa, a plastic surgeon. Since the birth of their children, Vanessa practiced part time, handling primarily aesthetic procedures, which didn't require her to be on call. Their children were involved in numerous extracurricular activities, which required Vanessa to shuttle them back and forth.

Ken came into therapy complaining that he felt "empty," that his life had become "stagnant and stale." He found himself quite attracted to one of the nurses who had recently joined his practice. He was contemplating having an affair with her. Although the feeling was energizing, he was terrified at the possible impact on his marriage and family.

Ken declined to ask Vanessa to join him in marital therapy, preferring instead to leave the option of the affair open. In the meantime, he began visiting online dating sites. There was one in particular that intrigued him. It was a highly publicized site for married individuals looking for a strictly sexual affair, no strings attached.

He registered on the site and responded to several profiles. The women who placed them appeared to be extremely attractive, educated, and intelligent. He began an e-mail flirtation with several of the women, but found that nothing ever developed in terms of actually meeting for a sexual encounter. Frustrated with the lack of response to his invitations, Ken did some online research and found a discussion board in which other men shared their opinions of this and other dating sites. Based on his research and his conversations with other men, Ken reluctantly concluded that the profiles might not be those of real website members, but rather were planted by the company as "promotional" and intended to generate interest and business.

Choosing Wisely

One of the secrets of a happy, healthy marriage is choosing the right partner. This does not mean that there's only one person on the planet who is a good match for you. Without a doubt, there is a pool of people, each of whom might be a good fit for you, under the right circumstances.

The key to a fulfilling relationship is to maximize the fit between you and a potential partner. This involves determining whether your core values match up. For instance, do you both value regular contact with family? How do you feel about money? Are you both savers, or do you both prefer to live for the moment, where your income is concerned? Does religion and faith play an important role in your lives? And what about children? If you have children from your first marriage, you might not be as eager to start over in the childrearing department. But your new spouse might feel differently.

Having discussions about these and other values is a critical step in making your second marriage as fulfilling as possible. One of the biggest challenges I encounter as a psychologist is working with spouses who never discussed their deeply held values and life goals. After 15 years of marriage, three children, a mortgage and credit card debt, and an affair, it can be difficult for them to view each other as partners and not combatants.

Shared Values and Interests

As mentioned previously, it's critical to have open and honest discussions about what you value and what you want out of life—before signing the marriage certificate. Finding out after the fact that your spouse would like to experiment with swinging or some other form of recreational sex, whereas you strongly value monogamy, is a prescription for trouble.

But do you need to have all interests in common? Absolutely not. Some couples do, and they enjoy spending all their nonworking hours together. They might shop and do yard work together on the weekend. They might have a weekly bridge date with other couples and attend church together every Sunday. And when they're not tending to errands or chores, they might be quite content to simply be in each other's presence, reading or watching TV.

Other couples prefer more emotional and physical space. When your spouse comes home, for instance, he might need to head out for a quick run before dinner. You might need a weekly girls' night out while your husband cares for your young children. Or the two of you might even decide to spend one weekend a year at a retreat with friends or family—without each other.

And then there are the couples who seem so independent and disconnected from each other that you wonder why they're even married. They might travel on business much of the time, spend evenings at the office, and have separate hobbies and interests. They might appear more like partners than lovers. Can these marriages work? Yes, but only if both spouses equally value that extreme degree of independence, are self-sufficient, and have a high degree of trust in each other.

Misc.

Long-Distance Relationships (LDRs)

Approximately 3 percent of marriages are considered long-distance relationships (LDRs), with about 10 percent having been an LDR at some time during the first three years. These relationships pose special challenges, but can be successfully managed with close attention to communication (for example, frequent phone calls, e-mails, texts, and instant messaging) and demonstrations of concern and affection (for example, occasional unexpected gifts). Of course, most relationships won't survive the long distance forever. And when couples are finally under the same roof, there is a period of adjustment. This is especially true for military families, where one spouse is exposed to combat, as well as a regimented lifestyle.

Mutual Respect

The importance of respect in a marriage can't be overemphasized. The vast majority of people pay lip service to respecting one's spouse, but, over time, slippage between what we say and what we do occurs. Several factors contribute to this.

One is the comfort factor. When we are in the early stages of an intimate relationship, we are generally concerned with impressing our partner. We are on our best behavior, we take great pains with our appearance, and we are likely to be respectful and solicitous where the partner's likes, dislikes, and wishes are concerned.

As we become better acquainted with each other, we begin to relax. Unfortunately, our concern for our partner and what's of importance to him or her might also relax considerably. For example, it doesn't matter that he wants to go see that new action movie. You want to see the romantic comedy your girlfriends are talking about.

The other is the "you're stuck with the real me now" factor. Vows have been said, the honeymoon is over, and now it's down to the business of day-to-day life. But this is no excuse for a radical change in the consideration you show your spouse. For example, just because your husband happens to be in the basement building some shelves for the garage doesn't make it appealing or acceptable for you to bellow down at him to bring the laundry up so you can fold it.

A third factor is the "familiarity breeds contempt" attitude. For many of us, unfortunately, exposure to our spouse's habits and quirks day in and day out can lead to irritation and even intolerance. His underwear lying on the floor every morning, the way she chews, his looking at the mail before he greets you, the way she laughs when she talks to her girlfriends—the potential list of offending behaviors is endless.

You know what those particular things are in your marriage that you find hard to tolerate. Be assured that your spouse has his or her list, too. If not managed carefully, these unspoken pet peeves can lead to contempt for one another. And contempt is one of the "seven deadly sins," where marriage is concerned.

Heartaches

Renowned marital researcher John Gottman believes, based upon his years of studying what leads couples to divorce, that contempt is the most destructive of the interactional styles that couples can engage in. Contempt conveys disgust for the other person. It effectively derails attempts to resolve conflict.

Respect is one of the relational "glues" that hold a marriage together. Both spouses want and need to feel respected, but lack of respect seems to be especially hard on men. Over and over, I hear from male clients that the respect of their wives is what empowers them to go out and do battle in the competitive world of work. They might struggle with physical infirmity or financial challenges, but their wife's respect gives them the confidence and the motivation to take on the challenges of the day. Without that, they feel lost and defeated.

When working with a couple in which one or both partners displays a high level of contempt and lack of consideration for each other, I often ask the following question: "Why is it that we are on our best behavior with our co-workers and friends, and frequently on our worst behavior with those we say we love the most?" Contempt was definitely a problem for Ellen and Will.

Ellen and Will divorced after 26 years. Will filed for divorce, claiming that Ellen became totally preoccupied with their children and made him feel unwelcome in his own home. He was no longer willing to tolerate her derision and sarcastic comments.

Unbeknownst to Ellen, Will had been having an affair for years with a woman who worked at his company's branch office. During their arguments about the divorce, Will blurted out, "At least she doesn't verbally castrate me." Ellen responded defensively, "Well, she doesn't have to put up with your absentmindedness and your self-absorption."

What Ellen also discovered, however, was that her contempt for Will was having a negative effect on their two daughters. Not only were the girls uncomfortable watching their mother make their father the butt of one cruel joke after another, but they were developing an unhealthy image of how spouses should behave toward one another. Instead of caring and respect, they were witnessing contempt and mutual withdrawal.

Although men are particularly sensitive to issues of respect, women seem to be very attuned to lack of affection on the part of their husbands. This involves not only feeling loved, but also feeling cherished and protected. When a husband withdraws emotionally, a wife might feel depressed, frightened, abandoned, even unlovable.

Making Love a Priority

Sex is another powerful "relational glue" that is widely misunderstood by men and women alike. Sex, of course, has been the subject of countless plays, poems, novels, songs, operas, and TV shows, just to name a few. It has been treated with the utmost seriousness, and it has been treated humorously and often crudely.

Stereotypes about men's and women's sexuality and attitudes toward sex abound in our culture. Men are held to be primarily interested in intercourse and climax, whereas women are considered to be more concerned with romance, displays of affection, and cuddling.

The reality is much more complex, and men's and women's sexual patterns and interests overlap considerably. It is true that many men seem to be more "hard wired" for sex than women, that they might be more visual in terms of what stimulates them, and that it, in general, takes less time for them to reach orgasm. For many women, the emotional tone of the relationship powerfully affects their interest in sex and the way they respond.

This simplistic view of men's sexuality is misguided, however. Their sexual behavior is strongly impacted by factors such as self-image and feelings about their marriage. The commonplace notion that men are just interested in "getting to the finish line" is highly questionable. Many of the male clients with whom I work want most of all to please their wives sexually and will work very hard to bring them to orgasm first.

Women's sexuality has come out into the open over the past few decades. It's clear that many women have strong sexual appetites and enjoy taking the initiative in sex. Although women often object to pornography's portrayal of females as sex objects, a growing number of them are enjoying watching erotic videos with their husbands, finding that it stimulates their sex lives.

Women are enjoying pornography in ever-increasing numbers. In 2007, one in three visitors to adult websites was female. A marketing executive at a major adult video company notes that women account for 56 percent of business at her company's stores. Laboratory research also indicates that women respond physiologically to pornography as rapidly as men do.

Whatever your (and your spouse's) preferences in sexual activities, making love is a critical ingredient in a happy and healthy marriage. Like verbal communication and shared activities, it helps couples stay connected, but on a deep, unspoken level. For when we bare ourselves—literally—to another person and give rein to our desires, we make ourselves vulnerable. Sex is an area in which it is paramount that we are gentle, understanding, and respectful of our spouse's individuality.

Marriage Is a Journey

It is perhaps a cliché to say that marriage, like life, is a journey, but the point can't be made often enough. You and your fiancé will make life plans and take your vows. You will try to map out much of your life. But inevitably, the unpredictable happens.

The job you were sure you were going to land falls through. You don't get into graduate school. You get pregnant. You must care for ailing parents. You're transferred to another part of the country for your job. You're promoted and must travel frequently on business. You get the picture. In other words, you need to expect the unexpected.

Marriage is also a journey of personal and couple development. Those who spend sufficient time in self-examination following a divorce fare far better than those who rush headlong into another marriage. For them, a second marriage can be a relationship in which they flourish and make meaningful discoveries about themselves. With patience, good humor, and a sense of curiosity, they can also gain valuable insights into themselves as an intimate partner.

A Partnership of Equals

Never forget that you and your spouse are partners in this marriage and, as such, you are equally important. One of you might do more around the house, and one might earn more money, but your opinions and wishes should be equally valued. You might work out a division of labor in which one of you handles the bill paying each month. But both individuals' opinions about household finances (whether to pay bills in full or carry a credit card balance, for example) should be considered.

The Power of "I" Statements

One of the biggest mistakes couples make is not taking responsibility for their own feelings. It's seductively easy to fall into a pattern of seeing our spouse as causing whatever unhappiness or displeasure we might feel. When this happens, we often lapse into the habit of making accusatory "you statements." These include statements such as "You make me so mad," "It's your fault I'm so miserable," and "If it weren't for you, my life would be great."

Honest communication requires that we "own" our feelings. Although this might sound like a pop psych expression, it's actually quite powerful. It has to do with the fact that a great deal of how we react to life circumstances emotionally is actually self-determined. We have much more control over our reactions than we realize.

We are in the habit of responding almost reflexively to our spouse's behavior and thinking that this is the cause of our emotional state (for example, anger, sadness, and frustration). But simply stopping to remind ourselves that we have some degree of choice in how we respond can make all the difference in our marriage.

> **Tried and True**
>
> The next time you're upset with your spouse, instead of framing the problem in terms of him or her causing your emotions, try the following. Say something like "When you do *a, b, c,* I feel *x, y, z.*" When you do this, you're still establishing a connection between your spouse's behavior and your emotional state, but you're not making him or her responsible for it. You're acknowledging that you can, to a large extent, decide how you interpret and experience life events.

Facing Challenges Together

Having survived infidelity, you are well aware that all marriages face challenges of one sort or another. When you take your wedding vows, it's almost impossible to predict what these will be. It might be illness, unemployment, job changes, or death of a cherished family member. Having worked your way through this book, the hope is that you will not face the heartbreak of infidelity again, but there are no ironclad guarantees.

Probably the best "insurance policy" you and your spouse have with regard to your marriage is a commitment to turn toward—rather than away from—each other during trying times. It's relatively easy to feel close and committed when things are going well. But when you hit hard times, the "or worse" clause in your marriage vows kicks in. Most of us think it will never actually happen to us, but it can and does, usually unexpectedly.

The trick to surviving these hard times is to remember that you and your spouse are partners, not adversaries. Turning away from the marriage is not the answer, and only increases the chances of damaging your relationship, if not destroying it outright. You need to turn toward each other in love and support. When you do so, you'll be amazed at what you can endure as a couple, and how your relationship can be deeper, richer, and more fulfilling.

Essential Takeaways

- Instead of viewing your divorce as a failure or a tragedy, you can choose to use it as an opportunity for personal transformation.

- Just as we create rituals to mark other life passages, it can be helpful to create a ritual to signify that you are moving into a new phase of your life after a divorce.

- Learning to love and trust again is a journey that requires time, patience, self-examination, and a willingness to walk away from a potential relationship that appears unhealthy.

- For a new relationship to succeed, it must be based on respect and a shared set of values and interests.

- A second marriage can thrive if you and your spouse treat each other as equals and take responsibility for your own emotions.

Appendix A

Affair Proofing Your Marriage

Is it really possible to affair proof your marriage? The truth is that there's no 100 percent, iron-clad guarantee that your spouse will never be unfaithful. But there are some steps that the two of you can take to strengthen your relationship and make it less vulnerable to infidelity. Here are a few tips:

Review your expectations about your spouse and your marriage.

When you and your spouse took your wedding vows, did you really expect "happily ever after"? Did you think that, after all the planning for the wedding day, the rest would more or less take care of itself? Did you think that love would be enough to keep your relationship alive? Did you expect your spouse to be all you needed in life once you were married? Did you and your husband- or wife-to-be sit down before the wedding—preferably before the engagement—and discuss the difficult topics of money, sex, children, in-laws, and religion, to name just a few of the things that often drive couples apart?

It may be helpful to create a "marriage fantasy versus reality" sheet. In one column, list the specifics of what you expected marriage would be like. For example, "I expected we'd come home from work and talk about our day," "I expected he'd handle 50 percent of the housework and childrearing chores," and "I expected she'd be as interested in sex after marriage as she was before." In the other column, list the reality. For example, "Some days, he just wants to come home and veg out in front of the TV," "He expects me to handle the bulk of the housework and child care," and "She doesn't seem to care as much about sex anymore now that we're married." Use this list to evaluate how realistic your expectations about marriage are, and to springboard into a discussion with your spouse and your therapist (if you're in marital therapy).

Set aside time to assess the "state of your union."

If you didn't have these open and honest conversations with your spouse before you married, don't despair. Any day is a perfect day to start improving your marriage. Talking is a critical part of this process. However, I don't recommend starting with the dreaded phrase, "We need to talk." Instead, try something like, "Honey, I'm so happy with you. I can't imagine life without you. I'd like us to do everything we can to keep our relationship strong, healthy, and exciting. What do you think about setting aside 15 minutes each week to touch base and see if we need to be working harder in any area of our marriage?"

Remember, however, that, in general, women are more talk-oriented than men. They can spend hours on end with their girlfriends dissecting the details of a conversation and its implications. Men, on the other hand, would rather minimize talk and just take care of the problem. So with that in mind, talk on a regular basis, by all means, but table the conversation for a later date if it feels like it's dragging on a bit. Sometimes less really is more. Just enjoy each other's company and be sure to have some interests and activities in common.

Don't do "one-stop shopping" where your spouse is concerned.

What this really means is that you and your spouse shouldn't expect the other to be the end-all and be-all where relationships and interests are concerned. You both had a life that included other people and activities before you met and fell in love. Why should this stop or change dramatically after you marry? Staying involved in activities and friendships outside your marriage not only enriches your personal life, but it enhances your marriage as well.

It's critical, of course, that you maintain appropriate boundaries in your activities. In other words, if you're a man, don't enroll in a yoga or Pilates class in which all the other students are women. If you want to take a French cooking class, ask your wife to join you. Likewise, if you're a woman, ask your husband to join you if you want to take up a male-dominated activity, like marksmanship or tournament fishing. Be mindful of activities and friendships where you may be misperceived as being romantically available or interested.

Do your part to keep your marriage fresh, exciting, and positive.

Although most of us know we need to put some effort into our marriages to keep them lively and interesting, the sad truth is that that's the area where we're most likely to "relax" once the knot is tied. To some extent, this is understandable. Our marriage should be a comfort zone, a haven in which we can be ourselves and share our concerns. But we need to remind ourselves occasionally that our marriage is our most cherished relationship, and our spouse deserves more than emotional "leftovers" at the end of the day.

So both of you need to put some thought and energy into planning outings or activities that will surprise and please each other. These activities don't need to be expensive or exotic, but there needs to be some occasional unpredictability. This is especially true in your sex life. Sex in marriage and long-term relationships can become highly predictable. This is what therapists mean when they talk about "maintenance sex." There is an expression that "new sex is good sex." Novelty is a powerful aphrodisiac, especially for men. So the challenge in marriage is introducing novel activities without introducing a new partner. Take advantage of the vast range of self-help books and online material in this area. Experiment and, by all means, have fun!

Keep your communication and problem-solving skills sharp.

Many couples mistakenly assume that arguing is a sign of trouble in a relationship. They couldn't be more wrong. Conflict is an inherent part of close relationships. The important thing is to know how to argue constructively and how to resolve differences. In therapy, I often work with couples on how to identify and define a problem in the marriage or family, how to generate possible solutions, and how to negotiate and compromise.

Effective communication skills are critical to a good marriage, yet most of us are never taught these. We learn by trial and error, or we don't learn them at all. We keep relying on the same toxic communication patterns, with the same unsatisfactory results. In my work with couples, whether infidelity is involved or not, I routinely assess their ability to own their feelings, to dialogue with each other, to pace their discussions of sensitive topics, and to partner with each other in devising solutions to problems in the marriage.

Fall in love with your spouse all over again.

I know, you may be thinking, "Sure, after 20 years of marriage, three kids, a job layoff, a cancer scare, and now my spouse's affair, just how am I supposed to do that?" The trick is to flex your "memory muscles" on a regular basis. Pick a time when you have as few distractions as possible. If this means you need to spend a few minutes in your car at lunch, away from phones, e-mail, co-workers, or children, then do it. Sit back, relax, close your eyes, and breathe slowly and deeply.

Think back to when you first met your spouse. Was it in high school or college? Church? On the job? At a friend's wedding? Volunteering with a local volunteer group? At a sporting event? Ladies, try to remember how he looked. And now for the gentlemen, do you remember what she was wearing? When did your spouse first notice you? Who approached whom? The more detailed your memories, the more effective this exercise is likely to be. The point is to recapture your spouse in as much sensory detail as possible. A question for the men: Was she wearing a perfume that you found particularly intoxicating? Ladies, did he have an aftershave or cologne that you couldn't resist?

Revisit that moment and others from the beginning of your relationship when you were fresh and new to each other, when you couldn't wait to be with each other again. Remember how exciting it was to get to know more about each other's likes and dislikes, hopes, dreams, and fears. Your spouse is the same person who ignited passion in you all those years ago. Let memories of that time create anticipation and appreciation for you now. You'll be amazed at the impact that falling in love again will have on both of you. We all crave the experience of being cherished and desired. As someone once said, "Have an affair with your spouse. If you don't, someone else will."

Resources for Surviving Infidelity

This appendix shares some of the better resources I've come across in working with clients recovering from infidelity. I've included books, online resources, and therapist referral sites. If you've located something that strikes you as particularly useful, I hope you'll feel free to contact me through my publisher and let me know about it.

Books

The following is a partial list of books that I have found useful in the clinical setting.

- Alan, Richard. *First Aid for the Betrayed* (expanded edition). Oxford, UK: Trafford Publishing, 2008.

  Alan shares his heart-wrenching story of learning of his wife's affair. He gives a detailed account of the devastation and whirlwind of emotions he experienced. He also addresses both the cheating spouse and the affair partner in brutally honest fashion.

- Bruns, J. R., M.D., and R. A. Richards II, D.D.S. *The Tiger Woods Syndrome: Why Men Prowl and How to Not Become the Prey.* Deerfield Beach, FL: Health Communications, Inc., 2010.

  Drs. Bruns and Richards explore the epidemic of relationships built on lies and illusions. They refer to these as "mirage relationships," trace the stages of a mirage relationship, and offer practical advice to both men and women for avoiding the "syndrome" and for attaining a new level of honesty in their relationships.

- Daugherty, Jonathan. *Secrets: A True Story of Addiction, Infidelity, and Second Chances.* Mustang, OK: Tate Publishing & Enterprises, LLC, 2009.

One man's personal story of the impact of pornography and cyber infidelity on his life and marriage, as well as his redemption from his secret life of shame.

- Forward, Susan, Ph.D., with Donna Frazier. *When Your Lover Is a Liar: Healing the Wounds of Deception and Betrayal.* New York: Quill, 2001.

Written specifically for women, Dr. Forward categorizes the lies that men tell, as well as the ways in which women tend to deceive themselves in unhealthy relationships. Additionally, however, she offers practical advice for confronting a partner who lies and for moving ahead in life.

- Frisbie, David, and Lisa Frisbie. *Moving Forward After Divorce.* Eugene, Oregon: Harvest House Publishers, 2006.

Practical and insightful advice to those struggling to regroup emotionally after divorce and chart a new course in life.

- Glass, Shirley P., Ph.D., with Jean Coppock Staeheli. *Not "Just Friends": Rebuilding Trust and Recovering Your Sanity After Infidelity.* New York: Free Press, 2003.

Glass points out that many affairs begin with people insisting they're "just friends." The problem is that boundaries in their relationships have been reversed, with "windows" between marriage partners turning into "walls" and windows opening up between affair partners, where there should be relational walls to protect the marriage.

- Kirshenbaum, Mira. *When Good People Have Affairs: Inside the Hearts & Minds of People in Two Relationships.* New York: St. Martin's Griffin, 2008.

  Kirshenbaum is a clinician who works with both individuals and couples struggling with an affair. She takes the reader through detailed steps that can help determine whether a spouse or a lover is a better love match for you. She also offers a description of 17 different types of affairs and tips on how to know which category yours falls into.

- Landers, Elizabeth, and Vicky Mainzer. *The Script: The 100% Absolutely Predictable Things Men Do When They Cheat.* New York: Hyperion, 2005.

  The authors outline the lines cheating men use and the behaviors they tend to engage in, time after time. They also reinforce to men that affairs are based on fantasy and that they rarely turn out as planned.

- Love, Pat, Ed.D. *The Truth About Love.* New York: Fireside, 2001.

  Dr. Love takes the reader through the stages of love and points out that we often mistake the transition to another stage as the end of the love relationship. She shares her own heartbreaking story of the unnecessary end of her first marriage.

- Love, Patricia, Ed.D., and Steven Stosny, Ph.D. *How to Improve Your Marriage Without Talking About It.* New York: Broadway Books, 2007.

  This book serves as a reminder that men and women connect in different ways. We tend to assume that talk is the answer to relationship problems. But there are other ways to strengthen your relationship, including shared interests and activities, as well as staying sexually connected.

- Neuman, M. Gary. *The Truth About Cheating: Why Men Stray and What You Can Do to Prevent It.* Hoboken, New Jersey: John Wiley & Sons, 2008.

  Neuman, a marriage counselor and a rabbi, presents the results of his interviews with men who had affairs. While emphasizing that he is in no way "blaming the victim," Neuman points out that most men cheat because of emotional dissatisfaction and gives wives specific tools that they can use to enhance their marriage.

- Snyder, Douglas K., Ph.D., Donald H. Baucom, Ph.D., and Kristina Coop Gordon, Ph.D. *Getting Past the Affair: A Program to Help You Cope, Heal, and Move On—Together or Apart.* New York: The Guilford Press, 2007.

  This work helps you deal with the intensity of your emotions immediately after revelation of your spouse's affair, get through the day, and make the decisions you and your spouse will need to make about your future. This applies regardless of whether you decide to end the marriage or go on together. There is a more technical companion book for therapists working with couples impacted by infidelity.

- Vaughan, Diane. *Uncoupling: Turning Points in Intimate Relationships.* New York: Vintage Books, 1990.

  Vaughan is a sociologist who looks at the dynamics of how intimate relationships unravel. She makes the interesting observation that the process begins when one member of a couple secretly begins to feel that the relationship no longer "fits" and that he or she would do better outside it.

- Vaughan, Peggy. *The Monogamy Myth: A Personal Handbook for Recovering from Affairs,* Third Edition. New York: Newmarket Press, 2003.

  One of the most popular self-help books for affair recovery, this grew out of Vaughan's devastating discovery that her husband, to whom she is still married, had had multiple affairs. Vaughan transformed her pain into helping others and also founded the

Beyond Affairs Network (BAN), which offers online information and support groups in several cities.

Online Resources

- www.beyondaffairs.com

  This website is run by Anne and Brian Bercht, who themselves overcame infidelity and went on to become writers, speakers, and relationship coaches. They have made countless media appearances. Their website offers articles, videos, and teleseminars, as well as links to relationship coaches and support groups.

- www.DearPeggy.com

  This is the site founded by Peggy Vaughan as part of her work in educating the public about monogamy and affairs. It contains Peggy and her husband James' personal story, testimonials, articles, synopses of books, and PDF downloads.

- www.divorce.com

  This site gives information related to the legal aspects of divorce at different stages of the process. It answers questions regarding the impact of infidelity on divorce, and includes state-specific information as well.

- www.infidelity.com

  This is a comprehensive site with advice on spotting a cheating spouse, discussion boards, referral to marriage and divorce professionals, and personal stories of those who have been traumatized by and overcome the devastation of infidelity in their lives.

A note about online resources: There is a tremendous amount of material about infidelity, affairs, marriage, and divorce on the web. It would be impossible to cover all of these in this space. However, my recommendation to you in assessing their value is to look at the source. The material comes from sources ranging from blogs to university professors to data released by the United States government. In general, the more authoritative the source, the more reliable the information.

Therapist Referral Sites

- The American Psychological Association (www.apa.org) and many state psychological associations have therapist referral services. In general, you can type in certain criteria you'd like met in your search—for example, a certain zip code or proximity to where you live or work. You may also be able to specify therapist gender, if you have a preference. Or you can use a drop-down menu to select the issue with which you'd like help, for instance "relationships."

- The popular magazine *Psychology Today* (www.psychologytoday. com) also offers a therapist locator service, which includes a statement by the mental health professional and indicates whether he or she is a licensed psychologist.

Index

F

G

H

I

J–K

L

M